D1384025

*Giuseppe Ferrari
and the Italian Revolution*

Giuseppe Ferrari
Courtesy of the Biblioteca Nazionale in Florence (Collezione Buonamici)

Giuseppe Ferrari and the Italian Revolution

by

Clara M. Lovett

THE UNIVERSITY OF NORTH CAROLINA PRESS

CHAPEL HILL

© 1979 The University of North Carolina Press
All rights reserved
Manufactured in the United States of America
ISBN 0-8078-1354-0
Library of Congress Catalog Card Number 78-24099

Library of Congress Cataloging in Publication Data

Lovett, Clara Maria, 1939–
    Giuseppe Ferrari and the Italian Revolution.
    Bibliography: p.
    Includes index.
    1. Ferrari, Giuseppe, 1811–1876.   2.   Italy—Politics
and government—19th century.   3.   France—Intellectual
life.   4.   Statesmen—Italy—Biography.   5.   Intellecuals
—Italy—Biography.   I.   Title.
DG552.8.F46L68   945'.08'0924   78-24099
ISBN 0-8078-1354-0

For C. J. L.
who always understood

Contents

Acknowledgments ix
Introduction xi

PART ONE   THE MAKING OF A RADICAL INTELLECTUAL

[1]   *Lombard Roots* 3
[2]   *Bittersweet France* 22
[3]   *The Crucible of 1848* 51
[4]   *Under the Bonapartist Eagle* 81

PART TWO   THE POLITICIAN

[5]   *Return to the Roots* 111
[6]   *The Art of Political Survival* 130
[7]   *Gadfly of the Chamber* 160
[8]   *The Twilight Years* 190

Conclusions 214
Notes 223
Bibliography 249
Index 269

Acknowledgments

ONE OF THE joys of researching and writing a book is to find at every stage of work colleagues and friends willing to give support and encouragement. The historians, archivists, and librarians, both in Italy and in this country, who earned my respect and gratitude while I was working on this project are too numerous to be thanked individually here. But I would be greatly remiss if I did not at least mention the invaluable assistance of three Italian scholars—Dr. Giulia Bologna, until recently Director of the Museo del Risorgimento in Milan, Dr. Emilia Morelli at the Istituto per la storia del Risorgimento italiano in Rome, and Dr. Clementina Rotondi at the Museo del Risorgimento in Florence.

Dr. Morelli not only facilitated my research in Rome but she also read and critiqued the entire manuscript, as did Professor Franco Della Peruta of the University of Milan. In this country, the following scholars read the entire work or parts of it and offered many helpful suggestions: Nancy N. Barker, Benjamin F. Brown, Marion S. Miller, Emiliana P. Noether, Frank Rosengarten, A. William Salomone, and Robert Wohl. Three of my colleagues at Baruch College—Carol Ruth Berkin, Edward Pessen, and Randolph Trumbach—contributed sharp questions, stylistic suggestions, and the emotional support necessary to overcome a very adverse institutional situation.

Financial support at the research and writing stages was provided by the Research Foundation of the City University of

New York, by the American Philosophical Society, and by the National Endowment for the Humanities. A generous publication subsidy was made available by Phi Alpha Theta, from which I received the Manuscript Award for 1976.

Finally, I wish to thank C. James Lovett, to whom this work is dedicated. His contribution was unique and, unlike all others, it can never be repaid.

C. M. L.
New York City
May 1978

Introduction

In THE LAST twenty years, Italian historians have produced a body of scholarship on the Italian Revolution of the nineteenth century (the Risorgimento) that compares favorably in its richness, depth, and diversity with the celebrated achievements of the *Annales* school in France and with the flowering of studies on seventeenth-century England. Among the most notable aspects of their work have been the rediscovery and interpretation of sources pertaining to the democratic and socialist currents in the Italian Revolution, which had been ignored or slighted by previous generations of historians.

Unfortunately, their work is still largely unknown outside of Italy. The language barrier and also, I believe, our traditional preoccupation with the Great Powers of nineteenth-century Europe account for the fact that most historians of modern Europe on this side of the Atlantic are familiar with only one radical leader of the Risorgimento, Giuseppe Mazzini. Only a handful of specialists are aware of those radical currents in the Italian Revolution that flourished alongside, and often in opposition to, both the moderate liberalism of Cavour and the democratic nationalism of Mazzini.

And yet, if we wish to understand the contemporary Italian Left, we should be very much aware of men like Giuseppe Ferrari, Carlo Pisacane, Giuseppe Ricciardi, and other dissidents who stood not only for Italy's independence but also for the radical transformation of her social structure and for the radical secularization of her culture. For better or worse, today's Italian radicals, socialists, and communists look upon those men, and not upon Cavour or Mazzini, as their intellectual forebears. I hope, therefore, that this study will provide for many scholars unfamiliar with recent Italian historiography an introduction to the ultraradical minority in the Italian Revolution.

Giuseppe Ferrari (1811–76) was a particularly interesting and important member of that minority and perhaps its most prominent spokesman in the Italian Parliament after the unification. The writings of Franco Della Peruta, Silvia Rota Ghibaudi, and others first brought him to my attention as a relentless and witty critic of the Mazzinian program before 1860 and of the policies of the *Destra storica* in the 1860s. An analysis of his published writings on the Italian Revolution, the French revolutionary tradition, the secularization of European culture, and other topics then revealed a political theorist no less interesting and original than his contemporaries and personal friends Leroux, Proudhon, and Renan. But much spadework in the unpublished Ferrari papers and much interpretive work remained to be done when I undertook this biographical study some five years ago.

Among the archival sources, the Archivio Giuseppe Ferrari at the Museo del Risorgimento in Milan was indispensable, because only a small portion of Ferrari's papers has ever been published. It must be pointed out, however, that the collection yields a wealth of material about Ferrari's public life and intellectual interests but little information of a personal nature. This is so because after Ferrari's death his friend and executor Michele Cavaleri complied, in part, with his wish that only items of significant scholarly or political value be preserved and be placed in the public domain. Fortunately, a few items of family correspondence have been preserved among the meticulous business records kept by Carlo Ferrari. And some glimpses of the young Ferrari in Milan and Paris can be caught in the correspondence of Carlo Cattaneo, Cesare Cantù, Giuseppe Massari, Lorenzo Valerio, and other contemporaries.

As the title indicates, a major portion of this work is devoted to Ferrari's view of the Italian Revolution and to his role in it. But he was more than just an important figure in nineteenth-century Italian politics. He spent one-half of his adult life in France and he wrote some of his most important works in French. Intellectually, he was as much a part of the European radical-socialist tradition as Proudhon and Marx. Thus, his cultural formation and personal experiences offer valuable insights into the making of a radical intellectual and activist at mid-nineteenth century. Ferrari's political experiences in France and in Italy closely reflected the radical movement's hours of glory in the 1840s, its crisis after 1848, and its gradual demise in the age of *Realpolitik*, mass parties, and imperialism. Further, his parliamentary career after the unification of Italy provides an excellent case study of the opportunities and challenges that awaited a European elected official in the days before universal suffrage, modern party organizations, and the mass media.

I have arranged the material for this book so as to preserve a certain natural symmetry in Ferrari's life. In the first part I shall discuss his family background and cultural formation in Habsburg Lombardy and his political education and radicalization in France through the last decade of the July Monarchy, the Revolution of 1848, and the Second Empire. And in the second part I shall discuss his decision to return to Italy at the time of unification and his role in the first Italian Parliament as an advocate of radical secularization, democracy, and social justice.

PART ONE
THE MAKING OF A RADICAL INTELLECTUAL

[1]

Lombard Roots

THE EARLY YEARS of the nineteenth century were troubled but exciting ones for the ancient capital of Lombardy. Milan, regarded since 1714 as one of the most splendid pearls in the crown of the Habsburg family, had become part of the Napoleonic Empire in 1807. The French did not find it easy to rule the city; memories of the Empress Maria Theresa and her sons and successors were still cherished among many segments of the population. In order to win supporters, the new rulers left a measure of autonomy to the city itself and to the surrounding countryside, and they made an effort to ingratiate themselves with powerful aristocratic families. As to the middle class, the French hoped it might be won over by the expansion of opportunities in business, in the professions, and in the upper echelons of the bureaucracy. Such expansion did, in fact, occur when Milan became the capital of a satellite state, the Kingdom of Italy.

But resentment against the new masters and a certain nostalgia for the old could not be suppressed. Disenchantment followed the French Emperor's seemingly endless military campaigns, to which Lombardy was expected to contribute heavily. Particularly at the time of the ill-fated Russian campaign, the politically conscious groups in Milan became uneasy, suspicious, and ultimately hostile to their French rulers. While prominent aristocrats entered secret negotiations with Vienna and St. Petersburg, middle-class leaders adopted a cautious, wait-and-see attitude, in some cases resigning from positions that identified them too closely with the French administration.[1]

Among those middle-class Milanese who, around 1812–13, were preparing themselves to face the possibility of a Habsburg Restoration, and who may even have desired it, were Francesco Ferrari, a small businessman, and his brother Giovanni, a staff physician at the Ospedale Maggiore. Although not very wealthy, the Ferrari brothers were coowners of rental properties in the city and of a small country estate—perhaps the land of their fore-bears—that provided cash payments and fresh produce from the tenants and a summertime refuge from the noisy and foul-smelling streets of Milan. The modest family fortune had been built over two or three generations partly upon the profits of landownership and partly upon those of a tannery.

At the time of the Habsburg Restoration, in 1814, both broth-ers were middle-aged men with families. The political changes did not affect them adversely. But Giovanni Ferrari hoped for a return to more stable conditions, since it was time for his elder son Carlo, born in 1795, to start thinking seriously about a career. The young man, in fact, entered the service of the Habsburg administration and gradually moved up through the ranks of its accounting section. As for the younger son, Giuseppe, born on 7 March 1811, time would tell. He might go into business with his uncle Francesco, who had no sons, or train for his father's occu-pation.[2]

In the early nineteenth century, the medical profession was neither prestigious nor very lucrative, and its scientific founda-tions were questionable. But Giovanni Ferrari seems to have been rather above average among the physicians of his day. He kept a laboratory at the Ospedale Maggiore and had an unusual private practice that made him famous among the wealthy people of his city. His specialty was the treatment of the physiological and emotional causes of impotence and infertility. His patients were men, or occasionally women, from prominent families, for whom sexual dysfunctions could have serious social and economic con-sequences.[3] While a few records of Giovanni Ferrari's profes-sional activities have survived, we can only speculate about his personal traits and his relationship with his family. It would seem that his scientific interests, intellectual curiosity, and willingness to defy convention had little impact upon his first-born, Carlo. Those qualities would one day be much more evident in Giuseppe, although the lad was only nine years old when his father died in 1820.

Giovanni Ferrari's wife, Rosalinda, was a cheerful woman who faced with courage many years of widowhood and the responsibility of raising her younger child with little help from others. Until her declining years she enjoyed a robust health and never lost her love of parties, good food, and merry company.[4]

In the 1820s it fell upon Carlo Ferrari, already established in his civil service career, to look after his mother and younger brother. Giovanni Ferrari's inheritance was sufficient to support his widow in a comfortable life-style, and, most importantly, it was adequate to provide for Giuseppe's formal education. In 1833 the family income was augmented by an inheritance from Francesco Ferrari, who wished thereby to reward Carlo for his services as a bookkeeper.[5]

Giuseppe Ferrari attended the prestigious Liceo Sant'Alessandro, a real breeding ground for the professional class of Restoration Milan. His father would almost certainly have approved of this choice, because the Liceo Sant'Alessandro had a distinguished faculty and also because the school was, for those times at any rate, quite free from clerical influence. Like many middle-class Milanese of his generation, Giovanni Ferrari had been a skeptic in matters of faith. And although his widow followed the traditional Roman Catholic beliefs and practices, their son Giuseppe grew up indifferent or hostile to organized religion. These attitudes already present within the family environment were probably strengthened by the intellectual atmosphere of the Sant'Alessandro, where the anticlerical and rationalist spirit of the Milanese Enlightenment and of the revolutionary period was still very much alive among the faculty in the 1820s. Ferrari showed special aptitude for the experimental sciences and in his last year at the school won a prize for excellence in physics. But upon graduation he chose not to follow in his father's footsteps;

instead, he chose to study law at the University of Pavia.

In the 1820s and 1830s, the Faculty of Law of that ancient and renowned institution was a kind of mecca for young men from the middle class who aspired to professional careers. It seems unlikely, however, that Ferrari chose the University of Pavia because he sought an opportunity for upward mobility. The relative affluence of his family, and the fact that there were no younger children to be provided for, left open to him a wider range of career options than was generally available to young men of his social class. It seems probable that Ferrari chose to study law because, given the curriculum at Italian universities at that time, it was a subject that he could learn easily and was closely related to his budding interest in historical and philosophical investigations. Besides, a law degree, particularly if earned at a prestigious institution, conferred upon its holder a respectability that was very important to the status-conscious middle class of that era, and was certain to please his family. He completed his studies at Pavia in less than four years, graduating in June 1832. It was a sign of the times that before he could be granted the degree he had to take a loyalty oath, denying that he had ever been involved in conspiracies or other antigovernment activities.[6]

In 1821–22, during the political trials that had resulted in the arrest and conviction of many well-known liberal intellectuals, there had been considerable unrest among the student population of Pavia. Since that time the Habsburg police had kept a watchful eye upon the university, and the presence of undercover agents among student groups had become commonplace. Police spies were again kept quite busy in 1830–31, when the news of the July Revolution in Paris and of attempted insurrections in central Italy led to student demonstrations and, briefly, to the closing of the university.[7]

There is no evidence that Ferrari during his student days joined underground political organizations; we know, however, that he met young men of advanced political and social ideas, among them Cesare Correnti, the future minister of the Kingdom of Italy, the brothers Cantù, the journalists Giacinto Battaglia and Michele Sartorio, and the cousins Giuseppe and Defendente Sacchi, both active in the reform of Milanese educational and charitable institutions. It seems probable that these contacts were established in Milan rather than through student organizations in Pavia, because Ferrari was in the habit of leaving his rented room near the university and heading for home whenever school was not in session.

In the autumn of 1832 the young graduate joined a law firm in Milan, a decision that certainly pleased his family. Intelligent, articulate, and well-connected with business and professional men, he seems to have had all of the qualities required to become a successful lawyer. But soon he found the routine of a law office insufferably tedious, and he left his position to seek intellectual challenge elsewhere.

Personal friends, including Carlo Cattaneo, soon to become the leading Lombard economist of that generation, were willing to introduce Ferrari to the world of editors and publishers. Ferrari was eager to explore that world and to try out for a new career as a man of letters, by beginning quite modestly as a reviewer of legal and philosophical works. Provided one had the proper connections, assignments were not difficult to come by— but financial rewards were quite another matter. The relative affluence of his family, however, made it possible for Ferrari to abandon the practice of law for a scholarly career better suited to his intellectual and emotional needs. After a great deal of haggling, Carlo Ferrari was persuaded to pay him an allowance out of their joint inheritance. The sum was apparently sufficient to cover Giuseppe's personal expenses, at least so long as he did not marry.[8]

Many contemporaries of Ferrari, including some who met him only in the 1860s and who abhorred his politics, described him as an attractive man, affable and eloquent, and fond of good conversation. The few photographs that have been preserved among his papers, although taken when he was well into middle age, also bear witness to his good looks and aristocratic bearing. A man with his personal qualities and good family background must have been regarded as a good match by young ladies of the

Milanese bourgeoisie of the 1830s. But if any of them tried to win his heart, they were obviously unsuccessful. Some negative remarks about marriage that Ferrari made in a letter of May 1860 to his friend Giovanni Carozzi seem to indicate that quite early in his life he made the decision not to marry. Despite occasional regrets, he never reversed this decision.[9]

It would be most interesting to know the reasons behind Ferrari's commitment to the single life. Unfortunately, the available evidence on this aspect of his life is so flimsy as to sustain little more than speculation. By all accounts, he made friends easily with both men and women, and he was certainly not a misogynist. Throughout his life, however, he showed a predilection for somewhat older women who possessed unusual intellectual gifts and who were (by the standards of the nineteenth century) emancipated. This pattern had already emerged in the 1830s when he met Anna Woodcock, the Irish-born wife of his friend Cattaneo.

But women like Anna Woodcock Cattaneo were rare indeed in the society of Restoration Milan. It is possible that Ferrari was simply not attracted to the idea of a lasting relationship with a young woman of more conventional education, values, and ambitions. And that was precisely the kind of young woman he was most likely to encounter in the parlors of middle-class families of that era.

Although the evidence concerning Ferrari's youth is not plentiful, it is possible to reconstruct the broad patterns of behavior that he followed consistently through the rest of his life. In sharp contrast to his father, uncle, and elder brother, he rejected the traditional career options of the Milanese bourgeoisie of his day—business, the professions, or the civil service—to seek personal fulfillment in the world of letters and philosophy. He also rejected, again in sharp contrast to his brother, the bourgeois ideals of marriage and family life. He did not actually break with his relatives, and he continued to live with his mother until his departure for France. Yet it is obvious, particularly from his correspondence with Carlo, that the family was not the chief source of the emotional support and intellectual stimulation necessary to his growth. These he found elsewhere.

Early in 1833, Ferrari was introduced to a close-knit group of philosophers and publicists who met in the home of Giovanni Domenico Romagnosi, a highly respected member of the Milanese intelligentsia and the editor of the *Annali universali di statistica*. Romagnosi's works reflected a desire to preserve the Enlightenment's concern with socially useful knowledge while at the same time remaining open to new ideas. He introduced his disciples to the writings of Vico and of the great German and British philosophers of the seventeenth century, but also to those of the eighteenth-century *philosophes* and of the Saint-Simonian school.

If Romagnosi's writings and his private library reflected broad intellectual interests, his personal life pointed to the narrow bounds within which those interests could be pursued in the 1830s. Implicated in the political trials of 1821, he had been barred from teaching and was watched closely by the Habsburg police. But this did not stop many young intellectuals from seeking his friendship and guidance. Their visits were a source of comfort for the old philosopher, whose only steady companion was an old servant, Angiolino Castelli.[10]

Since Romagnosi died in June 1835, it is obvious that Ferrari cannot have been as close to him personally as were others in the group, especially the Sacchis and Cattaneo. Yet this encounter had a profound impact upon him. In the Romagnosi circle, which bore no little resemblance to the philosophical groups of ancient Greece, he found role models of intellectual achievement and of political and social awareness unavailable within his own family and instrumental in his choices for the future.

The members of that circle, all active in the cultural affairs of their city, provided the first opportunities for him to publish the results of his readings and reflections in those magazines to which they had access. There was in those days no dearth of outlets for essays on nearly every subject except politics. The impressive number of serious journals published in Milan reflected its relatively high rate of literacy and its growing prosperity.[11]

A frequent topic of conversation in the Romagnosi circle was the revival of interest, in Italy and abroad, in the thought of Giambattista Vico. Ferrari read his works as well as the interpretations of his thought that were being published in the 1830s. Among these were Jules Michelet's introduction to a French translation of the *Scienza Nuova* and the writings of Jean-Louis-Eugène Lerminier, who taught the history and philosophy of law at the Collège de France.

Ferrari's first published essay, which appeared in *Il nuovo ricoglitore* toward the end of 1833, was a review of Lerminier's *Philosophie du droit.* The essay shows that he had already read voraciously in law, history, and epistemology, and that ever since reading Lerminier's works he had been mustering an array of arguments against his theories. Lerminier argued that laws originated not from experienced social or individual needs but from man's innate ethical conscience. Ferrari rejected this viewpoint, on the grounds that it seemed absurd to separate the study of law from the social sciences by making the law a branch of ethics. Man-made laws, Ferrari argued, were but an expression of the social contract; indeed, they were probably its most ancient and basic expression, because it was precisely the appearance of such laws that had marked man's painful transition from the savage and precarious state of nature to civilization.

His empirical approach to the philosophy of law showed the influence of Romagnosi, but it had radical overtones that are not found in Romagnosi's writings. Despite the absence of references and footnotes, Ferrari's critique of Lerminier suggests that he already had more than a passing acquaintance with Thomas Hobbes's *Leviathan* and with David Hume's epistemology. That he had read their works may have been due to the influence of Cattaneo, the authority on British philosophy and economic theory within the Romagnosi circle.

Impressed by Ferrari's first article, Romagnosi asked him to review, for the *Annali universali di statistica,* Pierre-Simon Ballanche's *Essais de palingénésie sociale* (1828–29). In preparation for this second article, Ferrari analyzed the intellectual debate between the conservative Ballanche and the followers of Saint-Simon and Fourier.[12] Ballanche recognized, as reactionary writers did not, that Restoration France could not set the clock back to the institutions of the Old Regime. But he rejected the social theories of Saint-Simon and Fourier on the grounds that they subverted the natural order of society created by God and known to man through the teachings of the Church. To Ballanche's main thesis that basic structural changes in a society cannot be contrived by man but must be left to Divine Providence, whose plans unfold slowly through a nation's historical development, Ferrari replied with a spirited defense of contemporary social theorists. It was easy to prove that the prophets of the new age were wrong in this or that particular judgment and unrealistic in their social planning; yet they, and not conservative thinkers like Ballanche, embodied the progress of European civilization. Future generations, Ferrari wrote, would remember Saint-Simon and Fourier not by the blueprints they had offered but by the questions they had raised. Two of Ballanche's closest friends, the poet Victor de Laprade and the painter Joseph Chenavard, learned about Ferrari through this article. Although they disagreed with his critique, they welcomed him upon his arrival in France and introduced him to other intellectuals who were, like themselves, from the Midi.[13]

Ferrari's article coincided with the publication in Milan of two works by the Italian Fourierist Giuseppe Bucellati.[14] Ferrari's acquaintance with French social theory at this early stage in his career was probably derivative, through the interpretations of men like Bucellati, rather than direct. But he was obviously moving briskly along the ideological path he was to follow in the next decade.

That Ferrari's literary career began with articles on Lerminier and Ballanche was due only in part to his budding interest in French social theory. His assignments were, in fact, typical of those given aspiring Milanese writers of his generation. The leading Milanese periodicals of the 1830s and 1840s devoted much space to reviews of British, French, and German works on nearly every subject except politics. This unofficial but widespread editorial practice reflected the attitude of the Milanese intelligentsia toward Lombardy's place in Europe. The leading intellectuals of the 1830s, and especially Francesco Lampato, founder of the editorial group Società degli Editori, regarded their native region as one whose cultural and economic development stood approximately halfway between the advanced countries of western Europe and the backward empires of central and eastern Europe. They perceived, correctly, that Lombardy was one of the most advanced provinces of the Habsburg Empire, although not quite as advanced as her neighbors to the north and west. Hence, they argued that to forge close cultural and economic ties with western Europe was to pave the way for progress in the whole Empire.[15]

The Austrian authorities in Lombardy supported this view and encouraged the adaptation to local needs of ideas born on French, British, and even American soil. The government in Vienna was less sanguine about such experiments. But in the early part of the decade it maintained a laissez faire attitude toward the Milanese intellectual community, under the condition that it should never openly discuss questions of political change. Indeed, at times the imperial government subsidized publications that had a strong European orientation, such as the *Biblioteca italiana*, on the assumption that they were sweeping away both the remnants of Lombard patriotism and the memories of the Napoleonic Kingdom of Italy.[16] The reading public of that era showed little curiosity with regard to other Italian regions, which it held, in any event, to be inferior to Lombardy. Even among the educated classes, few Lombards in the 1830s were able to identify with an Italian national culture. And those who did identify with it were often under the impression that Italy had not produced any significant artistic or philosophical works since the Renaissance.

Without denying that a prolonged crisis beginning in the sixteenth century had crippled Italy's political and economic progress, several Milanese intellectuals of the Restoration reacted against what they regarded as an overly pessimistic view of their country's history. It was true that in some respects the Italian states, politically weak and economically backward, had much to learn from foreign examples. But in the area of cultural achievements, Italians could find inspiration closer to home, in the works of Ludovico Muratori and Giambattista Vico, Pietro Giannone, Vincenzo Cuoco, Cesare Beccaria, the Verri brothers, and many others.

The members of the Romagnosi circle were particularly active in this attempt to identify and publicize the works of Italian authors of the seventeenth and eighteenth centuries. They were aiding a new generation of Lombards to discover cultural traditions that differed considerably from those of other parts of the Habsburg Empire. Unconsciously and unintentionally they were sowing seeds of disaffection between educated Lombards and their rulers, and they were paving the way for an Italian nationalist movement.

In the formative years of his life, Ferrari shared, through the Romagnosi circle, in the European orientation of Milanese culture, but he also learned to appreciate Italian authors. In fact, from about 1834 until his departure for France, he devoted much time to the study of Italian history and philosophy, thus preparing the ground for his own original contributions of the 1840s and 1850s.

Ferrari owed his introduction to contemporary Italian philosophy to the works of Terenzio Mamiani della Rovere, who represented the liberal-rationalist current, and of Antonio Rosmini-Serbati, the leader of a neo-Catholic revival.

Mamiani, a liberal aristocrat from Pesaro, had fled to France after an abortive insurrection against the papal government. Finding the French ignorant and contemptuous of Italian culture, he attempted to remedy the situation through public lectures at the Paris Athénée and through his book *Del rinnovamento della filosofia antica italiana.*[17] In his view, Italy was still far away from a political revolution, but she had entered an age of cultural progress, at the heart of which he saw a renewed interest in the philosophical traditions of the Renaissance. Among those traditions, Mamiani emphasized the use of the experimental method in the pursuit of knowledge.

Without going as far in his criticism as Cattaneo, who had ridiculed publicly Mamiani's "pathetic urge to parade the achievements of his countrymen before foreign eyes," Ferrari pointed out that ever since the Renaissance the experimental method had been used by foreign philosophers much more than by Italian ones. By stressing the validity of old native traditions, Mamiani was certainly providing inspiration for young Italian intellectuals. Yet was it not dangerous to predicate a revival of Italian philosophy only, or primarily, upon native traditions? One ran the risk of ignoring other countries' vital contributions and of adopting a reactionary position. In any event, Ferrari wrote, if Mamiani and other philosophers wished to build a revival of their country's culture upon native foundations, they were well advised to study the works of Vico, the only truly original Italian thinker of the last two centuries.

While pointing out the possible intellectual pitfalls of nationalist pride, Ferrari concurred with Mamiani that Italian culture was making progress, despite a thousand obstacles. Among the major ones he saw, even at this early stage in his life, the political power of the papacy and the intellectual influence of the Roman Catholic tradition. Around 1835 he became particularly alarmed by the popularity of Rosmini's works in Milan. Like other philosophers of the Restoration, Rosmini rejected the culture of the Enlightenment because it led inevitably to the ruin of the established Church. And he attempted to forge a new synthesis between Catholic doctrine and contemporary thought, particularly Hegelian Idealism. The philosophical revival that he promoted was diametrically opposed to Mamiani's emphasis on the traditions of the Renaissance. Whether or not he understood the long-range implications of these philosophical differences for the future of Italy, Ferrari did not hesitate to take sides. He wrote:

Rosmini's reputation [in Milan] grows more and more each day; unless someone stops him, in this climate of universal ignorance it will be easy for him to infect our schools, our youth with his doctrines and his bigotry. His purpose is to set us back to the times of San Carlo Borromeo. . . . The medals of Santa Filomena for the populace, Abbot Rosmini's books for the schools, the Teatro alla Scala for the world, and censorship presiding over all things . . . and so we travel posthaste back to the Middle Ages![18]

Ferrari had obviously grown impatient with the limited opportunities for intellectual growth and the omnipresent censorship of Habsburg Milan. But this sarcastic outburst also shows that he was already committed to the militant anti-Catholicism that is one of the hallmarks of his thought. Indeed, in his distrust of the Roman Catholic Church and of everything connected with it, he went far beyond other members of the Romagnosi circle; even Cattaneo's anticlericalism seems mild by comparison. As an antidote to Rosmini's influence, Ferrari proposed the rediscovery and reevaluation of those Italian thinkers who had labored outside of or in opposition to the Roman Catholic Church. His own contribution to this endeavor was a six-volume critical edition of Vico's writings. With this work he continued the dissemination of Vichian philosophy that the Neapolitan emigré Vincenzo Cuoco had begun during the revolutionary period. And thus he helped shape the cult of Vico that became commonplace among Risorgimento intellectuals, a cult that was often based more upon national pride than upon philosophical analysis.[19]

That his project was well received in Milan can be inferred from the fact that very soon thereafter eager imitators published their own partial or complete editions of Vico. But in the long run these unpleasant developments did not undermine the importance of Ferrari's work, which received almost unanimous critical acclaim.[20] Volumes two and three of Ferrari's edition, which included all but one of Vico's Latin tracts, came out in the spring of 1835. But the publication of the remaining volumes was delayed due to the death of Romagnosi on 8 June of that year.

Romagnosi had left to his friends a fine library, a large collection of letters, and some unpublished essays. It was decided to prepare these manuscripts for publication, along with a new edition of out-of-print works, as a tribute to him. As coeditors of this project, Cattaneo and Ferrari were responsible for finding a publisher and for negotiating with Angiolino Castelli, the legal custodian of the materials.[21]

While working on Romagnosi's manuscripts, Ferrari found time to write an essay in his honor, *La mente di Giovanni Domenico Romagnosi*. From a young man whose education and career owed much to Romagnosi and his circle, one might have expected a eulogy, not a critical assessment of the man and his work. But such was not the case. Ferrari's intellectual portrait of

Romagnosi—one that recent scholarship has by and large confirmed—was surprisingly devoid of flattery.

Romagnosi, Ferrari wrote, had not been an original thinker. His contributions to epistemology were no match for those of Condillac or Hume and his writings on law and criminology were not as significant as those of Bentham and Beccaria. But during his lifetime, in his successive roles as an administrator, a legislator, and an educator, he had succeeded better than many of his talented contemporaries in achieving a synthesis of these various fields of inquiry. Better than any man of his generation, Romagnosi had embodied the principal moving force of his century—the struggle for equality before the law—and he had done much to determine its positive outcome in Italy. But during the last decades of his life, new historical questions had come to the fore. For instance, once a society had established the principle of the equality of all citizens before the law, could it tolerate other kinds of inequality, such as the ones based on property? This, Ferrari wrote, was precisely the kind of question to which men of the nineteenth century were beginning to address themselves and which could not be answered on the basis of Romagnosi's synthesis—hence the need for new directions.

But to point out the limitations of Romagnosi's synthesis was not to belittle his contribution to the progress of Italian society. Indeed, Ferrari argued, historical progress required two kinds of great minds: those who blazed new intellectual paths and those who organized the new knowledge into laws, principles, and policies for the common good. Ferrari's scholarly interests suggested an obvious comparison between Vico, an example of the isolated creative genius, and Romagnosi, an example of organizing genius.

To this theme of the role of genius in history Ferrari returned in a lengthy introduction to his edition of Vico. It appeared in 1837 as volume one of the series, under the title *La mente di G. B. Vico*. He wrote:

Glory is the prize that mankind awards to the works of the great; admiration is the hallmark of discovery, the currency by which intellectual achievements are measured. . . . A man who after years of hard work finds no other reward than the sarcasm of the intellectual community or the supreme indifference of his contemporaries may feel that he has lived in vain, that he has wasted his talents in aberrations. Such was the fate of the greatest thinker in modern history.[22]

Learned men in Italy and abroad were discovering in Vico one of the great philosophers of the seventeenth century. But why had recognition come so late? Vico had not been indifferent to worldly honors and riches; on the contrary, he had sought them with a pathetic eagerness. His failure to achieve recognition during his lifetime could only be understood by analyzing his theories and the intellectual atmosphere prevailing in his country at the close of the seventeenth century.

The historical function of the creative genius, Ferrari wrote, was to lead mankind in the exploration of new frontiers of knowledge. But his mission could not be fulfilled unless some of his contemporaries recognized his intellectual leadership and joined him. One could say, in short, that the creative genius must be both of his age and ahead of his age. Vico had challenged the predominance of Cartesian philosophy in the academic circles of his day, denounced its reliance upon mathematical abstractions, and asserted the scientific value of studying human institutions, religions, and languages. In so doing, he had anticipated the intellectual preoccupations of the early nineteenth century. But he had moved so far ahead of his own contemporaries that they had failed to see the new horizons opened up by the *Scienza Nuova*. Instead of exploring the laws governing the development of human civilizations, they had continued to dismiss history as a catalog of past errors to be overcome by the application of pure reason.

Italy's unstable political situation and the intellectual impact of the Counter-Reformation had hindered the acceptance of the *Scienza Nuova*. By contrast, in other European countries the contributions of creative minds had not been wasted. France, in particular, had been in the vanguard of progress ever since the early eighteenth century.

In *La mente di Vico* we can already trace several intellectual themes that Ferrari pursued after his departure for France. Vico's suggestion of recurring cycles in human history sparked his interest in discovering the laws of historical change. The study of Vico's career led him to investigate Italy's seventeenth-century political and intellectual crisis. And finally, Ferrari hinted that in his view the heritage of the French Revolution contained the seeds of progress for Europe and therefore also for Italy.

Ferrari's essay on Vico was an intellectual statement that showed the first signs of tension between adherence to the rationalist tradition of the Enlightenment, with its belief in historical progress, and a more contemporary pessimism of Romantic inspiration concerning human nature. But it was also a camouflaged political statement of dissatisfaction with the relative backwardness of Italian culture and with the stifling political climate of the Lombard capital in the 1830s.[23] In Ferrari's portrait of Vico as the solitary genius whose wings had been clipped by the indifference and the dogmatism of his contemporaries it was not difficult to recognize Romagnosi, whose career in public administration and teaching had twice been crippled by political reaction. Romagnosi's young disciple was determined not to suffer similar misfortunes.

Because Ferrari's departure for France early in 1838 was perhaps the single most important event in his life, it would be interesting to know in detail the circumstances that led up to it. Unfortunately, the evidence on this matter is circumstantial and not plentiful.

In the summer of 1835, two events left him dispirited and restless—the death of Romagnosi and Cattaneo's prolonged absence from Milan preceding his marriage to Anna Woodcock. The demise of the Romagnosi circle probably made Ferrari more acutely aware of his dissatisfaction with the cultural and political climate of his native city. He was not left completely adrift, because in the autumn Cattaneo and his bride opened their home to him. Many years later, in fact, he still remembered fondly the hours spent in the Cattaneo home in front of a blazing fire, talking and arguing late into the night.[24] But he began to think seriously about an extended trip abroad, although his editorial responsibilities and the difficulty of obtaining a passport precluded an immediate departure.

There were other worries. With the death of Romagnosi, Cattaneo found it difficult to continue collaborating with the *Annali universali di statistica*, because he disagreed with Lampato's editorial policies. Since he depended upon Cattaneo for good assignments, Ferrari was adversely affected by this new situation. He and Cattaneo then made plans to launch their own philosophic-scientific journal, to be called *L'Ateneo*, but their application for a government license was rejected.[25] In the 1830s Cattaneo was known as an advocate of economic liberalism and an admirer of the British system of government. But he was also loyal to the Habsburg administration, whose confidence he enjoyed until the eve of the Revolution of 1848.[26] It seems improbable that permission to launch *L'Ateneo* was denied because the authorities had suddenly become suspicious of his intentions. If the refusal was politically motivated (and we cannot be certain that it was), it was directed primarily against the younger Ferrari, whose activities the police had indeed been watching for some time.[27]

During the Restoration it was not at all unusual for young intellectuals to have a secret police dossier. Journalists, editors, teachers, and others from the educated middle class were watched closely by the Habsburg administration, especially if they were young, because precisely among such people liberal and nationalist ideas were slowly but surely gaining ground. Some liberal demands, provided they were accompanied by protestations of loyalty to the dynasty, were tolerated in Milan, if not in Vienna. But liberal demands coupled with dreams of Lombard separatism or of an independent and united Italy posed a mortal threat to Habsburg interests. Particularly dangerous in the eyes of the Habsburg government was the nationalist and democratic propaganda of Giuseppe Mazzini's Young Italy movement.[28]

The first political trials against members of that movement had taken place in Milan in 1832–33, just as Ferrari was beginning to move around in the city's intellectual circles. Ever since those days he had been an obvious target for police surveillance.

He was not personally involved with Young Italy, but by social background, education, and personal interests he matched the profile of the political rebel of that era. Police spies, try as they might, were unable to establish any connection between him and specific opposition groups. But in a report forwarded to Governor Franz von Hartig in 1837 they mentioned that he was under surveillance as a former disciple of Romagnosi and as a close friend of Carlo and Alessandro Porro, members of a distinguished Milanese family of known liberal sentiments. They recommended that Ferrari's request for a passport be denied. In his application he had stated that he wished to travel to Paris to make arrangements with the publisher Eveillard for a French edition of Vico's writings. Governor von Hartig decided that this was a valid reason for travel abroad and that the evidence of Ferrari's subversive tendencies was not substantial enough to warrant rejection of his application. That the governor decided to discount the unfavorable police reports on Ferrari may have been due to the influence of his secretary, Karl von Czoernig, who was a good friend of Cattaneo and an enthusiastic patron of literary and scientific projects.

Despite von Hartig's enlightened attitude, the unfavorable police reports suggest that if Ferrari had remained in Milan during the decade 1838–48, when the growth of liberal and nationalist opposition to the Habsburg government was matched by increased bureaucratic rigidity and by political repression, he might well have faced serious difficulties. His departure for Paris and his subsequent decision to settle there provided an escape, if not from persecution or harassment, at least from an increasingly tense situation that limited his freedom of action and endangered his peace of mind.

We do not know how long he intended to remain abroad when he left Milan; very probably he did not know himself. In fact, he packed only a few personal effects and books, leaving the rest at his mother's apartment, and he arranged with Carlo to have the usual allowance paid to him in Paris through the banking house of Antonio Gargantini. While abroad he kept in touch with old friends and with the Società degli Editori, and he continued to work with Cattaneo on the edition of Romagnosi's works. His letters of 1838–39 to family and close friends reveal neither a reluctant, unhappy exile nor an angry rebel who rejected his native land, but simply a restless young man eager to see more of the world, to meet interesting people, and to broaden his intellectual horizon by leaving, for a time, the relatively provincial environment of his city. And what better place was there than Paris, the intellectual capital of Europe and the hub of political and social experiments, to continue his education? He would soon learn, however, that if life in Paris was more exciting and free than in Milan, it was also more demanding, more complex, and quite likely to take unexpected turns.

[2]

Bittersweet France

ON HIS WAY to the French capital, Ferrari stopped briefly in Turin and Lyon. The Cattaneos, the Piedmontese scholars Amedeo Peyron and Lorenzo Valerio, and Ballanche's friends in Lyon gave him letters of introduction to Parisian intellectuals, publishers, and political figures. Ferrari already had contacts of his own with the publisher Eveillard and the exiled Mamiani. By April 1838, he had reached Paris and had settled in small but comfortable quarters on the rue Jacob in the VIè arrondissement. It was an excellent choice for a young man who wanted to explore the city and to study. The rue Jacob, recently widened and flanked by elegant new buildings, was located about halfway between the Tuileries and the Luxembourg Gardens and within easy walking distance of the Sorbonne, the Collège de France, and the Ecole des Beaux Arts.[1]

The next several months were among the happiest in Ferrari's life. Like the protagonist of Flaubert's *Education sentimentale*, he was completely captivated by the historic sights, the shops, the cafés, and the theaters of Paris, all of which made his native Milan seem hopelessly dull and provincial by comparison. At the same time, he did not forget that he had come to Paris in order to continue his literary and philosophical education. Above all, he was eager to meet the proponents of advanced social and political ideas, who enjoyed considerably more freedom in the France of Louis-Philippe than in Habsburg Lombardy.

His intellectual curiosity and his desire to make interesting friends were quickly and handsomely rewarded. Peyron's letter of introduction made it possible for him to meet Victor Cousin and other notables at the Collège de France and at the Ministry of Public Education. He also received a warm welcome in the home of Augustin Thierry, thanks to his friendship with Anna Woodcock Cattaneo; the eminent French historian had courted her in the 1820s. To Anna, moreover, Ferrari owed introductions to Mary Clarke, a learned Englishwoman whose salon attracted well-known writers and scholars, and to Hortense Allart, a novelist and a feminist whose defiance of bourgeois morality rivalled the exploits of her more famous contemporary, George Sand. Anna's friends found Ferrari charming, articulate, and handsome; for several years thereafter, they included him among a select group of guests who met at their homes to talk about literature, the performing arts, and politics.[2]

Through his French publisher, Ferrari met François Buloz, the editor of the *Revue des deux Mondes*, a magazine still young in years yet destined to become a literary and cultural landmark. Soon he became a regular contributor, along with Sand, Sainte-Beuve, Lamartine, and other distinguished writers of his generation. Buloz was known to be quite selective in his choice of contributors to the *Revue*. That Ferrari, only recently arrived from Italy, was asked to write an essay for the magazine was certainly due to his growing reputation as the editor of Vico's works.[3]

To George Sand, then one of Buloz's most valuable collaborators, Ferrari probably owed an introduction to the socialist theorist and reformer Pierre Leroux. Already well known in radical intellectual circles as the editor of the *Encyclopédie nouvelle*, Leroux had just published an important work, *De l'égalité*. The central theme of the book was Leroux's belief that his own generation was destined to implement through concrete economic and social reforms the principle of equality proclaimed in universal and abstract terms by the great revolutions of the eighteenth century.[4] The young Ferrari was unusually receptive to this argument. In fact, the idea that his own generation had a

special responsibility to turn the principles of the eighteenth century into political and social realities was well attuned to what
he had learned within the Romagnosi circle, and it became a
recurring theme of his later writings. Around 1840 he was invited to contribute to the *Encyclopédie nouvelle*, and thereafter
he kept regularly in touch with Leroux and his coeditor, Jean
Reynaud.[5] Over the years, they showed on numerous occasions
that they regarded Ferrari as a talented publicist and a kindred
soul. Leroux not only solicited from him contributions to his
journals but also defended him, as we shall see, during the harrowing Strasbourg affair.[6] And Reynaud helped Ferrari in March
1848 by recommending him to his friend Hippolyte Carnot, the
Minister of Public Education in the Provisional Government.[7]

Piedmontese friends of Ferrari had suggested that he should
get in touch with Laurent (or Lorenzo) Cerise, a physician who
had migrated to France in 1831.[8] The two men met sometime in
the summer of 1838 and soon discovered that they shared a deep
admiration for things French and an interest in the problems and
the future of the emerging industrial society. Cerise was a pleasant and dynamic man who maintained a thriving medical practice, wrote scientific tracts, and also found time for an active
commitment to the circle of Philippe Buchez, the Société des
Amis du Peuple.

Trained, like Cerise, for a medical career, Buchez as a young
student in Paris had been attracted by the egalitarian theories
of Gracchus Babeuf and later by the teachings of the Saint-
Simonians. But his association with Bazard and Enfantin, the
high priests of the movement in the 1820s, had not been entirely
happy. He had broken with the Saint-Simonians in the fall of
1831 and had founded his own circle for the purpose of recon-
ciling socialist reforms and Christian thought. Unlike other figures in the Christian Socialist movement of the 1830s, Buchez
was a republican and a democrat. He had no ideological objections to monarchy per se but he saw little hope of democratic
progress under the July Monarchy, noting that the stability of
that regime depended upon an intimate partnership between political power and wealth.[9]

Such were the ideas that Buchez and his friends expressed, to the extent that police surveillance and censorship permitted, through the columns of *L'Européen* in the 1830s and the *Revue nationale* in the 1840s. Cerise, who contributed articles on science and public health, introduced Ferrari to Buchez himself and to his chief collaborators, Auguste Ott, Frédéric Arnaud, and Henri Feugueray. Ott and Feugueray were not merely theorists of reform. They maintained close ties with workingmen's organizations, which sometimes held their meetings in the headquarters of the Buchez circle. Moreover, they acted as advisers to such organizations on a variety of problems, from the printing and distribution of a newspaper, *L'Atelier*, to the establishment of mutual assistance funds, to the best way of avoiding harassment by employers and police. The Buchez circle also included radical artists, such as the actor-playwright Hippolyte Auger, who were critical of the Romantic slogan "art for art's sake" and who searched for new modes of expression, particularly in the performing arts, that might appeal to the masses.[10]

The friendship with Leroux and the introduction to the Buchez circle marked a real milestone in the social and political education of Giuseppe Ferrari. The ideas and activities of those men enhanced his awareness and understanding of the social question of his times, prompted him to reflect upon the social and cultural effects of economic modernization, and eventually led him to challenge the notion, held firmly by many of his friends in Lombardy, that economic and political liberalism were the keys to progress for all nations and for all social classes. It was the beginning of a long process of radicalization that shaped his outlook and career, with occasional interruptions, from his arrival in France to the Paris Commune of 1871. For several years, however, Ferrari's emerging radicalism was reflected only in some of his writings and in letters to his friends. In the 1840s, the notion that one day he would try to implement his ideas about political and social change in the service of his native country would have seemed utterly absurd to him and to all who knew him.

After a few months in Paris, Ferrari informed his family and friends that he had resolved to stay on indefinitely. While protesting to Cattaneo that his heart was in his native land, he admitted that he was happy and excited about his new surroundings and that Paris was more than living up to his expectations.[11] His family agreed to continue paying him a monthly allowance through the Gargantini banking house. This sum, plus an occasional fee for magazine articles and royalties from the French edition of Vico, freed him from financial worry and even allowed him a few luxuries, such as tickets to plays or the ballet (of which he was especially fond), stylish clothes, and the services of a valet.

In the span of three or four years, Ferrari became completely immersed in French culture and customs, he began a career within the Université, and he obtained French citizenship. Indeed, had it not been for the war of 1859 and the subsequent unification of Italy, he might well have remained in France to the end of his life. In contrast to those Italians of his generation who were driven from their homeland by political persecution and repression, Ferrari chose to remain abroad primarily for personal reasons—he found France intellectually more exciting and congenial than Italy.[12]

There were at least three reasons behind his decision to become an expatriate. He wished to explore further the various currents of the French socialist movement and he was justly proud of his association with the promising *Revue des deux Mondes*. But in addition he had become quite enthralled with two charismatic figures of the French academic world, Claude Fauriel and Jules Michelet.[13] The latter, in particular, dazzled Ferrari with his erudition and oratorical gifts.

Ferrari was initially attracted to the Collège de France by the desire to hear Lerminier, the philosopher whose works he had once reviewed. But, inevitably, he was also drawn to the lectures of Fauriel, whose scholarly reputation and pro-Italian sympathies were well known in Milan, and of the younger Michelet, who had publicized Vico's *Scienza Nuova* in France. Fauriel's lectures on Romance philology and literatures taught Ferrari to appreciate popular dialects and folklore and to establish connections between these and the web of a people's social and political institutions. Inspired by Fauriel's teachings, he set out to study the most important Italian dialects and regional literary traditions. Already well disposed toward France, Ferrari could hardly resist Michelet's contagious enthusiasm for the French Revolution and his appeal to the young generation to understand and to continue the democratic principles that had emerged in 1792–93. He recognized the same burning desire to influence the young in Michelet's closest friend, Edgar Quinet, who was in Paris during the summer and fall of 1838, preparing himself to take a new chair of Romance literatures in Lyon. Soon after his arrival in Paris, Ferrari resolved to follow in the footsteps of these fascinating men.

In those days the road to success in academic circles, in France as elsewhere, bristled with obstacles: the interplay of personal and party rivalries among the men at the top, a series of demanding examinations, a scarcity of jobs, and meager financial rewards for the chosen few. Ferrari could not have faced his new career without the help of knowledgeable men. Fauriel, Lerminier, Michelet, and Thierry were generous with advice and encouragement. And, of course, it did no harm at all to have acquaintances at the Ministry of Public Education.

In 1838–39 Ferrari's deliberate efforts to associate with leading French scholars, social theorists, and artists contrasted sharply with his lack of interest in the company of fellow Italians. There were, of course, a few exceptions, such as Cerise, Mamiani, and two Lombard ladies whose beauty and intelligence charmed Parisian society. Cristina Trivulzio di Belgiojoso, a refugee from the boredom of aristocratic life in the Lombard countryside and from an unhappy marriage, and Bianca Milesi Mojon, a friend of the liberal conspirators of 1820–21 and the Cattaneos, were in those days the patron saints of the Italian residents in Paris.[14] In their homes, which Ferrari visited frequently, encounters with other expatriates or with exiles were unavoidable, if not always welcome.

The Italian community in Paris was numerous and visible. In the late 1830s it consisted of three groups: a few older men who had served the governments of revolutionary or Napoleonic France in Italy; a larger group of expatriates, like Cerise, who had migrated in the 1820s in search of greater political freedom and opportunities for personal advancement than they had enjoyed in Italy; and, finally, the refugees of the unsuccessful liberal movements of 1820–21 and the early 1830s.[15]

From the beginning of his sojourn in France, the relationship between Ferrari and the Italian community, especially the political refugees of recent years, was marked by tension, mutual suspicion, and even outright hostility.[16] Some of the exiles had lost their fortune along with their citizenship and were reduced to eking out a miserable living as tutors, clerks, or translators. They resented Ferrari's comfortable circumstances and his apparent indifference to their plight. For his part, he found them clannish, too prone to self-pity, and insufferably provincial. To Cattaneo, who urged him to try to get along better with his countrymen, he wrote:

I must describe for you the type of Italian that one finds in Paris. He arrives here convinced that he is a great politician or a great poet, but he produces nothing more than hot air and sonnets; the great man of 1821 or 1830 is received with honors; the French are excessively polite and incredibly ignorant when it comes to Italian affairs. . . . Within a year or two, the great man is ever so politely rebuffed; people know him, they can evaluate his actual ability; wrapped up as he is in his Italian prejudices, he cannot become French, he associates only with other Italians. Within three years he finds himself alone, isolated; then he remembers the good old days in Italy, he adores his country for selfish reasons; he loathes everything about a country where he could live for a thousand years without ever finding the least sympathy for his bad ideas.[17]

This letter reveals that, quite apart from personal animosity, there were differences in political outlook that precluded friendship between Ferrari and the Italian exiles in Paris. The problem was that most of them had developed a high level of nationalist consciousness, while he had not. Nothing was more odious to them than his outspoken admiration for French civilization and his obvious ambition to succeed in a foreign land.[18]

These hostile feelings were brought out into the open by the publication of Ferrari's *Vico et l'Italie*, a revised edition of the essay published in Milan two years earlier. The central theme was again the paralysis of Italian culture and political life in the seventeenth century and the country's isolation, reflected in the work of Vico, from the mainstream of European history.[19] A storm of indignant protest followed its publication. Some reviewers, for instance Cattaneo in *Il Politecnico*, were critical of Ferrari's interpretation, yet their remarks were kept within the generally accepted bounds of a scholarly controversy. But among the Italian exiles in Paris the response to Ferrari's essay was extremely negative and emotionally charged. The mathematician Guglielmo Libri led the assault with a vitriolic article in the *Journal des savants*. He attributed Ferrari's stark portrait of Italian isolation and backwardness to his ignorance of Italy's traditions and, worse, to his desire to find favor among prejudiced foreigners. Not all of the exiles found fault with Ferrari's historical analysis. What really aroused their anger was the fact that he had called the attention of foreigners to a painful and embarrassing problem that was best discussed and solved among fellow Italians.[20]

Ferrari was hurt and confused by this criticism. He was willing to debate the fine points of Italy's seventeenth-century crisis and of Vico's *Scienza Nuova*. But how was he to deal with the charge—so obviously meaningless for him—that he had slandered the fatherland?[21] A second round of the same controversy was fought upon the publication of "De la littérature populaire en Italie," an essay in which he presented a thesis about the relationship between national and regional literature that modern scholarship has by and large confirmed.[22]

The Italian people, he wrote, could boast a national literary tradition that had produced great works of art, from Dante and Machiavelli to Ariosto and Tasso. Yet in the atmosphere of cultural stagnation that had followed the Renaissance those works had been read only by an educated elite. Regional and local literary movements, however, had continued to flourish, reflecting the everyday concerns of the Italian people through a variety of folksongs, poems, and novellas, and through the *commedia dell'arte*. Far from being unworthy of scholarly attention, the so-called popular literature based upon regional or local dialects was rich, vibrant, and perhaps more valuable to an understanding of Italian civilization than all the musty tomes of the academies.

Italian literature, Ferrari argued, differed in several important ways from that of other European countries. First of all, by the nineteenth century Italy's popular literary traditions appeared more viable and important than the national tradition. Second, Italy had developed a highly decentralized culture, with several centers instead of one great capital like Paris or London. And finally, her rich popular traditions constituted a bond— possibly the only strong one—that existed within the various regions between literates and illiterates, between upper and lower classes, and between city and countryside. The national literary tradition tended to exacerbate differences of social background and education, because it appealed only to the educated few. But the popular literatures, grounded in regional or local dialects, were the common heritage of all social classes. Ferrari concluded that those who were working for a cultural revival in Italy could succeed only if they built upon the existing popular traditions and if they recognized the diverse and decentralized nature of Italian culture. This essay, which reflected the influence of Fauriel's teachings and the interests of a Romantic mind, represented Ferrari's first tentative step in the development of his federalist conception of Italian culture and politics, which will be discussed throughout this work.

Ferrari's critics objected strongly to the suggestion that the national literary tradition was academic, lifeless, and divorced from the lives of most Italians. And they interpreted his emphasis on the decentralized character of Italian culture to mean that he denied the possibility of an Italian nation-state.[23] As had been the case when *Vico et l'Italie* was published, Ferrari could not quite understand his critics. But in trying to refute them he became active in the debate concerning Italy's future. In the next several years he interpreted the history and the culture of his native homeland for the French reading public in much the same way as his fellow expatriates Adam Mickiewicz and Heinrich Heine were interpreting Poland and Germany respectively. But his involvement with the Italian Question was slow and gradual, because in 1840–41 other matters demanded his attention.

In the summer of 1840, Ferrari approached with trepidation the first of the competitive examinations (*concours d'agrégation*) required of aspiring academicians in France. For nearly two years he had studied rhetoric, philosophy, and history, and he had written the two mandatory dissertations. The first one, on the utopian thought of Tommaso Campanella, shows his continuing interest in the Italian philosophical tradition, with an emphasis on those aspects of it that had flourished in opposition to the Roman Catholic Church.[24] It also offers the first example of an approach to the study of the human past that pervades all of his subsequent historical works. Ferrari did not investigate the past because it was interesting in itself nor did he simply ask, in Rankean fashion, what actually happened. Instead, he began with the attitudes and problems of his own day and he sought to understand their origins. Men, ideas, and methods were almost invariably judged according to what they had contributed to the shaping of the contemporary world. Thus, Campanella earned high praise because, Ferrari wrote, he had dealt with the question of human happiness in a way that anticipated modern thought. Breaking with the tradition of the medieval church, he had dared suggest that human happiness and justice on this earth were a legitimate concern of the philosopher and of the legislator. In Ferrari's work Campanella emerged as a kindred spirit and a precursor of modern social theorists, such as Saint-Simon, Leroux, and Buchez.

Ferrari's second dissertation was a survey of the relationship between truth and error as interpreted by leading Western thinkers from Plato to the Idealists of the nineteenth century.[25] As others have noted, in evaluating the epistemological position of various thinkers Ferrari outlined his own framework more clearly than had been the case in his Milanese writings.[26] He believed, with Malebranche, that man could not attain absolute truths but only probable truths or "probabilities." But his philosophical skepticism was tempered by his belief in historical progress, defined as the movement from error to new probabilities. The knowledge that we can never be free of error, he argued, should be not a reason for despair but an incentive to continue searching for truth.

In September 1840 Ferrari's name appeared in the *Journal général de l'instruction publique* among the successful candidates in the *concours d'agrégation*.[27] Because a university lectureship, to which he aspired, was not available for the academic year 1840–41, he accepted a position at the lycée of Rochefort-sur-Mer, near Poitiers. In November 1840 he applied to the Ministry of Justice for permission to reside in France permanently while maintaining his Habsburg citizenship. An investigation of his personal and professional conduct produced a very flattering portrait.[28] But he regarded this as a temporary arrangement, and he was prepared to leave at the earliest opportunity. Rochefort-sur-Mer was a pleasant and picturesque town, yet its charm and the tranquil beauty of the surrounding countryside were no match for the excitement of the capital. Fortunately, his friends in Paris had not forgotten him. Letters with the latest political and literary gossip and requests from Buloz and Leroux for articles arrived now and then to brighten the humdrum life of the Rochefort schoolteacher. In academic circles, Claude Fauriel and Théodore Jouffroy, whose unorthodox religious views were similar to Ferrari's, were looking out for him in the event that a more desirable position became available.

Fortune smiled upon their efforts: in the fall of 1841, their protégé was appointed *professeur suppléant* in the Faculty of Letters and Philosophy of the University of Strasbourg.[29] Although this appointment was a temporary one, with little or no chance of ever obtaining a chair, Ferrari accepted it without hesitation. The University of Strasbourg was one of the oldest and most prestigious in France, and the town itself, although nearly as far from Paris as Rochefort-sur-Mer, was larger, more prosperous, and culturally alive. Upon his arrival, Ferrari set immediately to work on a series of lectures, because the new academic year was about to begin. As the theme of his course he chose a historical survey of the intellectual foundations of the nineteenth century. In his opening lecture he outlined what he regarded as the milestones of the modern age: the Renaissance, the discovery of the Americas, the invention of the printing press, the Lutheran Reformation, and the scientific revolution of the seventeenth century. The lecture was well attended and, he thought, well received.[30]

The scholarly stature of the new lecturer was obviously not what had attracted over one hundred students and townspeople to his opening lecture. The main reason for the high level of interest was the reputation of his predecessor, the Abbé Louis-Eugène-Marie Bautain, who had been forced to resign following a confrontation with the reactionary bishop of Strasbourg, Mgr. J.-F. La Pappe de Trévern. Ferrari's audience wanted above all to find out where he stood on the issues that had precipitated Bautain's resignation. With little or no warning the newcomer found himself in the eye of a political maelstrom.

For years the Abbé Bautain had been a driving force behind a revival of Catholic thought that had begun in Strasbourg in the early 1820s. His courses had been a rallying point for young Catholics in their long-standing political and intellectual struggle against the Université. Bautain's activism and popularity had created resentment among Protestant students and townspeople, some of whom had complained to the Ministry of Public Education. But since his personal integrity and professional competence were above reproach, he had continued to teach as he wished. Ironically, his ecclesiastical superior had succeeded where the defenders of Protestant opinion and of state control over education had failed.

Mgr. La Pappe de Trévern had appreciated Bautain's spirited defense of Roman Catholicism in a town where religious differences mattered more than anywhere else in France. But as a Legitimist and a former emigré, he had been angered by the political leanings of the controversial abbé. Shortly after the revolution of 1830, Bautain, a Liberal Catholic, had called for a reconciliation between the Roman Catholic Church and the new regime. After years of tension, the bishop had finally invoked the principle of ecclesiastical discipline against him. Bautain had submitted, but, not wishing to alter the content of his courses, he had also resigned from the University.[31]

Ferrari's first lectures, on the relationship between the political philosophy of Plato and Aristotle and that of the Italian Renaissance, did not arouse overt opposition, although his anticlerical leanings did not go unnoticed. Those conservative elements who had supported Mgr. La Pappe de Trévern against Bautain were obviously unhappy with the appointment of a layman of foreign birth and undetermined religious affiliation. As for the followers of Bautain, they had hoped for the appointment of another Liberal Catholic. Ferrari's lectures on the Renaissance, with their emphasis on the separation of religion and philosophy, showed the new lecturer to be not merely a critic of the Roman Catholic Church but also an atheist. By the end of 1841, therefore, the opposing Catholic factions within the university began to work together for Ferrari's dismissal. Careful notes were taken of the content of his lectures and of any comments that he made in response to questions from the audience.[32]

His lectures on the Lutheran Reformation, delivered in December 1841, set the stage for what was to be known in French academic circles as the *affaire Ferrari*. Catholic students and auditors reported that he had praised Luther for having "emancipated" some forty million Germans from the papal yoke. Letters of protest were sent to the Rector of the university, Louis Magloire Cottard, and to the Minister of Education, Villemain.[33]

Then, on 23 January 1842, an indictment of Ferrari's teachings and a call for his immediate dismissal appeared in the columns of Louis Veuillot's *L'Univers*, an ultramontane newspaper well known for its polemics against state control over education.[34] With Veuillot's intervention, the controversy over Ferrari's philosophy course could no longer be attributed to the rather unusual intellectual and religious environment of the Alsatian capital. The *affaire Ferrari* was clearly part of a larger struggle over the issues of church-state relations and of academic freedom. Both issues, but especially the first one, loomed large in the history of Ferrari's two homelands. It was inevitable that they should affect his outlook and career.

Faced with an increasing number of complaints, Villemain upheld Cottard's decision to place Ferrari on temporary suspension and ordered a thorough investigation of the Faculty of Letters and Philosophy. In fact, while Ferrari's lectures on the Lutheran Reformation had been the immediate cause of Catholic remonstrances, there had also been complaints against his colleagues Frédéric-Guillaume Bergmann and René-Gaspard Taillandier of the Faculty of Letters. The former, an Alsatian Protestant by birth, was said to have Masonic and Saint-Simonian connections.[35] A young man from the Midi and a disciple of Edgar Quinet, Taillandier had a mystic temperament quite different from the rationalistic tendencies of Bergmann and the uncompromising atheism of Ferrari.[36] That all three came under attack at this time was due not to an identity of philosophical outlook but to their adherence to a notion of academic freedom that was completely at variance with the Catholic position. What that notion was can be seen clearly in Ferrari's case from his correspondence with the ministry and with Veuillot.

To the charge that his lectures on the Reformation had offended the sensibilities of his Catholic students, Ferrari answered with an apology. He had certainly not intended to antagonize anyone. As to the statement attributed to him that Luther had "emancipated" his fellow Germans, he denied having made it. But although he repudiated the one statement that his critics had singled out as an example of inflammatory "Protestant" rhetoric, Ferrari did not modify his overall interpretation of the Reformation. Finally, to the charges that he believed in the separation of philosophy and religion and that he was personally indifferent to Roman Catholic practice, Ferrari pleaded guilty. But he denied that his convictions, although they might differ from those of many students, made him unfit to teach. Those who called for his dismissal, he stated, must demonstrate either that his philosophical preparation was inadequate for the task at hand or that he had been somehow remiss in the scholar's first duty, the constant search for truth.[37] In a private letter to Villemain, Ferrari pointed out with obvious bitterness that he had been under scrutiny almost from the day of his arrival. He was convinced that he was being made a scapegoat for long-standing Catholic grievances against the Université and against the liberal regime of Louis-Philippe. But he expressed confidence in the outcome of the investigation ordered by Villemain.[38]

In a sense his confidence was justified. The investigators stressed his command of his material and his genuine enthusiasm for teaching. They did find weaknesses in his performance. His exuberant temperament and his limited experience as a lecturer accounted for a certain lack of restraint in his presentations. At times he had not weighed his words quite as carefully as he should have done when presenting sensitive or controversial material to an admittedly difficult audience. But on balance they concluded that he was an asset to the Faculty of Letters and Philosophy.[39]

Not surprisingly, Ferrari's Catholic opponents dismissed the investigation as a ministerial whitewash. In February 1842, the *affaire Ferrari*, which thus far had been aired in public only by *L'Univers*, became the object of a well-orchestrated campaign by lesser Catholic newspapers, especially in Alsace. His name was mentioned as a particularly shocking example of the threat to the education of French youth that would persist as long as the state maintained control over the universities. Calls for his dismissal were now accompanied by demands for the resignation of Cottard and Villemain.[40]

Because Ferrari's lectures on the Reformation had precipitated this crisis, one might have expected the Strasbourg Protestant community to defend him. As a professed atheist and a foreigner, however, he found no more favor among Protestants than among Catholics. Indeed, the only influential person to plead his case (and then only privately in his correspondence with the ministry) was the beleaguered Cottard.[41] The Rector had made many friends in Strasbourg over the years, especially among the Protestant and Jewish minorities, for his defense of religious toleration. But in the face of mounting pressures even he was forced to abandon any thought of reinstating Ferrari.

The decisive factor in Cottard's decision to suspend Ferrari indefinitely appears to have been the threat of violent demonstrations on the part of Catholic militants at the university. While privately expressing his sympathy to Ferrari and promising a future appointment elsewhere, Villemain upheld Cottard's decision. They all knew that this course of action was tantamount to dismissal.[42]

The Strasbourg experience had a lasting impact upon Ferrari's intellectual orientation.[43] First of all, the Catholic opposition that had brought about his suspension strengthened the anticlerical bias he had internalized as a youth. The controversy over his philosophy course convinced him that the influence of the Church was a powerful obstacle to intellectual and political modernization everywhere, not just in Italy. From 1842 until the end of his life, in his writings and in his political activities, Ferrari fought an uncompromising battle to diminish the intellectual, social, and political role of the Roman Catholic Church in the modern world.

Second, the Strasbourg experience opened his eyes to the limitations of the liberal state as it existed in France under the July Monarchy. The regime did permit greater freedom than its Habsburg counterpart, but it was a far cry from the intellectual and political promised land that this impatient expatriate had apparently hoped to find. He did not become disillusioned with French culture, nor did he contemplate a move back to Lombardy. But thereafter he assumed a more critical attitude toward the French political leadership, and particularly toward Cousin.

Third, this experience made him aware, for the first time in four years, of the fact that he was vulnerable as a foreigner. His background had not really mattered as long as he had moved in the cosmopolitan literary and academic circles of the capital. But Paris was not France. There was no escaping the unpleasant fact that all of his critics in Strasbourg had made much of his foreign birth. Finally, the crisis of 1841–42 exacerbated his already difficult relationship with the Italian exiles in France. A bitter animosity between him and his countrymen resulted from a letter on the *affaire Ferrari* that Vincenzo Gioberti sent to the editor of

L'Univers. In those days, Gioberti was establishing a reputation as an important interpreter of Catholic philosophy and a theorist of Italian nationalism. In his letter he stated that Ferrari was unworthy of the sympathy usually accorded to political refugees because he had left Milan of his own free will and because, far from being proud of his heritage, he had rejected it to pursue the chimera of success in a foreign country.[44] While it seems improbable that Gioberti's letter influenced the decisions of Cottard and Villemain, it had a devastating impact upon Ferrari's already low morale. Angry, and for the time being quite helpless, he nursed thoughts of revenge.[45]

When he learned that this controversy had cost Ferrari his position, Gioberti felt some pangs of conscience. In public, he complained that his letter to *L'Univers* had been edited in such a way as to make it harsher than he intended. In private, he admitted that he was not interested in the specific content of Ferrari's lectures. He had intervened in the controversy not to defend the Roman Catholic Church but "to strike a blow against a bad Italian."[46] Several Italian exiles in Paris deplored Gioberti's intervention against a man who was already under severe stress. But they too hoped that Ferrari might at long last realize how closely his destiny was tied to theirs. Once again, he disappointed them by remaining aloof.

If the Strasbourg controversy had opened his eyes to the enduring influence of the Church in postrevolutionary France, Gioberti's attack strengthened his belief in the political backwardness of the Italian exiles and alerted him to the potential appeal of those neo-guelph political tendencies of which the Piedmontese publicist was the outstanding spokesman. From then on, Ferrari followed with great interest the career of this opponent, whom he hated but never underestimated.

After his quarrel with Gioberti, Ferrari avoided more than ever the public places patronized by Italian exiles. But he continued to be a welcome guest in the homes of Thierry, Mary Clarke, and the princess Belgiojoso, where the brightest lights of the French intelligentsia often gathered to dine and match wits with illustrious foreign visitors. He was particularly impressed by his encounters with Leopold von Ranke, Lord Elgin, and Michele Amari, the historian of Arabic civilization.[47]

Occasionally Ferrari also enjoyed an evening with Leroux and his circle of friends, but he was careful not to become too closely identified with them and their new journal, the *Revue indépendante*. He realized that a close friendship with the ebullient socialist thinker could be the kiss of death for a man like himself who wished to succeed within the intellectual establishment of Orleanist France. Moreover, he knew that since 1841, when George Sand had broken her contract with the *Revue des deux Mondes* in order to work full-time with Leroux, Buloz had regarded all the contributors to the *Revue indépendante* as his personal enemies—hence the need for caution.[48]

In these various circles, Ferrari found not only sympathy for his recent misadventures but also curiosity concerning his controversial lectures at the University of Strasbourg. He decided to capitalize on that curiosity by publishing those lectures in which he had discussed the influence of Greek political thought on the Italian Renaissance.[49] At the same time, he wrote a longer work on the philosophy of history, using as the core some of the lectures that he had not been able to deliver. Although very awkwardly written, Ferrari's *Essai sur le principe et les limites de la philosophie de l'histoire* is an important work. At the heart of his theory concerning the nature and uses of historical knowledge was a basic distinction between what he called positive history, i.e., the factual reconstruction of some episode of the human past, and ideal history, by which he meant the philosophy of history. For Ferrari, positive history was a fascinating intellectual exercise of limited value to civilization. Basically, it provided information about isolated moments in the history of mankind, but it could not provide meaningful clues to the general trends of historical progress through the centuries. The philosophy of history, however, could be useful in forecasting the future course of a civilization. Its synthetic and abstract quality enabled its practitioner to transcend the idiosyncrasies of time, place, and culture and to understand the broad patterns of history. Thus, according to Ferrari, the philosopher of history could perform an extremely valuable social function. His insights, provided they were at some point accepted by the ruling groups and transformed into actual policies, could help his society to grow in the direction in which the universal history of mankind was moving, thus assuring its survival. There were, of course, limitations within which Ferrari's hypothetical philosopher of history must operate. His mission was not to predict the future in every detail but to suggest directions. Therefore, whenever he received public recognition, he must take care not to become conceited or, worse still, subservient toward those who honored him. And he must resist the temptation of facile syntheses in which disparate and even contradictory elements from various stages of civilization were artfully blended together. It was not difficult to detect in these warnings to future philosophers of history an attack against the eclectic school of Victor Cousin. Ferrari's criticism perhaps reflected his knowledge that Cousin had recently opposed his candidacy to a second *concours d'agrégation*.

If the *Essai sur le principe* did little to improve the relationship between its author and Cousin, it was generally well received. Villemain showed his appreciation (and perhaps his desire to atone for his role in the Strasbourg debacle) by endorsing Ferrari's successful application for French citizenship. Ironically, just as Ferrari was making this political commitment to France, he had to turn his attention once again to the problems of his native country. Buloz had entrusted to him a new series of articles concerning the most recent philosophical and political trends across the Alps.

Ferrari's first piece for the new series, an essay on the revival of Catholic thought in Italy, placed him at the center of yet another heated controversy.[50] The philosophical tradition of the Enlightenment and the political ideals of freedom and equality introduced by the French Revolution had not entirely disappeared from Italy, he wrote, but they had suffered a decline. Contrary to the expectations of liberal thinkers like Mamiani, the Italy of the 1840s did not seem very conscious of her Renaissance heritage. Under the influence of Romantic ideals, her leading artists and writers looked to the Christian culture of the Middle Ages for inspiration. In a similar vein, her most significant thinkers were attempting to bring about a revival of Catholic thought. Recognizing the importance of this revival, Ferrari discussed at length the leading Italian Catholic philosopher of his day, Antonio Rosmini-Serbati. His appraisal, although still very critical, was a far cry from the youthful outburst of scorn by which a decade earlier he had assailed Rosmini's influence.

At the heart of Rosmini's philosophical system was an attempt to create a synthesis between Tomistic and modern thought, particularly the various theories of historical progress that had been formulated since the eighteenth century. Ferrari, who had questioned the viability of such a synthesis in his previous essays, wrote a detailed refutation of Rosminian philosophy. As he suggested in a letter to Lorenzo Valerio, such a refutation was designed not only to serve the interest of philosophical truth, but also to expose and to counter the political implications of the neoguelph revival.[51] Indeed, "La philosophie catholique en Italie" is more important as a political document than as a philosophical essay.

For all its contradictions, he wrote, Rosmini's thought represented a very serious attempt to place Italy once again into the mainstream of European culture. The Catholic philosopher proposed to accomplish this through the modernization of theology and the training of a new elite capable of shaking Italy out of her intellectual and moral inertia. But, Ferrari thought, the new role of intellectual and moral leadership that Rosmini claimed for the Church might well lead to political dominance. This was especially true given the weakness of the Italian states, the absence of political or military figures of a stature comparable to the pope, and the primitive level of political organization even among the educated classes. If the leading member of the Catholic philosophical revival shied away from the theocratic implications of his system and professed satisfaction with the political status quo in Italy, lesser figures in the movement were not equally reticent. Among those followers of Rosmini who looked to the Church for political leadership Ferrari singled out, as a rather extreme example, the Dalmatian Niccoló Tommaseo, whom he had met in Paris. Finally, Ferrari discussed his recent antagonist Gioberti, now an exile in Brussels. Much more politically minded than Rosmini, Ferrari wrote, Gioberti showed considerable interest in the emergence of a neo-guelph party. In pursuit of political influence he did not hesitate to flatter his countrymen with the absurd notion of a "primacy" of Italian civilization in Europe, which would become apparent in a new political order under the hegemony of the pope. Fortunately for Italy, Ferrari concluded, most advocates of political change could read through Gioberti's ambitions and were choosing other alternatives:

Fortunately, an already large group is forming that shall be able some day to rally the Italians to a truly fruitful principle of unity. This party does not seek Italian unity . . . in ecclesiastical utopias destined to die in some vestry. No, this party seeks a focus and a foundation for a national movement in European ideas, in the religion of the modern state, in that constitutional ideology that Italy finds irresistible. This party is not afraid to open Italy up to foreign ideas, because it knows that in the application of such ideas the Italian genius shall always take the upper hand.[52]

The Italian community in Paris reacted swiftly and angrily to Ferrari's essay. His barely veiled accusations against Gioberti, which could not be proved, exposed the editor of the *Revue des deux Mondes* to the risk of a libel suit. Under the circumstances, many readers of the *Revue* assumed that Ferrari was simply trying to get even with Gioberti for the insult suffered in 1842.

No one who had shared with Ferrari the frustrations of the Strasbourg experience could doubt that thoughts of revenge had indeed been lurking in his mind. But Ferrari's critique of Gioberti was inspired not just by personal antagonism but also by a genuine fear of a successful neo-guelph movement in Italy. In Gioberti he saw a skillful polemicist who might convince the Italian people that the pope held the key to their political progress as well as to their spiritual welfare. As long as Gregory XVI, a man who distrusted change in any form, sat on the papal throne, Gioberti's political dreams seemed likely to remain just that. But the incumbent was getting on in years. What if Gregory's successor were to be a man of political ambition, or perhaps simply a weak man who could be manipulated by others? A nationalist-clerical coalition in Italy was a real, if dreadful, possibility—hence the need to watch the political scene closely.

In 1844, Ferrari resolved to visit Lombardy in order to gather firsthand information about the political situation there and to see his family and friends. But his trip would have to be brief; he did not wish to lose touch with French politics. Always hoping for an academic reinstatement, he followed with enthusiasm the campaign that Quinet and Michelet were waging against clerical influence in the universities.[53] His departure for Italy, scheduled for the summer of 1844, was postponed to the end of the year because of bureaucratic hurdles in obtaining a visa for Lombardy and also because of Fauriel's death in August.[54]

While he was in Milan, the *Revue des deux Mondes* published his second article on the Italian Question, "La révolution et les révolutionnaries en Italie." It was a model of historical analysis and political insight that has stood well the test of time. Italy, he wrote, was a country of paradox. After fifty years of revolutionary turmoil she was still under the heel of Austria and the Holy See. Given French laws during the Great Revolution, she had made no effort to reject them; deprived of them in 1815, she had made no effort to defend them. She had known insurrections that had succeeded too easily and repressions unrestrained by popular resistance.[55]

The obvious contradictions in Italian politics, such as the constant revolutionary tensions without a revolution, could be traced back to the years of French domination. The changes imposed by the French had split politically conscious Italians into three distinct parties, which had continued to exist after the Congress of Vienna. The absolutists, as Ferrari called them, had opposed both the ideals of the French Revolution and the hegemony of France in Italy. After the defeat of Napoleon, the political and military might of Austria and the appalling ignorance of the populace had made possible their return to positions of power. But they were constantly challenged by the other groups. The Italian democrats (as Ferrari called the Jacobins) had known a fleeting moment of glory under French protection. But they had paid dearly for it. In the eyes of many Italians they had become identified with heavy taxation, with the Napoleonic wars, and with outrages against the pope. Finally, between the absolutists and the democrats a third force had emerged, which Ferrari called the national party. The nationalists had been hostile to the French Empire. But they accepted two cardinal principles of the French Revolution, constitutional government and equality before the law. No friends of the Jacobins, they were cast in the mold of moderate French or English liberals. For all their differences and rivalries these three groups shared an important feature: none of them had a basis of support among the Italian masses, who remained largely indifferent to politics.

What did the future hold for these emerging parties? According to Ferrari, the days of the absolutists, already driven to excesses of cruelty and repression by an endless chain of conspiracies and insurrections, were numbered. Because the absolutists were, for the most part, members of the aristocracy or the clergy, they had once enjoyed a distinct advantage over their opponents: the masses, particularly the peasantry, had traditionally looked up to them as natural leaders. But during the Restoration the absolutists had managed to dissipate this initial advantage by neglecting the material needs of the masses. They had abandoned the practices of enlightened despotism in favor of despotism pure and simple.

Although his sympathies were clearly with the Italian democrats, Ferrari acknowledged that their future was not bright. He was convinced that a revolutionary program could not succeed in Italy if it remained restricted to one social class, in this case the educated bourgeoisie, or at least that part of it that had broken with the Church. In 1844, at any rate, a democratic revolution did not seem feasible. The really significant developments of the decade seemed to be taking place within the national party.

In 1815 the nationalists had been forced to go underground. But they had not disappeared. Indeed, from the Congress of Vienna to the early 1830s, they had been the chief critics of the status quo in Italy, sometimes the promoters of rebellion, and very often the victims of repression. But over the years the heavy prison sentences meted out by the governments to their intellectual critics and the unmitigated failures of rebellion had dictated important changes in nationalist tactics. Turning away from dreams of an independent Italy and of a direct confrontation with Austria, the nationalists had focused their attention upon less ambitious goals, such as the improvement of trade relations among the Italian states, the exchange of scientific and technical knowledge, and the refinement and promotion of the national literary language. These initiatives had set the country on the path of much-needed economic modernization and had fostered a climate of national unity. But, Ferrari observed, by the early 1840s all of the progress that could be achieved within this context had been achieved. A new generation of nationalists, more self-confident and less tried by disappointments and persecutions, realized that further modernization required a political solution of the Italian question. But to alter the political status quo in Italy meant war with Austria. Where would the Italian nationalists find an ally? Ferrari concluded his essay with a discussion of the various alternatives that seemed available to the Italian nationalists.

There was, first of all, Gioberti's curious marriage of nationalist and clerical interests. Because in Ferrari's view modernization was synonymous with secularization, he found it absurd to hope that the papacy would preside over a development contrary to its teachings and to its interests. The Piedmontese writer Cesare Balbo offered a second alternative, an alliance between the nationalists and the House of Savoy. Such an alliance, Balbo hoped, would eventually put pressure on Austria to relinquish control of northern Italy and to find compensation in the Balkans at the expense of the Ottoman Empire. A clever plan, Ferrari observed, but a dangerous one. In the rather unlikely event that Austria took the bait, it would result in a substantial aggrandizement of Piedmont-Sardinia. As a Lombard and a French citizen, Ferrari saw in Balbo's *Le speranze d'Italia* a sort of trial balloon of Piedmontese ambitions; and as such he denounced it.

He much preferred a third alternative, the program of Giuseppe Mazzini, which combined nationalist and democratic principles: "Fiery, impulsive, animated by the faith of a martyr combined with the feverish activity of a conspirator, he found no question too difficult to tackle; . . . to continue the mission of the men of 1793, to join hands with Young France, Young Germany, Young Poland; to break with the aristocracy, with royalty, with the papacy, with the past; such was the program outlined by Mazzini in the first issue of his *Young Italy*."[56]

Ferrari's portrait of Mazzini, a sympathetic and sensitive one, paid high tribute to his courage and self-denial. It also praised the Mazzinian program as the only one that required a sharp break with Italy's past and was attuned to the contemporary intellectual and political trends in Europe. At this time, Ferrari even sympathized with Mazzini's goal of a centralized and republican form of government for an independent Italy. The events that eventually led him to criticize Mazzini from a federalist perspective were still a few years away.[57] But his positive evaluation of the Mazzinian movement was tempered by some misgivings concerning its future. Although unsuccessful, insurrections such as those of 1831 and 1834 had exposed the relative weakness of the Italian states and had called the Italian Question to the attention of foreigners. But, Ferrari wrote, unless the Mazzinians could somehow move beyond these heroic and desperate tactics they would ultimately fail to free and to unite their country. Mazzini blamed his own cadres for their inability to arouse the populace. Apparently he did not realize that the leadership could transmit to the masses specific ideas or directives but not the spirit of revolution, which must arise independently and spontaneously. The Italian people for the most part lacked that spirit, because they saw no advantage to themselves in the moral and political revolution to which Mazzini had devoted his life. In Ferrari's words: "If [material] means without ideas cannot arouse the masses, ideas without means are worthless weapons. Mazzini relied on ideas and he proclaimed liberty to rally the people. Unfortunately, he forgot that the only enduring liberty is that which corresponds to the true needs of the masses."[58]

In this essay Ferrari did not really explain what he meant by "the true needs of the masses." Presumably he meant the social and economic needs of the lower classes, which Buchez regarded as the central mission of the Christian in the nineteenth century and which the socialist Leroux regarded as the logical concern of the intellectual and political heirs to the French Revolution. At any rate, Ferrari had not yet developed a full-fledged critique of the Mazzinian program from a radical-socialist perspective. The necessary stimuli for such a development came later, through the revolutionary experiences of 1848–49 and through his encounter with Pierre-Joseph Proudhon.

While working on the articles discussed above, Ferrari became much more interested in the affairs of his native country than he had been upon his arrival in Paris. His new attitude did not change his relationship with the Italian exiles, who continued to ostracize him, but it strengthened his friendship with Cristina di Belgiojoso. The relationship between Ferrari and the princess was the source of some gossip within the Italian community in Paris.[59] While there is no evidence that he ever became her lover, he certainly admired her and he enjoyed the atmosphere of sophisticated luxury that surrounded her, complementing her legendary beauty. Brought up in the comfortable but austere world of the Milanese bourgeoisie of his day, Ferrari had learned over the years to appreciate the more refined life-style of well-to-do Parisians. Unfortunately, in the pursuit of refinement his expenses began to outrun his income.

In the fall of 1845, Ferrari wrote to his brother that he wished to meet with him and negotiate a new settlement concerning their joint properties.[60] The high cost of living in Paris was only one reason why he was asking for a new settlement. He also wanted some capital of his own to invest in the real estate speculations that were then sweeping through the French business community like an epidemic fever. Around 1845 speculators were especially active in the X^e arrondissement, where rail lines were being built leading into the Gare de l'Est and the Gare du Nord. Ferrari had his eye on some properties in that area. Eventually, on the advice of his banker Gargantini, he purchased two buildings which provided him with an income for the rest of his life. The necessary capital came from the inheritance of Giovanni and Francesco Ferrari, but arranging for a permanent division between himself and Carlo proved to be difficult.[61]

In the spring of 1846, news that his mother was ailing and pleading for his return added a new urgency to his travel plans. But before leaving Paris he had to finish another assignment for the *Revue des deux Mondes*[62] and obtain a visa for Lombardy. The Habsburg government had acknowledged Ferrari's change of citizenship and had classified him as a voluntary emigrant from the Kingdom of Lombardy-Venetia. As a property owner, however, he had retained the privilege of returning to his native city whenever his business affairs required his presence there.[63] Thus, he was shocked to learn in July 1846 that a new visa would not be forthcoming from the Austrian embassy in Paris. His brother and his friend and attorney Alessandro Porro counseled patience. They pointed out that his right to return to Milan was clearly protected under Habsburg law, and they attributed the delay to bureaucratic ineptitude.[64] Taking their advice, Ferrari remained in Paris a little longer. Meanwhile, he followed the ups and downs of the Paris Bourse and the real estate market.[65] Prices were falling with the onset of the economic crisis that would soon spell trouble for the regime of Louis-Philippe. Convinced that the time was right for purchasing property in Paris, Ferrari fretted over his brother's reluctance to proceed with a permanent division of their inheritance and over the inexplicable silence of the Austrian embassy.[66]

In 1844 the Habsburg authorities had not objected to Ferrari's return to Milan, but much had changed in only two years. The deteriorating political situation within the Kingdom of Lombardy-Venetia was making them more cautious and suspicious than ever before. By September 1846 even the optimistic Porro concluded that the inactivity of the Austrian embassy in Paris was politically motivated.[67] Although Ferrari had truthfully stated in his application that he was returning to Milan to settle his private affairs, it was easy for the Habsburg authorities to suspect that he might also have other motives. But Austrian law clearly granted him the privilege of conducting business in Milan—hence the unexplained delays instead of the outright refusal of a visa. Ferrari's only recourse was a petition to prince Metternich himself, in which he asserted his rights as a property owner but also pleaded for the privilege of embracing his mother.[68] Before any decision had been reached in Vienna, he learned that her health had taken a turn for the worse. He departed immediately for Lugano, but she died before he even got to the Swiss border.[69]

He remained in Lugano from mid-November 1846 to mid-March 1847, four months that seemed like four years. Each day he waited anxiously and in vain for a word from the imperial government. Shrouded in the winter fog, the bare hillside orchards and vineyards and the grey waters of Lake Lugano matched his mood of sadness and despondency. The tidbits of political information that came from Italy tantalized his curiosity. The news was encouraging one day, disconcerting the next, but always interesting. As to France, this was no time for Ferrari to be away. His friends wrote of stormy debates in the French Parliament, of the possible fall of Guizot, and of mounting opposition to the regime. The political changes that he had awaited for five years now seemed in the offing. He resolved to leave Lugano as soon as the Alpine passes were free of fresh snow, even though the new property settlement had not been made final.

The most exciting and frustrating news awaited him in Paris. Edgar Quinet had recommended him for a position as *professeur suppléant* at the Collège de France. The faculty of the Collège had approved the appointment, but the ministry had refused to concur.[70] There is no doubt that this new disappointment contributed to the political radicalization of Giuseppe Ferrari. By the summer of 1847, he could be counted among those intellectuals who had lost hope in the ability of the Orleanist regime to reform itself along democratic lines.

To his chagrin, another trip to Lugano became necessary, between August and October 1847, in order to prod the ever-reluctant Carlo into a final settlement. After a heated argument, the two brothers agreed that Giuseppe's share of the joint properties would be sold at a public auction. But, perhaps because of the general economic crisis of that year, no serious bidders could be found. In the end, Gargantini, from whose Paris bank Giuseppe Ferrari had already borrowed a substantial sum, came to the rescue by buying him out. The resulting cash settlement enabled him to pay his debts, make a down payment on the Parisian properties mentioned earlier, and furnish his apartment.[71]

During this second trip to Lugano he was seized by an intense desire to see his native city. But a letter from Porro, smuggled across the border amidst legal papers, gave him a very pessimistic account of the current crisis in the Kingdom of Lombardy-Venetia and warned him not to attempt an illegal entry.[72] Ferrari recognized that this was indeed a friend's advice, and he returned to France posthaste. Back in Paris by early November 1847, he was quickly caught up in the heady atmosphere of the political banquets. For nearly ten years he had studied the social and political system of Orleanist France. But despite his friendship with politically active men like Buchez, Leroux, and Quinet, he had remained very much on the sidelines. The events of 1847 prepared him, it seems, to become directly involved in the political tragedy that was about to unfold.

[3]
The Crucible of 1848

FOR FERRARI, as for most radical and socialist thinkers of the nineteenth century, the last decade of the July Monarchy was a time for learning, for experimenting, for thinking about the whole range of issues that confronted European civilization as the first industrial revolution quickened the pace of change. During that period of ideological and political preparation, Ferrari became acquainted with some currents of French socialism, he learned to look critically at the liberal monarchy of Louis-Philippe, and he began a lifelong crusade against the intellectual and political influence of the Roman Catholic Church. Moreover, he began to reflect seriously upon the Italian Question. For him as for many others of his generation, the Revolution of 1848 was the great crucible in which ideas and experiences were tested. At the end of the revolutionary period, his philosophical and political position was articulated in a series of important works around three interrelated principles: secularism, socialism, and federalism.

That by 1847 Ferrari could be counted among the left-wing opponents of the Orleanist regime can be inferred by the government's veto of his appointment to the faculty of the Collège de France. At that point he abandoned his previous reluctance to associate with Leroux and became a contributor to the *Revue indépendante*.[1] Within the Leroux-Sand circle he met two well-known republican opponents of the regime, Louis Michel of Bourges and Pascal Duprat, as well as Victor Schoelcher, the abolitionist, and the maverick theologian Félicité de Lamennais.[2] In his criticism of the liberal monarchy Ferrari did not go as far as these men. Certainly he did not anticipate its sudden collapse in February 1848. At the first signs of serious unrest in Paris, he reported for duty with the National Guard, as was expected of any good bourgeois. But upon the abdication of Louis-Philippe he sided unequivocally with the advocates of a democratic republic. Given the Assembly's reluctance to accept a regency under the duchess of Orleans, this seemed the only acceptable alternative.[3]

His views at the beginning of the revolution were expressed in three editorials that he wrote for Le Peuple constituant, a democratic-republican newspaper founded by Lamennais and Duprat. The monarchy, he wrote, had created a gulf between the few who had political and economic power and the many who had nothing. A republic based upon universal suffrage could unite the French people, heretofore divided. But it was important to avoid new rifts in the body politic while trying to heal the old. Pointing out the increasing antagonism of the Parisian workers toward the bourgeoisie at a time of high bread prices and high unemployment, he stressed that the new republic must be built upon two principles: the sanctity of private property and "the organization of labor." By this he meant new legislation to curb the exploitation of the workers and limited state intervention in times of severe economic distress. The ideal republic, he wrote, was one built upon an alliance of National Guard and populace, of bourgeoisie and workers. His was a Jacobin position, not a socialist one; he was arguing for the principles of 1793, updated to include a greater awareness of the social conditions of contemporary France and expanded to allow for direct participation by the workers in the political process.[4]

Although he did not anticipate the fall of Louis-Philippe, toward the end of 1847 Ferrari watched with eager expectation the swelling of a revolutionary tide in Italy. He analyzed the Italian situation in two articles for the Revue indépendante, the first of which dealt with a favorite topic of his, the Italian Renaissance. For all its achievements, he wrote, the Italian Renaissance had ended with a political catastrophe. The most widely accepted interpretation of Italy's decline after a period of European prominence held that the Italian states, small and at odds with one another, had succumbed to the ambition of stronger powers. But this interpretation raised more questions than it answered. In the first place, Ferrari pointed out, the Italian governments of the Renaissance had not been the innocent victims of aggression. To some extent, their own policies had invited foreign intervention. Besides, in medieval times independent communes like Milan had successfully resisted any outside threats to their liberty. If the Signorie of the Renaissance had failed to do so it was not because they had lacked the means, but perhaps because they had lacked the will to resist. He wrote:

Such was the Renaissance; it was a new Italy arising from the ruins of the old. In politics she demanded the independence of an Italian confederation; with her Greco-Roman culture she protested against feudal theocracy in Europe; she wanted to submit to the rule of reason even the papal and imperial traditions that had survived in Italy. It was obvious that the future belonged to the Renaissance. Unfortunately, on the soil of the peninsula the Renaissance defeated the principles of the Middle Ages without destroying them; it oppressed the old Italy without killing her.[5]

Confident in the wisdom and power of the new ideas, the intellectuals and the statesmen of the Renaissance had ignored or ridiculed the persistence of traditions deeply rooted in the country's past. By the early sixteenth century, the old allegiances to pope and emperor had once again surfaced; the moral principles of the papacy had triumphed over the secular spirit of the Renaissance, and the myth of a universal political community had triumphed over the emerging consciousness of national differences. With the victory of what Ferrari called "the imperial and papal restoration," sixteenth-century Italy had parted ways with the rest of western Europe:

The Renaissance was then forced to abandon . . . Italy, but she continued her great mission in exile. In Germany she became the Reformation, and there she made a great revolution against papacy and empire in the name of faith. Later on, and still in exile, she became the century of Louis XIV in France, . . . theocracy gave way to absolutism; Europe attained a universal language. Finally, eighteenth-century France proclaimed the religion of mankind; then the Renaissance became the French Revolution in the world and it marked the beginning of a universal regeneration. Having accomplished this, the Renaissance knocked once again at Italy's doors.[6]

In the liberal movement of his day Ferrari saw—to use his metaphor—the Italian Renaissance returning to its ancestral land after an exile of three hundred years.[7]

His second contribution to Leroux's journal appeared on 10 January 1848, just as the first reports of revolutionary outbreaks in southern Italy were reaching Paris. "Italy wants to awaken from centuries of enervating slumber," he wrote. "Two paths are open to her: the path of reform or that of revolution. The reforms strengthen absolutism and abandon the future of the peninsula to it; the revolution breaks the yoke of traditional authority and entrusts Italy's future to the genius of her people. . . . Reforms or constitutions, absolutism or revolution: this is Italy's dilemma."[8]

As prince Metternich had understood so well in 1815, centralization of government functions, modernization of the bureaucracy, and liberalization of ancient legal codes were the best guarantees of political stability. For that reason Vienna had pressured the Italian governments of the Restoration to move ahead with moderate reforms. Only one of them, the papal government, had dragged its feet. But now, in a curious reversal of roles, the reforming impulse came from the Rome of Pope Pius IX, and not from the Vienna of the inept Ferdinand I. The popularity of the pope in Italy obscured the fact that he was doing essentially the same things that Metternich had done in the 1820s. He was prolonging the life of the Old Regime by making it more tolerable. To Ferrari's chagrin, many Italian liberals misinterpreted the purpose of the papal reforms and of the changes that were taking place in Milan, Turin, and Naples. But he hoped that the revolutionary elements of whom he had written in 1845 might resist the lure of reform. He wrote: "First of all, the revolution must renew the social contract in each of the states. If she wants to begin her task by the attainment of unity, she is doomed. Italian unity exists only in the realm of literature and poetry; in that realm one cannot recruit armies or organize a political system. Let us eschew the realm of poetry, or we shall slip on the blood of the Bandiera brothers.[19] With this reference to the Bandiera brothers, who had sacrificed their young lives to the dream of a free and united Italy, Ferrari began a critique of Mazzini's ideas and methods.

First of all, while he recognized that cultural and political nationalism had made much progress in recent years, he felt that to subordinate the pursuit of liberty to the attainment of a united Italian state was to prolong the supremacy of Austria and the papacy. A political revolution, he wrote, could be carried out within each of the Italian states without leading immediately to unification. Second, Ferrari criticized Mazzini's reliance on secret societies. He had already expressed reservations on this subject in his essay of 1845. Secret societies not only invited repression, with the inevitable loss of lives and talents, but they also restricted the numbers of potential supporters of the revolution. If they had been useful to spread revolutionary ideas and to train cadres in the early days of the liberal movement, by the late 1840s they were becoming a liability to the cause of political progress. There was, Ferrari wrote, an outlet for liberal propaganda that was more effective and less risky: "Let the liberals transform the [advisory councils] into legislative bodies; let them put men from their own ranks in positions of power. They should not seek such men amidst the debris of secret societies and Carbonarism; they should rely upon the unique power of publicity."[10]

Anticipating Mazzinian objections that separate revolutionary initiatives in the various Italian states were bound to split the liberal movement, Ferrari argued that the main liberal aspirations (a constitution, representative government, and freedom of the press) were essentially the same everywhere in Italy. Once liberal elements had taken control of their respective states, an Italian federation would surely arise out of the need to defend the liberal movement against Austrian pressure. A federation of liberal governments would be able to raise a citizens' army to defend the revolution, just as the French Republic had done in 1792. And he was confident that the Italian liberals would receive help from other countries if and when they were ready for a war against Austria.[11] Was a federation of constitutional states to be the terminal point of Italy's political development? Perhaps not, but any talk of unification, he insisted, was premature as long as the Italian people did not enjoy political freedom.[12]

In January and February 1848, the reports from Italy seemed to justify Ferrari's moderate optimism. Everywhere the Italian liberals were asking for constitutional government and freedom of the press. Aided by unrest among the populace, the "conspiracy in broad daylight" that he advocated seemed to be making steady progress. But ironically, the crisis of the Orleanist regime thwarted his hopes for gradual change in Italy. News of the Parisian revolution encouraged radical groups to call for the immediate overthrow of the Italian governments in an atmosphere of popular excitement and confusion.[13]

Had Ferrari remained in Paris during the spring of 1848, he might have discovered how far removed France was from his ideal republic of democratic harmony and social compromise. But by the end of March he had already returned to the University of Strasbourg. The revolution of February 1848 brought to power political leaders more in tune with his ideas and less likely to heed Catholic objections to his teaching. By a stroke of luck, Hippolyte Carnot, a close friend of Reynaud, became minister of Public Education in the Provisional Government, and he reappointed Ferrari as *professeur suppléant* at Strasbourg.[14]

To the pleasure of greeting again the ancient Alsatian capital was added the excitement of a letter from his friend Giulio Caimi describing the recent Milanese insurrection against Habsburg rule.[15] From occasional hints in Porro's letters Ferrari already knew that Milan had been seething with political discontent. But the news of the successful uprising took him by surprise. It seemed oddly out of character for the placid burghers of Milan and for its usually docile populace to have taken up arms against Radetzky's soldiers. It was truly hard to believe that the scholarly Cattaneo had played a major role in the insurrection. And there were disturbing rumors of a forthcoming union between Lombardy and the Kingdom of Sardinia. Ferrari's curiosity grew enormously, and he resolved to leave Strasbourg as soon as the university closed for the Easter recess. By 24 April 1848 he was back in his native city.

Although his relatives had made preparations for his visit, he spurned their hospitality, preferring instead to stay with friends. Carlo Ferrari was hurt by his brother's behavior, because he had awaited an opportunity for reconciliation after the recent family quarrels. Giuseppe held no grudge against his family, and he was fond of his nephews Giovanni and Cristoforo and his niece Giuditta. But the political events of 1848 had exacerbated the old differences between the Ferrari brothers. The elder, a conservative by temperament and conviction, mourned the loss of political stability and feared the loss of his livelihood, while the younger plunged with the zest of a neophyte into the turbid waters of Milanese politics.[16]

Only one month had elapsed since the extraordinary victory of the Milanese people against Radetzky's army. But already the popular enthusiasm that had sustained the insurrection seemed to have waned. Ferrari found an apathetic and demoralized populace and leaders bitterly divided by social and political conflicts. The middle-class radicals who had led the fight on the barricades urged preparations for the defense of Lombardy, and they called for a constituent assembly and for an alliance with republican France. But the moderate liberals whose control of the Lombard Provisional Government had been gained through their social and political prominence feared the implications of placing guns and ballots in the hands of the masses. They much preferred to entrust the defense of their region to the army of King Charles Albert, whose intervention they had solicited. As for the future, a union with Piedmont-Sardinia was more palatable to them than an independent and perhaps democratic Lombard state.[17]

Ferrari's background, his growing political consciousness, and his identification with the French revolutionary government hardly allowed him to remain a passive spectator. If he regretted having to choose between friends, he could not fail to back the radicals.[18] Given his commitments in Strasbourg, he was unable to spend much time in Milan. But during his brief visit he helped Cattaneo and Enrico Cernuschi, a younger man who had made a name for himself during the insurrection, to raise money for an independent newspaper that was intended to counteract the pro-Piedmontese line of the official *Ventidue marzo*. More important, he arranged a meeting between Cattaneo and Mazzini, who had arrived in Milan surreptitiously at the end of April 1848.[19] A few days in his native city had convinced Ferrari that his radical friends faced an uphill battle. They needed allies, and Mazzini seemed the obvious choice. He might be persuaded to call upon his Lombard supporters to aid in the overthrow of the Provisional Government. And he might be willing to help raise volunteer forces in other parts of Italy for a revolutionary war in the North.[20] It was not easy to persuade Cattaneo to attend the meeting. He regarded Mazzini as an intruder and he was hostile to the *programma unitario*. But Ferrari was very persuasive, and the meeting took place on 30 April 1848. Many years later Ferrari still remembered it as one of the most wretched days in his life.[21]

Far from unleashing his followers against the Provisional Government, Mazzini urged cooperation with it and the postponement of plans for a constituent assembly until after the end of the war. Moreover, he was adamantly opposed to French intervention. An alliance with France, he argued, must come only after Italy, or at least its northern portion, had achieved independence. From Ferrari's viewpoint all this was disappointing enough. To make matters worse, Cattaneo lost his temper and accused Mazzini of being in the pay of Charles Albert. It was an unjust insult, one that Mazzini never forgot.[22]

Early in May, Ferrari journeyed back to France. He was disgusted but not surprised when he heard of the referendum by which Lombardy was virtually merged with the Kingdom of Sardinia. In France he found an equally bleak situation. The elections of April 1848, held on the basis of universal manhood suffrage, had produced a moderate to conservative majority in the National Assembly. At the same time, misery and frustration had increased among the Parisian poor and among workers from other parts of France who had been lured to the capital by the prospect of a job in the National Workshops. Reports from Paris raised grave doubts in Ferrari's mind as to the stability of the French Republic, and he concluded that a future intervention in favor of the Italian radicals was most improbable.[23]

This unsettled political climate affected him personally in various ways. Because the university had been closed briefly following the February revolution, the Rector postponed the end of the academic year. Ferrari had contemplated a return to Paris and then a trip to Milan in June or early July, but he was forced to change his plans. As a result of the persisting economic crisis, some of his tenants had fallen behind in their rent payments. Although for the time being he could live on his academic salary, he was understandably concerned about the future of the French economy in general and of his Parisian properties in particular.[24] But to be relatively isolated from the turmoil of French politics and from the war in northern Italy was not without advantages. Ferrari found time to reflect upon the recent events and to resume his political writings. During this period of relative tranquillity in Strasbourg, he finished a long essay on Machiavelli and wrote an outline for an interpretive work on the French Revolution.

But in June 1848 his peaceful life was shaken by reports of the Parisian workers' uprising and of Cavaignac's repression. The editorials in the local newspapers and the letters of his agent Pierre Charpenne gave him the impression that this uprising, like the republican one of 1839, had been inspired by a few agitators and that Cavaignac had acted in the best interests of the democratic republic.[25] Because he believed that the survival of the new political order depended upon an alliance between bourgeoisie and workers, Ferrari was troubled by these reports. But the full extent of the uprising and the consequences of Cavaignac's actions became clear to him only after he returned to Paris at the end of that summer.

The letters from Lombardy were even less comforting. News that Enrico Cernuschi had been imprisoned as the alleged leader of a plot to overthrow the Provisional Government and that Cattaneo himself was in political trouble were soon followed by reports that the war against Austria was going badly. Early in August, as Charles Albert's army was retreating from Lombardy, a desperate appeal for help came from the newly formed Committee of Public Safety.[26] Ferrari, who was preparing to go back to Paris, was deeply touched by it. Despite his love for France, he cared about his native region, and he was proud of what the people of Milan had done in March 1848. It was going to be difficult, he wrote, to convince the French government to negotiate with an independent Lombard delegation. Nonetheless, he was willing to try, provided he received the appropriate credentials from the Committee of Public Safety.[27] He waited in Strasbourg for a few more days, but the credentials that he had requested did not arrive. After Charles Albert's capitulation the Committee was unable to organize the defense of Milan. By 6 August 1848 the Habsburg eagles were flying once again over the Sforza Castle.

The Lombard revolution ended tragically for Ferrari's family and for many of his friends. His nephew Giovanni, who had enlisted in the Piedmontese army, was in a military hospital in Turin, severely wounded and without hope of ever returning to Milan. The Cattaneos had fled across the border to Lugano with little more than the clothes on their backs. So had Giovanni Carozzi and his sister Luisa, the wife of Antonio Gargantini. And the Porro brothers, now in exile, were punished for their role in the revolution by the confiscation of their property. Ferrari himself was directly, if less severely, affected. In view of his meddling in Milanese politics, the Habsburg authorities revoked his right of reentry into the Kingdom of Lombardy-Venetia.[28]

By mid-August 1848 he was back in Paris at last. From the Italian exiles who arrived by way of Switzerland he learned that Mazzini had formed a national committee with headquarters in Lugano. The founder of Young Italy was now willing to espouse Cattaneo's concept of a *guerra di popolo* against Austria and Ferrari's contention that the help of France was necessary to the success of the revolution in Italy. As a gesture of reconciliation toward the Mazzinians, Cattaneo traveled to Paris as one of three representatives of the committee.[29]

The French political climate had changed dramatically since March 1848. The country that had then proclaimed the principles of political democracy 'and revolutionary solidarity was now turning away from both under the de facto dictatorship of General Cavaignac. The personal experiences of Ferrari's own friends were a good indication of how much things had changed. Despite his moderate editorials and his support of Cavaignac, Duprat had been forced to suspend the publication of *Le Peuple constituant* in July.[30] Jean Reynaud, who had worked closely with Hippolyte Carnot in the reform of the primary schools, had been dismissed from the Ministry of Public Education.[31] In the spring of 1848 the Provisional Government had accepted a proposal by the painter Chenavard to transform the church of Sainte-Geneviève into a shrine of the new revolution. But the Cavaignac government refused further support for the project, which it judged offensive to the Catholic faith. Impoverished and politically disgraced, the artist chose to live in exile.[32]

As yet untouched by the chilly winds of reaction, Ferrari reflected over the meaning of the June Days. The only bright spot in this gloomy atmosphere was the presence in Paris of Cattaneo, who had decided to stay just long enough to write a book on the Milan insurrection. Ferrari urged him to settle in Paris and so did Anna Cattaneo's sister, Isabelle Brénier, who was married to a French diplomat.[33] But in October 1848 Cattaneo returned to Lugano, where his wife lay gravely ill.

Shortly after Cattaneo's departure Ferrari returned to Strasbourg. Preoccupied with politics, he had given little thought to his courses for the new academic year. But the events of November–December 1848 were such that he had little reason to regret his negligence. His career was once again disrupted when Carnot's successors at the Ministry of Public Education decided to restructure the Université. Seven districts were suppressed, while others were strengthened through the addition of chairs or the upgrading of existing lectureships. The University of Strasbourg was among those that were expanded and strengthened. But for

Ferrari these reforms by Cavaignac's ministers had disastrous consequences.[34]

He was not pleased to hear that his position was to be upgraded, because this meant facing another *concours d'agrégation*, for which he was inadequately prepared. He knew that his reinstatement in March 1848 had not been a reward for outstanding academic achievements, but was simply a sign of Carnot's appreciation for his radical political views and a belated compensation for the injustice suffered earlier. He also knew that he could not compete with men like Paul Janet or C. M. Jourdain who had held teaching positions for years. But since there was no real alternative, he appeared reluctantly before the board of examiners.[35]

As he had expected, he was unsuccessful. The new chair of philosophy at the University of Strasbourg went to Janet, a former teacher at the lycée of Bourges. Ferrari protested his dismissal. But his case was weak, particularly because he had previously admitted in a letter to Cousin his reluctance to face the *concours*. In his report to the ministry, in fact, Cousin used Ferrari's confession against him. Another examiner, Charles de Rémusat, later wrote that he had found Ferrari's presentation eloquent, original, and provocative, but not sufficiently solid for an aspiring academician.[36]

Although Ferrari recognized the weaknesses in his own preparation and the excellence of his successor's credentials, he suspected that Cousin, always the unreconstructed Orleanist, was using his influence to eliminate from the Université the supporters of the democratic republic. His suspicions obviously stemmed from the bitter memories of his previous dismissal from the University of Strasbourg. He had no hard evidence of Cousin's partisanship. And yet he was perhaps closer to the truth than he realized. In his report on the *concours*, in fact, Cousin praised the successful candidates for the sober balance with which they had treated controversial questions. He stressed, significantly, that they had said nothing offensive to morality, religion, or the state. Nearly one year after the fall of Louis-Philippe, conformity to the ideal of the *juste milieu* remained, it seems, an important prerequisite for academic appointments.[37]

Even if Ferrari had known the content of this report, his charges would have sounded hollow. It was a well-known fact that his friend Carnot during his tenure as minister of public education had forced the resignation of Legitimist and Orleanist professors from the Collège de France.[38] Ferrari, who had not protested Carnot's policies, was hardly in a position to complain now that the shoe was on the other foot. The ministry, in any event, was not entirely indifferent to his plight. As an alternative to unemployment he was offered Janet's former position at the lycée of Bourges. He accepted it, although he was reluctant to leave Paris, especially now that the mysterious figure of Louis Napoleon Bonaparte, victorious at the polls, loomed large on the political horizon.

Ferrari remained in Bourges from January to June 1849. His fears that in a provincial town he would be bored and isolated from politics proved completely unfounded. Political harassment, not boredom, made him miserable during his sojourn in that city. His reputation as a protégé of Carnot and a friend of Louis Michel, who represented his native Bourges in the National Assembly, assured him of a cordial reception in local republican and perhaps also in socialist circles.[39] But that reputation did not serve him equally well with his superiors at the lycée and with the prefect of the Department du Cher. They watched him closely from the very beginning.

Ferrari's troubles began with unfavorable reports on his teaching that the principal of the lycée forwarded to the ministry.[40] These reports contrasted sharply with the accounts of his performance at the lycée of Rochefort-sur-Mer. It was true, of course, that he had taken this new position reluctantly and that he hoped to return to university teaching. And it is also possible that over the years he had lost the art of inspiring an adolescent audience. But other aspects of Ferrari's experience in Bourges suggest that political as well as educational considerations lay behind the criticism.

Not only did he associate with the local radical circles, but he made no attempt to hide his political views from his colleagues and students. By early March 1849 his political ideas and connections had obviously come to the attention of the authorities. His superiors came under pressure from prominent citizens who threatened to withdraw their offspring from the lycée unless he and other allegedly subversive teachers were removed. By April or May it was clear to all concerned that he was persona non grata to many local notables. But the worst was yet to come.

The Parisian demonstrations of 13 June 1849 in support of the democratic republic and against the Roman expedition of General Oudinot were accompanied by similar incidents in other parts of France. In Bourges, demonstrations by radical and socialist clubs led to numerous arrests. Under questioning, one of the demonstrators told of an agitator who had allegedly come to Bourges from Paris, had blonde hair, long sideburns, and spoke with a foreign accent. This description fit Ferrari closely enough to warrant his suspension from teaching and a subpoena to appear before the magistrates who were investigating the left-wing clubs. Fearing the worst, Ferrari departed hastily for Paris. In July 1849 a new subpoena was issued along with a warrant for a search of his apartment in Paris. The authorities in Bourges then learned that he had moved his belongings to an unknown location and had crossed the border into Belgium.[41]

Ferrari remained in Brussels until December 1849. The material and psychological rigors of exile were made more tolerable by the friendship of a wealthy fellow Lombard, Giovanni Arrivabene, who had lived in Belgium since the 1820s.[42] Ferrari felt very bitter toward the leaders of the Université, and particularly toward Cousin. But political persecution and exile made him more open and compassionate in his dealings with past political adversaries, including Mazzini. At this point, both men seemed willing to forget the unfortunate confrontation of April 1848. Mazzini advised: "How can you . . . continue to preach that *hors de la France point de salut*? We cannot call for the intervention of France such as she is today. You must overthrow the present system, you must put the Mountain into power, but it must not give birth to a mouse. . . . Let them at the same time organize a republican movement, then we shall invite our *frères*. For the time being you must wage war against those who have betrayed the republic."[43] Within his limited means, Ferrari was more than willing to follow Mazzini's advice. But before returning to the political struggle in France he had to await the outcome of the Bourges trials. Fortunately for him, all charges against the demonstrators of June 1849 were dropped, and he was able to return safely to Paris. Yet this time even the sight of the familiar and beloved streets of the Left Bank could not lift his spirits.[44]

In February 1850 he was again involved in a political trial. The opposition newspaper *La Liberté* had published three articles suggesting that a coup d'état was in the offing. Charged with inciting popular sentiment against the government of the republic, its editor had named Ferrari as his source. At the trial Ferrari stated that a highly placed official had indeed spoken to him about plans for a coup, but he refused to give the official's name. His source may have been Cattaneo's brother-in-law, Alexandre-Anatole Brénier, a moderate conservative who later sided with Bonaparte and was rewarded with important diplomatic posts.[45]

From the early months of 1850 until the Bonapartist coup of 1851, Ferrari struggled to understand the political tragedies that had crippled his two homelands. As always, he found solace in writing. His work in the quiet solitude of his Paris apartment was frequently interrupted by the arrival of refugees from Italy. The compassion that he displayed toward them contrasted sharply with the aloof and contemptuous behavior of his first years in Paris. Obviously, life had taught him a few hard lessons.[46] The exiles who came by way of Switzerland brought messages from both Cattaneo and Mazzini. The former had settled in the Lugano area, where he had found a business partner, the publisher Alessandro Repetti, for a series of works on the Italian Revolution, the *Archivio triennale delle cose d'Italia*. For this project Cattaneo solicited the help of Ferrari, whose opinions he respected and whose company both he and Anna enjoyed.[47] Appeals of a different nature came from Mazzini. Convinced that the recent events represented only a temporary setback for Italian nationalism, he was busy raising funds for a newspaper and trying to float an Italian national loan to finance a future revolution; he solicited Ferrari's help for both of these projects.[48] Disappointed that Cattaneo had decided not to move to Paris, Ferrari was eager to join him in Lugano and to help with the editing of the *Archivio triennale*. But he turned a deaf ear to Mazzini's request for cooperation. In October 1850, having just read the latest proclamation of the Italian National Committee, he wrote:

My dearest Mazzini,
    I have been very unhappy with your manifestos; . . . I respect you, I make no accusations against you personally; but if you persist on the same path, you will lose your honor.
    We Italians made three mistakes in 1848: we listened to the Church; we disregarded France; and we failed to proclaim independent republics [in northern Italy]. You made *all* of those mistakes. When it was imperative to resist the false influence of Pius IX, you supported him; when it was imperative to invoke the help of France, you accepted the password of the moderates, *"L'Italia fà da se"*; when it was imperative to proclaim independent republics, you restrained the republican initiative for the sake of a plan for unity that subordinated it to the whim of a king. Your message was ambiguous, monarchical-republican, revolutionary-Catholic. . . . What are you doing now? You are making the same mistakes, you seem determined to lay the foundations of a new catastrophe.
    Your ambivalence is even more disturbing when you talk about political institutions. . . . The word "republic" disappears. . . . You sacrifice it to unity, unification, fusion. . . .
    These are harsh words, my dear Mazzini; they are an unkind response to your friendly inquiries. But I told you the truth, I owed you this much. Should Italy be freed by means of intrigue; should she accomplish her revolution without regard to truth and justice, I shall never wish to see her again.[49]

Within a year, with the publication of Ferrari's *La Federazione repubblicana* and his *Filosofia della Rivoluzione*, the rift between him and Mazzini became irreparable and public.

Ferrari spent the better part of 1851 in the Lugano area. Like Cattaneo, he hoped to see Repetti's publishing firm, the Tipografia Elvetica, prosper as a center of anti-Piedmontese and anti-Mazzinian propaganda.[50] In the summer of 1851 he began to make plans for a political party with a republican, socialist, and federalist program, and he contacted potential supporters among the Italian exiles in various countries. In Paris he could count upon Cernuschi, Carozzi, and the Tuscan exile Giuseppe Montanelli; in Turin, upon Angelo Brofferio and Gino Daelli, a former manager of the Tipografia Elvetica. But Cattaneo could not be persuaded to help. He objected to Ferrari's socialist sympathies, and he was generally eager to avoid political commitments because he feared expulsion from Switzerland.[51]

During Ferrari's absence from Paris, Lamennais, badly shaken by the failures of 1848, had attempted to establish a federation of French radical-republican groups in order to keep the revolutionary tradition alive. He and Ferrari's friends Schoelcher and Michel had also opened a political dialogue with fellow radicals in Spain, and they had established a Franco-Spanish Democratic Committee with headquarters in Paris. Their efforts had greatly annoyed Mazzini, whose European Democratic Central Committee, newly founded in London, claimed to represent the most important democratic groups in Europe. Agents of Mazzini in Paris had then tried to persuade Lamennais to join their organization. In order to counter this Mazzinian move, Montanelli and Cernuschi had proposed to Lamennais the expansion of the Franco-Spanish committee to include an Italian contingent. These negotiations had led to the founding of the Latin Democratic Committee, whose Italian members were hostile to the *programma unitario*.[52] Ferrari was well disposed toward this new multinational committee though critical of some aspects of its program. He wrote:

The manifesto [of the Latin Democratic Committee] is a masterpiece of deception. . . . It argues against religion, yet it stands for deism, the starting point of every religion; it fights against sectarianism, yet it does not assert the primacy of science, the only principle that can defeat it; it defends the Latin tradition against a common enemy, but it does not say whether this enemy is Catholicism or the Northern tradition; it is not clear whether it preaches a racial solidarity that would be inferior even to Christianity or a human brotherhood superior to that of Christ. The manifesto makes claims of socialism, yet it is underwritten by men who are strangers to the socialist tradition and hostile to it. . . . [53]

During the last months of 1851, Ferrari tried hard to unify the leadership and to publicize the goals of the committee. He faced innumerable obstacles. Both Lamennais and Montanelli were troubled and erratic men, who were neither easy to deal with nor likely to agree with Ferrari's atheistic views. Sympathizers like Cattaneo and Daniele Manin, the hero of the Venetian Revolution of 1848, shied away from active involvement. Quite often, the Italian and Spanish members of the committee complained about the overwhelming influence of the French. But the most serious obstacle of all was the murky political situation in France. The constitutional crisis that developed around the issue of a second presidential term for Bonaparte gave Ferrari cause for concern. His feelings were reflected in a manifesto in which he outlined the position of the Latin Democratic Committee concerning the Italian Question.[54]

The European revolutionary movement had been temporarily halted. Even so, Ferrari hoped that the Italian people would not accept insurrections or a war of national liberation as substitutes for a revolution. Political freedom and social justice, not unity, he argued, must be the goals of the Italian revolutionaries and their supporters throughout Europe.[55] But if his views were clearly and forcefully expressed, they were not destined to become popular. Any chance that he might have had to attract supporters was destroyed at the end of 1851 by adverse political developments in Switzerland, Turin, and Paris.

Following the arrest of the book smuggler Luigi Dottesio, the Tipografia Elvetica suffered a financial collapse from which it never recovered.[56] Gino Daelli, who was planning a newspaper in line with Ferrari's program, was forced to give up the idea for lack of adequate financing but also because of the tightened political censorship in Piedmont-Sardinia.[57] And finally, the Bonapartist coup of 2 December all but destroyed the fledgling Latin Democratic Committee, whose leaders were either proscribed or in other ways silenced.[58] Thus, Ferrari's first foray into the world of politics came to a sudden and inglorious end. He had played only a minor part in the revolution, but the events of 1848–51 affected his subsequent writings on the French revolutionary tradition and on the Italian Question. Those writings, more than his political activities, earned him a place among the French radical-socialist intellectuals of his time and among the theorists of Italy's Risorgimento.

The experiences of 1848–49 prompted Ferrari to reinterpret both the French revolutionary tradition and the Italian Question. In his mind and, of course, in his writings, the two issues were closely intertwined. But it is possible to treat his interpretation of the French Revolution of 1848 separately from his appraisal of the revolutionary events in Italy; and clarity of exposition makes it advisable to do so.

In *Le Peuple constituant* Ferrari had greeted the downfall of Louis-Philippe from the viewpoint of a latter-day Jacobin, committed to political democracy and republicanism, although open to the influence of humanitarian socialism. Within a year, however, he published a radical critique of both moderate liberalism and Jacobin democracy.[59] This dramatic shift was due to the course of events in Paris and in Milan during the spring and summer of 1848 and, to a lesser degree, to the influence of Proudhon's writings on property.[60]

The first pillar of Ferrari's Jacobin faith to be shaken by the events of 1848 was the belief that universal suffrage was synonymous with political democracy. The first elections to the French National Assembly held under the republican constitution were reason enough to doubt the usefulness of universal suffrage as an instrument of democratic progress.[61] But what really undermined Ferrari's confidence in this great political reform was the result of the referendum on the union of Lombardy with the Kingdom of Sardinia. From direct observation and from Cattaneo's writings, he learned how universal suffrage could be manipulated by powerful special interests, especially when the electorate was inexperienced or indifferent.[62]

Republicanism was the second great principle of the Jacobin tradition to be called into question in 1848. "Monarchy has divided the people; the republic can unite it," Ferrari had written. But when he returned to Paris in August 1848, he found a republican government headed by the impeccably republican General Cavaignac and a people more deeply divided along class lines than they had been under the July Monarchy.[63]

The June Days, above all, required a reevaluation of his position. The accounts that his friends gave him, and perhaps direct observation of the Parisian scene, made him aware of the gulf that existed between bourgeoisie and workers. He concluded that the June uprising had not been merely a traditional "bread riot" that had somehow gotten out of hand and resulted in unusually severe repression. Rather, it had been evidence of the workers' rejection of a political order dominated by the bourgeoisie. And it had revealed the fear among the propertied classes that the political revolution of February, initiated by middle-class intellectuals, might be followed by "a revolution by the poor." He wrote:

On the evening of 24 February 1848, Paris was sad, the streets of the fashionable districts were deserted; after the demise of Louis-Philippe, the bourgeoisie felt that the social revolution was imminent. It must be stopped, and it was stopped by reducing the new revolutionary movement to the same vague generalities that had paralyzed the [First] French Republic. . . . Three months were enough time to organize a bourgeois counterrevolution. During the democratic heyday of the new republic the bourgeoisie feigned clemency, generosity; . . . but meanwhile, the bourgeoisie kept its powder dry. The results were seen during the June Days . . . ; the bourgeois repression was a thousand times more effective than the most odious actions of the Old Regime; it brought together the supporters of three deposed regimes in order to consolidate and to use economic and religious freedom for its own ends.[64]

The Second Republic, in short, had not gone much beyond the illusion of democracy that had existed under the previous regime. And yet, the revolutionaries of February 1848 had sincerely believed that the republic meant political progress for all Frenchmen. What could explain the quick transition from the solidarity of February to the horrors of the class struggle in Paris? In search of an answer to this question, Ferrari began a restrospective analysis of the French revolutionary tradition from the fall of Louis-Philippe to the Enlightenment.[65]

The revolution that was the subject of his work was a revolution of ideas, the intellectual revolution that had given birth to modern Europe.

The revolution is the triumph of philosophy called upon to govern mankind. Without philosophy there is no revolution; reason is not free, science does not hold sway; religious worship dominates society and reason, it dictates laws and it governs mankind.

It was the philosophy of Locke that defeated Christianity, that bound man's destiny to this earth, that called upon every man to be his own pope. And yet, ever since the day when the revolutionary movement was stopped by the two reactions of the Bourbons and of Louis-Philippe, every conquest of the human mind has been in doubt.[66]

Which "conquests of the human mind" had the French Revolution proclaimed among the peoples of Europe? And why the "reactions" of the nineteenth century, which threatened to rub out those conquests? According to Ferrari, "The principles of the revolution [could] be narrowed down to two: the reign of science and the reign of equality; all other principles [were] simply means to arrest or to hasten the progress of those two. Inaugurated on the eve of the French explosion of 1789, the two principles [were now] so closely identified with France that they [could] no longer be discussed apart from that nation's destiny."[67]

The French Revolution as the proclamation of the reign of science and the reign of equality—this theme of the *Filosofia della Rivoluzione* is of crucial importance in the development of Ferrari's ideology. His reign of science is undoubtedly what we would call a secular culture. According to Ferrari, there were various ways of recognizing such a culture; one way was to examine its theories of knowledge. All civilizations, he wrote, went through three epistemological stages: the religious one, in which all knowledge was thought to be a gift of the gods; the metaphysical one, in which all knowledge was thought to be the manifestation of innate ideas; and, finally, the scientific one. Europe's first breakthrough in this area had occurred with the advancement of scientific inquiry in the seventeenth century.[68] But the advent of the reign of science had been delayed, he argued, by the popularity of deism. The glory of Descartes's *cogito ergo sum* had been tarnished by the French philosopher's belief (perhaps dictated by fear) that mathematical knowledge was the domain of human reason, while moral knowledge must come from God.[69]

By the early eighteenth century, however, a small group of revolutionaries were espousing a deism that was no longer "the neutral ground upon which theology and metaphysics could embrace, . . . but a system that fought Christianity and cursed the unjust God of Adam, of Abraham, of Christ."[70] Those men had attained real freedom by their total rejection of God. But their atheism had remained on an abstract level; it had not developed into a social system that could replace the one based upon religion. Thus, it had been easy for theology "to use the weapons that had been left in its hands; it proclaimed its alliance with property; and while throne and altar were reestablished, theology asserted its claims within the universities. . . . And so the redeemers, despised by the people, were defeated and left with no other resource than an indomitable right to think, a right forced to languish in solitude until such time as a new atheism came to rescue man from the follies of deism and Christianity."[71]

The atheists of the early eighteenth century had been doomed to failure because they had attacked religion (the spiritual domain) without realizing that it was supported by property (the temporal or material domain). A generation later, this error had been repeated by Voltaire, and through his influence it had occurred again during the French Revolution. What Voltaire, despite his deist equivocations, had done for the reign of science, Rousseau had done for the reign of equality. Ferrari defined the reign of equality as a society in which the equality of all men in the state of nature had been proclaimed and carried to its logical conclusion, in the form of equal legal, political, and economic rights for all its members.[72] In the pages of Rousseau, he found "the poet of justice, pitted against the old social order that oppresses and torments him and that he wants to destroy at any cost, even if he must destroy property in order to attain the reign of equality."[73]

The events of 1789–91 in France, he wrote, had opened up for the first time in Europe the prospect of a secular and egalitarian society. The Constituent Assembly had turned the French clergy into ordinary citizens, destroyed the legal basis of aristocratic privilege, and proclaimed the sovereignty of the people. Every one of these actions had been but the logical consequence of the previous assertion of human reason and natural equality.[74] The Declaration of the Rights of Man and of the Citizen should have freed the French people from the tyranny of throne, altar, and property. Unfortunately, before long the Assembly had undermined the strength of its own declaration by "swaddling it in layers of equivocation."

Instead of promoting the complete secularization of French society, consistent with its affirmation of human reason, the Assembly had espoused the American concept of freedom of worship. While making Roman Catholics, Protestants, and Jews theoretically equal before the state, Ferrari wrote, the Assembly had in fact left in the hands of the dominant religious establishment an immense reservoir of influence and power that was eventually used against the revolution.

Moreover, while establishing the premises for legal and political equality in France, the Constituent Assembly had fallen into a gross equivocation in the area of economic equality. It had espoused Adam Smith's then popular notion of economic freedom, "that Protestant freedom that leaves every property right to every property owner." But far from producing equality, that spurious freedom had produced a greater gap between rich and poor than had existed under feudalism.[75]

What was the source of the economic inequality that stood in the way of a truly egalitarian society? Some contemporary economists, like Proudhon, singled out the *rente* as the main problem, and they advocated the cancellation of all leases and contracts and the introduction of such measures as interest-free loans guaranteed by the state. Others, like Etienne Cabet, advocated the abolition of individual property. Ferrari focused his critique upon the existing inheritance laws. The reign of equality, he argued, would never be attained if some members of society, through no effort or merit of their own, enjoyed from birth a headstart over others. As a necessary step toward equality, he suggested changes in the existing laws and the redistribution of wealth, particularly landed wealth, acquired through inheritance. It should be pointed out, however, that by economic equality Ferrari did not mean absolute equality of income or wealth among all citizens, but rather equality of economic rights. Among these rights, the most important, he thought, was the right of access to capital. The liberal regimes of the nineteenth century in theory recognized that right, but in reality the existing inheritance laws and economic practices allowed a privileged few to have disproportionate access to capital resources, while the many had no access at all.[76]

The "double equivocation over religious and economic freedom" had been painfully evident, Ferrari wrote, in the Jacobin phase of the French Revolution. Robespierre had thundered against archbishops and cardinals, but he had not even attempted to uproot religion. On the contrary, he had juxtaposed a cloak of deism upon the traditional Catholic beliefs. With regard to property rights, his position had been even more contradictory than that of the Constituent Assembly. He had recognized that the abolition of feudal obligations and the extension of civil rights to the masses made little difference in the lives of the poor. And he had realized that only a new revolution could change their situation. But the revolution by the poor that he envisioned "must be gentle and nonviolent, it must be accomplished without frightening the propertied classes and without undermining justice." In practice, Robespierre's social revolution had been reduced to "a patchwork of expedients, which were useful, but peripheral, and which left the base of the old society virtually untouched."[77] Because the religious and economic foundations of French society had not been changed, Ferrari wrote, it was not surprising that the republican experiment had failed. In the rise of Napoleon Bonaparte he saw the triumph of all these contradictions: secular education and the Concordat, economic freedom and the Continental System, republicanism and monarchy. Nonetheless, the French Revolution, whose creature Napoleon was, had continued and had become a European phenomenon.[78]

Ferrari concluded that, on balance, the French Revolution

had been a major step toward a society free from religion and metaphysics and compatible with natural equality. Yet the attainment of the reign of science and equality remained in the distant future. The revolutionary tradition, of which he felt very much a part, was the constant struggle to attain those goals. In the mid-nineteenth century, the enemies were no longer monarchy, feudal rights, and aristocratic privilege (all of which had been successfully undermined by the French Revolution), but rather religion in all its forms and property, i.e., the unrestrained economic freedom that was permitted, indeed encouraged, by the liberal governments of that era.

In the light of his interpretation of the revolutionary tradition, the two episodes that had shocked him most deeply in 1848–49—the June Days and the Oudinot expedition against the Roman Republic—turned out to be two sides of the same coin. As in the past, religion and property had supported each other; to these pillars of the existing social and political order in France and in Italy he opposed two equally inseparable ones, *irreligione* (secularism) and *legge agraria* (the regulation of private ownership of land).

Ferrari's concern with economic inequality and his critique of laissez faire liberalism justify the decision by Italian Marxist scholars to place him within the socialist tradition of the nineteenth century.[79] While discussing his ideology, however, we should bear in mind that for him the attainment of the reign of science was as important as the attainment of the reign of equality. And indeed, later on in his career he came to regard the secularization of culture as a more important objective than social and economic justice. If Ferrari's concept of equality can be traced back to the writings of Locke and Rousseau, his concept of *irreligione* harks back to those libertine sects of the early eighteenth century whose members had "cursed the unjust God of Adam, of Abraham, and of Christ." In his strong preoccupation with secularism, Ferrari differed from Buchez, who attempted to make Christianity relevant to the emerging urban-industrial society, and from Leroux and the Saint-Simonians, whose political and social ideals were usually expressed in religious terms. And he obviously differed from Marx, who regarded the bourgeois hegemony over culture, in its religious, artistic, and literary forms, as of secondary importance vis-à-vis bourgeois domination of the means of production. For Ferrari, religion in whatever form was not a superstructure, but the equal partner of property in the social order of his time. He argued that it was absurd to fight one and not the other.

Although he chided the French republicans of 1848 for their failure to carry on the revolutionary crusade against religion and property, Ferrari defended them against Italian critics. Despite the mistakes of 1848, he argued, France was still years ahead of Italy on the road that led to the reign of science and of equality.

The France of February [1848] has been indicted; there goes the adulterous one; well, then, let the people who are without sin cast the first stone. What can Italy possibly say? She is not even capable of understanding the errors of France. The French *repubblica formale* is a perfidious abstraction; I have already said it, but it is at least a veil cast upon medieval traditions. [Formal] liberty is a phase through which the old society is rearranged, rationalized, converted to reason, emancipated from [ascriptive] authority. Italy has not yet reached this phase, this error; on what grounds, then, can she complain about France?[80]

If the June Days and the Oudinot expedition prompted Ferrari's reappraisal of the French revolutionary tradition, the events of 1848 in Lombardy led him to rethink the Italian Question. At the beginning of the year of revolutions he had urged all Italian liberals not to waste their energies in the pursuit of distant dreams of independence and unity but to subvert the existing political order from within. But his moderate and optimistic suggestions had not taken sufficient account of several problems which had emerged clearly during the Revolution of 1848. One such problem had been the popularity of Pope Pius IX, whose advent to the papal throne in 1846 had revived the hopes of the neo-guelph movement. Another had been the reluctance of the Habsburg government to accede to liberal demands in its Italian territories.[81] And last but not least, there had been the expansionist aims of the Sardinian government in northern Italy.

Ferrari acknowledged his previous failure to weigh all of

these factors carefully. But he argued that the failures of 1848 could not be explained away as the result of papal, Sardinian, and Habsburg influence. The real tragedy of 1848 had been the inability of the republican revolutionaries to develop an independent program truly responsive to their country's past history and present conditions. The Mazzinians had forfeited the leadership of the Italian movement, to which they were entitled in view of their democratic ideas and past sacrifices, because their chief goals, national independence and unity, were out of step with Italy's historical traditions.

The Mazzinian theory of independence, Ferrari thought, was based upon two assumptions, both of which had been disproved in 1848–49. One was the assumption that Italy's most powerful enemies were external (Austria and France). In fact, as elsewhere, internal enemies, religion and property, stood in the way of progress. Another was the assumption that Italy could develop in isolation from the revolutionary tradition, which Ferrari regarded as inseparable from the destiny of France. That the theory of Italian independence was irrelevant to the egalitarian and secular trends of European civilization, Ferrari quipped, was proved by the fact that the partisans of the pope and of Sardinia had eagerly adopted it in the late 1840s.[82]

The Mazzinian theory of unity, he argued, was not applicable to Italy, whose history had been shaped by the papacy and by the Roman Empire and its medieval successors. Both papacy and empire represented universal and federal principles; they could never be the basis for national unity. Mazzini's theory assumed the existence of a sense of unity among the Italian people. Once again Ferrari voiced a deep skepticism on this point. Over the years he had become convinced that a distinct Italian culture did exist, but he doubted that it could be turned into a political force.[83] Some elements in the population might some day be attracted to the Mazzinian theory of unity and mobilized in favor of it. The commercial and industrial bourgeoisie, in particular, might see advantages in the creation of a national market and a national government. But what advantages did the Mazzinian program offer to the other social classes? In 1848 Mazzini had been silent on this point. "[He] had promised a war without a revolution; and after the war, a peaceful revolution in which philosopher and priest, noble and bourgeois, privileged and underprivileged would live happily together."[84] Mazzini's dangerous utopianism was summed up by his favorite slogan, "God and the People." Did he not realize the danger, especially in Italy, of clothing a political program in religious terms?[85]

In the closing chapters of *La federazione repubblicana*, Ferrari outlined some alternatives to the Mazzinian theory of independence and unity. His outline was essentially the program of the political party that he was attempting to organize in the summer of 1851, when this book was published.[86] As the first priority of any revolutionary movement in Italy, he mentioned "war against the pope, against the Roman Catholic Apostolic Church enthroned in Rome and dominant elsewhere in Italy. . . . No equivocations, no uncertain halfway doctrines, semi-Catholic, semi-Christian, semipapal. . . . The religion of the revolution is that which deifies man, his reason, his rights unrecognized and scorned by the Church."[87]

Because the alliance between throne and altar was the mainstay of the Restoration, the second highest priority of the Italian revolutionaries must be the elimination of all dynasties and the establishment of democratic republics in each of the existing states. These goals, Ferrari insisted, deserved much higher priority than any plans for unification. A federation of the new republican regimes was certain to arise in any event, out of a common need to defend the revolution. These suggestions did not depart significantly from those that he had made in January 1848 and that Cattaneo had more recently articulated in the *Archivio Triennale*. What made Ferrari's program of 1851 unique and extremely controversial among his contemporaries was his application to the Italian Question of the two great principles of the revolutionary tradition, *irreligione* and *legge agraria*.

He advocated not merely the elimination of the Papal States and of clerical influence in Italian politics, but also the radical secularization of Italy's educational and cultural institutions, to be carried out by ruthless dictatorial means if necessary. Only a sharp break with the past, he thought, and an uncompromising fight against religion in all its forms could bring Italy into step with the modern age. But how could a small revolutionary force take on such a gigantic task? It could not, Ferrari argued, if it persisted in the Mazzinian abstractions, unity, independence, the nation. But it could win the uphill battle if it rallied the Italian masses to its banners. To this end, he urged the Italian revolutionaries to give serious thought to

the right of necessity, which strikes at the vices of the rich on behalf of the hungry poor; this is a law that all peoples, all lawmakers recognize aboard a ship in peril. . . . Some day this right will cease to be a juridical abstraction. . . . This right has no other source or limits than those dictated by necessity; and the necessity that all contemporary economists, beginning with Malthus, recognize is that the greatest part of mankind is gnawed by hunger, while a privileged few luxuriate in superfluous amenities. And the more we progress, the greater the necessity, because the capitalist oppresses the worker, the landowner oppresses his tenants, and they in turn oppress the day laborers.[88]

With the exception of the Neapolitan Carlo Pisacane, Ferrari was the only major figure of the Risorgimento to argue openly that a cultural and economic revolution was necessary to the political modernization of Italy.[89] His contemporaries were almost uniformly critical of his two revolutionary principles. The moderate liberals feared him as an agent of French socialism, whose ideas were alien, pernicious, and irrelevant to his native homeland. Mazzini, while recognizing in him a fellow supporter of democratic republicanism, recoiled in horror at the very thought of turning the nationalist crusade into a revolution for and by the economically oppressed classes. Cattaneo agreed with Ferrari's critique of the *programma unitario*, with his emphasis on secularism, and, in part, with his belief in the revolutionary leadership of France. But even Cattaneo reacted negatively to *La Federazione repubblicana*. From his standpoint as a liberal economist, he disapproved of Ferrari's suggested changes in inheritance laws. As for a redistribution of inherited wealth, Cattaneo opposed it because he thought that it would prevent the rapid accumulation of capital necessary to economic modernization. This disagreement between the two friends was never resolved. Ironically, it foreshadowed an equally unresolved debate among interpreters of modern Italian history over the Gramscian view of the Risorgimento as a *rivoluzione mancata*.[90] Cattaneo envisioned a revolution by the liberal bourgeoisie, although one open to the growth of political democracy. The events of 1848 convinced Ferrari that the predominantly middle-class revolutionary groups in Italy were neither strong nor advanced enough to fight a war on three fronts, against the papacy, Austria, and Sardinia. Only a mass movement, he thought, could accomplish that. But such a movement was not likely to occur unless the disinherited masses were given concrete incentives to participate in the Italian Revolution. He wrote that "liberty, sovereignty, independence are nothing but lies wherever the rich oppress the poor, wherever the poor exist only to enhance the comforts of the rich, wherever a poor man can feed his family only by toiling hard to build palaces, to build a world of luxury to which he can never aspire."[91] From this viewpoint, the unification of Italy as it occurred in 1859–60 was certainly a *rivoluzione mancata*. As a member of the Italian Parliament from 1860 to 1876, Ferrari came to accept the Sardinian monarchy and the unitary state, but he maintained that the survival and progress of the new Italy in the modern era demanded the secularization of culture and the extension of political *and* economic rights to the masses. His political program, criticized by contemporaries as extremist, impractical, and too closely patterned after French ideas, had little impact upon the Risorgimento, but it lived on in the radical and socialist ideals of later generations.

[4]

Under the Bonapartist Eagle

ALTHOUGH HIS OWN safety and well-being were not at stake, Ferrari was emotionally shaken by the Bonapartist coup d'état. Many French leaders whom he had met or worked with during the revolutionary years were imprisoned, while others joined the ill-starred insurgents of his native Milan in involuntary exile.[1] A few days after the coup he resolved to leave again for Switzerland. There he would be able to write about the recent political crisis without fear of government reprisals and he would enjoy the companionship of old friends.

Cattaneo and the staff of the Tipografia Elvetica welcomed his return. They were making plans for a newspaper that reflected their republican, democratic, and federalist ideas. But this project fell through because the Tipografia Elvetica was unable to finance it.[2] When Gino Daelli contacted other possible publishers in Turin, he found them hostile to the Capolago group and indeed to all democratic nationalists.[3] But he reported that Ferrari's *Filosofia della Rivoluzione* was selling briskly, if illegally, in the Kingdom of Sardinia, and he encouraged the successful author to write other essays on the Italian Question.[4]

During this second sojourn in the Lugano area Ferrari edited his articles of the 1840s for the Tipografia Elvetica and wrote the first draft of a new work on the Bonapartist coup. By mid-March, however, business affairs called him back to Paris. Unfortunately, his departure interrupted a dialogue between himself and Cattaneo concerning the significance of 2 December 1851 for French democracy and for the Italian Question. The two friends continued to exchange ideas on this subject by correspondence, but a dialogue by mail was a poor substitute for the intimate conversations held by the glow of a fireplace in Cattaneo's modest hillside home.[5]

At the end of March 1852, Ferrari completed *L'Italia dopo il colpo di stato del 2 dicembre 1851*.[6] Repetti accepted the manuscript, but he asked the author to forfeit any expectation of royalties and to help with the editing of the work. It was the fear of impending bankruptcy rather than avarice that led the publisher to drive such a hard bargain. Ferrari accepted these terms, but his return to Capolago was marred by sad news from Turin.[7] Giovanni Cattaneo, a distant relative of Carlo, had been arrested on charges of having smuggled into the Kingdom of Sardinia inflammatory political works, among them Ferrari's *Filosofia della Rivoluzione*. Ferrari wanted to cry out against Sardinian censorship, but he realized that any public pronouncement on his part would do the accused more harm than good. Reluctantly he held his tongue, and he tried to allay his sense of guilt by a gift of money to the unfortunate man's needy family.[8] He also got in touch with Cattaneo's attorney and attempted to enlist the support of Sardinian intellectuals for the accused.[9] He rejoiced in November 1852 when he heard that Cattaneo had been given a ten-month suspended sentence, much less than the maximum penalty prescribed by law.[10]

The trial of Giovanni Cattaneo had a strong emotional impact upon Ferrari. Like most authors, he wished to be read and appreciated, but he could not bear the thought that others might suffer personal injury or political harassment in the attempt to disseminate his ideas.[11] If he did not lack the courage of his convictions, he certainly lacked the ability to use and to manipulate others in the pursuit of some all-important objective. Thus, in contrast to his contemporaries Mazzini and Cavour, he could not be more than an articulate and controversial theorist as long as being a political leader meant engaging in illegal, secret, dangerous, or even violent actions. Only when the unification of

Italy made it possible for him to play an active role within a legitimate, peaceful, and open framework did he learn to practice the art of politics and even to enjoy it.

At the insistence of the author himself, Repetti and his associates were extremely cautious in distributing Ferrari's *L'Italia dopo il colpo di stato*. Indeed, even political friends like Pisacane in Genoa complained of delays in obtaining a copy of the pamphlet through the usual smuggling network.[12] Repetti's cautiousness avoided a repetition of the tragic incidents of 1851–52, but it also restricted, of course, the sale of Ferrari's work. It was read only within the small circle of the author's political friends in Italy and in France; by the time of Italy's unification it had been all but forgotten. And yet, as an analysis of Louis Napoleon's role in French history and of his possible impact upon Italian history, it deserves to be rediscovered and compared with the better-known interpretations by Marx, Proudhon, Hugo, Tocqueville, and Bagehot.[13]

Ferrari shared with Bagehot and Tocqueville the desire to understand the background of the Bonapartist coup, to predict its impact upon the future of France, and to interpret it for his contemporaries. In contrast to Bagehot, Ferrari experienced this event as a French citizen who had been directly involved in the troubled history of the Second Republic. And, unlike Tocqueville, he was very concerned about the future of the revolutionary movement in France. But his background led him inevitably to emphasize those aspects of the Bonapartist coup which were most directly pertinent to the Italian Question.

The events of 2 December 1851 had not only wrecked his last remaining hopes of a new academic post; they had also placed him in a very embarrassing position vis-à-vis his Italian nationalist friends. Since the early 1840s he had argued that political change in Italy could only come through the leaven of French revolutionary ideas. But very few Italian nationalists had shared his belief, indeed his fixation, concerning the historical relationship between France and Italy. Mazzini, above all others, had been critical of his theses from the very beginning.[14] As Ferrari well knew, the events of 1849–51 in France had greatly strengthened the case of his Italian critics. How, they asked, could he continue to repeat *"hors de la France point de salut"* after the repressions of June 1848 and May 1849, after the French occupation of Rome, and after the rise of Louis Napoleon Bonaparte? Obviously, Ferrari wrote *L'Italia dopo il colpo di stato* as much to defend his political posture against these criticisms as to educate the Italian reading public.

What was the meaning of 2 December? What did the future hold for Bonaparte, for his country, and for Europe? These were the questions that his pamphlet attempted to answer. Many radical leaders of 1848, like Duprat and Schoelcher, mourned the death of their movement. On 2 December 1851, they charged, the revolutionary spirit had succumbed to the false glitter of Bonapartism, to empty promises of social peace and international prestige. Basically, they expected the nephew to emulate the policies of the uncle. This would mean the gradual erosion of civil and political liberties for the sake of national unity and the pursuit of international successes at the expense of domestic reforms and prosperity.[15] A moderate liberal, Tocqueville agreed with this pessimistic appraisal of the coup, but he blamed the French radicals and socialists as much as Bonaparte for the demise of the Second Republic. Their actions, he claimed, had divided the supporters of the February Revolution and had destroyed the possibility of a gradual transition to a democratic society. The radicals and socialists had sown the seeds of discord; Bonaparte, a skillful and unscrupulous opportunist, was now harvesting the fruits.[16]

But were these, Ferrari asked, tenable explanations of the political crisis in France? Did it make sense to portray Louis Napoleon as a reactionary? Against the theses of his liberal and radical contemporaries Ferrari argued: "Louis Napoleon does not embody reactionary principles. Before 2 December he was, indeed, the leader of a reactionary movement, which he channeled and exploited to his own advantage; but after 2 December he can no longer play that role. . . . His type of democracy may well be a travesty; but that travesty is built upon the rejection of Legitimism."[17] It was no secret, he added, that influential men in business, clerical and military circles had been Bonaparte's silent accomplices on 2 December. But Ferrari was convinced that these political alliances were temporary and quite weak. Once the radical-socialist currents within the republican movement had been reduced to silence, he argued, Bonaparte's new friends would revert to the older, more comfortable traditions of Legitimism or Orleanism. Unable, as a Bonaparte, to preside over a resurgence of either Bourbon or Orleans power, Louis Napoleon might then turn to the only possible alternative, an alliance with the surviving liberal-democratic forces.[18]

Ferrari's analysis of the Bonapartist coup offers an interesting contrast to the thesis of Karl Marx's *The Eighteenth Brumaire of Louis Bonaparte*. Both of them had interpreted the Revolution of 1848, and particularly the June Days, from the perspective of a class struggle between bourgeoisie and workers. They agreed that the propertied classes had been frightened by the rhetoric, if not by the actual threat, of social revolution. And both believed that this fear had turned many supporters of the February Revolution into supporters of the coup d'état. But the similarities between their respective positions ended here.

In his appraisal of Louis Napoleon's ability, prospects, and ambitions, Marx differed less from his liberal and radical contemporaries than he cared to admit. He profoundly despised the new ruler of France, whose power was based, he charged, upon the memories of his uncle's great military talent, the support of the Parisian *Lumpenproletariat*, and the political backwardness of millions of French smallholders. For all his bitter sarcasm toward bourgeois liberalism, Marx also regretted the collapse of the Second Republic.[19] But Ferrari disagreed. He believed that although Louis Napoleon lacked the mettle of his famous uncle, he could not be dismissed as a lucky adventurer or as a mere tool of the French bourgeoisie. "The coup d'état destroyed nothing but the possibility of waiting until 1852, that messianic hope of a revolutionary millennium," Ferrari wrote. "What have we lost, we who did not pin our hopes on 1852? We lost our inadequate resources, our errors, misconceptions, and illusions; we faced a thick jungle that had to be cleared with a hatchet; should we bewail its sudden destruction by lightning?"[20] In this essay Louis Napoleon was cast in the role of an avenging angel whose flaming sword was dispelling the fog that had been generated in France by the sudden birth of the democratic republic and by its equally rapid demise. It was a surprising and paradoxical interpretation indeed for a man who was identified with the radical-socialist factions in French politics, who had lost a much-coveted job at the onset of reaction in 1849, and whose friends had recently been jailed or proscribed.

In the vast literature on the Bonapartist coup, only one interpretation, Proudhon's *La révolution sociale démontrée par le coup d'état*, comes close in at least some respects to Ferrari's. The similarity is not accidental; we know that the two authors exchanged ideas on the political events of 1849–51 and read portions of each other's manuscripts. Like Ferrari, Proudhon argued that a future alliance between the new ruler of France and the advocates of social democracy was inevitable, if Bonaparte wished to offset challenges from Legitimist or Orleanist interests. He too condemned his fellow republicans for their abstract notions of political freedom. And, like Ferrari, he refuted the charge that the French radicals and socialists were to blame for the Bonapartist resurgence. This refutation was directed at French liberals like Tocqueville, but also at foreign critics, and above all at Mazzini.[21]

When Ferrari's and Proudhon's works on the Bonapartist coup were published, a bitter feud had already erupted in London between Mazzini on the one hand and Leroux and Blanc on the other. The two Frenchmen had reacted vigorously to Mazzini's charge that their plans for social revolution had driven the middle class and the land-owning peasantry into the arms of Louis Napoleon.[22] Proudhon, who had never been known to lavish praise upon these socialist leaders, this time came to their defense.[23] And so did Ferrari. He argued that the nephew of Napoleon I could not be indifferent to the treaties of 1815. If his regime lasted, he would some day move against the conservative powers of Europe, thus opening up new opportunities for Italy.[24]

Ferrari and Proudhon knew that their writings might be interpreted as attempts to court the favor of the new French government. Such an interpretation was especially likely for Proudhon, who appealed to Louis Napoleon himself for permission to publish *La révolution sociale*.[25] But even Ferrari, whose book was published abroad and had a much smaller circulation, expected and received his share of criticism from the adversaries of Bonaparte.[26] The wording of Proudhon's appeal and his later dealings with such influential Bonapartists as Morny and Persigny seemed to justify the suspicions of his critics. But Ferrari definitely did not deserve to be labeled a Bonapartist. His letters to Cattaneo, Cernuschi, and Carozzi show clearly that we must distinguish between his analysis of Louis Napoleon's historical role and his personal feelings toward the new ruler and his entourage.[27] After the proclamation of the Second Empire, he reported to his Italian friends that the influx of former Orleanists in the administration was changing the nature of the regime and weakening the position of Bonaparte himself. Only a war, he wrote, could sustain the rule of "that rotten gang of crooks, speculators, and high-born adventurers." He made the same prediction the following year, when he reported from Paris that the regime was threatened by Legitimist conspiracies.[28]

But within two years of the Bonapartist coup, Ferrari and Proudhon had to face up to unpleasant realities. As they had predicted, Bonaparte was indeed being challenged by supporters of the previous monarchial regimes. But he did not seem at all inclined to offer an olive branch to the leaders of French democracy, or at least not yet. Any hopes for change seemed to rest more and more upon the outbreak of an international crisis that might tempt or force the imperial government to wage war.

Ferrari and Proudhon had known of each other's work ever since the early 1840s, through their mutual friend Bergmann.[29] During the Second Republic they moved in the same radical-socialist intellectual circles. However, Ferrari's role in the French Revolution of 1848 was limited to his collaboration on Duprat's *Le Peuple constituant*. But Proudhon, not satisfied with the editorship of the extremist newspaper *Le Représentant du peuple*, also served briefly in the Assembly.[30]

Both men suffered from the reactionary tide that followed

the presidential election of December 1848. As Ferrari, dismissed again from the University of Strasbourg, came to grips with the hostile atmosphere of the Bourges lycée, Proudhon faced even greater dangers. His scathing editorials and his prediction that a second Bonapartist empire loomed on the horizon enraged not only the newly-elected prince president, but also a majority of Proudhon's own colleagues in the Assembly. Deprived of his parliamentary immunity and brought to trial in 1849, he was sentenced to three years in prison, most of which he spent in the Parisian fortress of Sainte-Pélagie.[31]

To the historian familiar with the more sophisticated cruelties of the twentieth century, Proudhon's incarceration seems mild indeed. He was allowed to visit his wife at her rented quarters nearby; he could receive books, clothing, and food from the outside; and he entertained visitors nearly every day.[32] In 1850, upon his return from exile in Belgium, Ferrari joined a small group of friends who gathered regularly in Proudhon's cell. It included the Russian exile Alexander Herzen, the revolutionary painter Gustave Courbet, Charles Beslay, a future leader of the Paris Commune, and the young Alfred Darimon, soon to be known around Paris as one of the republican "Opposition Five" in the Corps Législatif.[33]

A warm friendship grew between Ferrari and Proudhon within the austere walls of Sainte-Pélagie. After Proudhon's release from prison, Ferrari visited him at home and became quite fond of his family. His devotion was such that he nursed them, at grave risk to himself, during the cholera epidemic of 1853.[34] Ferrari and Proudhon were brought together by a common interest in radical politics and by shared adversity. But despite this common ground, it is surprising that they ever became close friends, for in many ways they were at opposite poles. The Milanese expatriate, even while writing revolutionary tracts, remained true to his urban, bourgeois origins in his demeanor, tastes, and attire. Free of family responsibilities and financial worries, he enjoyed the cultural attractions of city life and sought the company of cosmopolitan men and emancipated women. It would be quite impossible to imagine Ferrari decked in the *blouson* and *sabots* that were Proudhon's trademark, and equally impossible to imagine him as an authoritarian paterfamilias. Proudhon was proud of—indeed he flaunted—his peasant origins and the gruff, simple ways of his native Jura mountains. A maladjusted city dweller often forced to live in miserably cramped, unhealthy quarters, he seemed happy only within the circle of his own very traditional family.[35] Perhaps Ferrari enjoyed the company of the Proudhons precisely because their life-style was so different from his own. Moreover, he established a warm rapport with Proudhon's children, as he had in the early 1840s with the children of Antonio Gargantini.[36]

But personal friendship aside, there is ample evidence that the intellectual and political relationship between Ferrari and Proudhon was important to the development of their similar outlooks. The evidence emerges indirectly from a comparison of some of their published works and directly from their correspondence, from Proudhon's *Carnets*, from the testimony of mutual friends like Darimon, and from a moving evocation written by Ferrari in 1875, on the tenth anniversary of his friend's death.[37] What direct evidence has been preserved can give us only a limited view of the intellectual exchange that occurred between two men who visited each other frequently for nearly a decade. But even so, three major themes emerge from their dialogue: the meaning of freedom and equality in modern society, the policies of Napoleon III (particularly his foreign policy), and the nature and applications of federalism. Both Ferrari and Proudhon were men of lively curiosity and wide-ranging interests; they wrote almost without respite (perhaps too much), constantly shifting their position to include this or that new insight or a new bit of evidence gathered from their latest readings. It is very difficult, therefore, to compare their ideas without falling prey to distortion and oversimplification. But the essence of their critique of the liberal state is clear; it can be captured in a few sentences.[38]

Proudhon by the early 1840s and Ferrari sometime during the Revolution of 1848 became convinced that the rights for which fellow radicals in France and elsewhere were fighting (freedom of the press, freedom in the academy, and universal suffrage) were illusory so long as glaring economic inequalities allowed some citizens to dominate the lives of others. Political rights were only meaningful when they were truly exercised, and they could not be exercised so long as wealthy citizens had greater access to the levers of power than poor ones. François Guizot had perceived this dilemma, but his classic piece of advice— *"enrichissez-vous"*—was obviously impractical for the great majority of ordinary citizens, who had no access to capital. If Guizot's advice was irrelevant to their needs, how else could the masses achieve that measure of economic freedom that must go hand in hand with political rights?

Over the years, Proudhon suggested a number of more or less practical measures, such as the introduction of interest-free loans guaranteed by the state. In the *Filosofia della Rivoluzione* and in later works, Ferrari advocated the elimination of inherited fortunes and the limitation of the amount of real property that any individual might own. If their suggestions were vague and utopian, their intent was clear: they believed that unrestricted economic freedom for the capitalists was not compatible with the ideals of political equality and social justice that were the hallmarks of modern European society. Neither of them, however, ever advocated the elimination of the private ownership of capital or the inevitability of a class struggle for control over the means of production.

If Proudhon's ideas helped shape Ferrari's outlook on economic problems, the reverse was true with regard to the role of the Church in modern society. Both Ferrari and Proudhon had rejected Roman Catholicism in their youth. They were both opposed to clerical censorship of the press. But while Ferrari during the 1840s had moved from a simple, emotional form of anticlericalism to the development of a full-fledged secular ideology, Proudhon had not. He made the transition nearly a decade later, and clearly under Ferrari's guidance, as a result of the Mirecourt incident. In 1855, the ultramontane writer Eugène de Mirecourt, who specialized in attacks upon socialist theorists, published a very damaging, scurrilous pamphlet on Proudhon. Ferrari urged his irate friend not to retaliate in kind, but to write instead a serious critique of Catholic political philosophy, comparing the Christian concept of justice to the concept that had emerged through the French revolutionary tradition.[39]

Proudhon took his advice; the result was *De la Justice dans la Révolution et dans l'Eglise*, published in April 1858. The book clearly reflects the influence of two important concepts that Ferrari had developed in his *Machiavel* and in the *Filosofia della Rivoluzione*. In the first place, Proudhon argued that Christian ethics, particularly in their Roman Catholic form, and the principles of the French Revolution were irreconcilable, because they were grounded in mutually exclusive views of man's nature and of his place in the universe. Second, he argued that the liberal principle of freedom of worship, though useful and commendable in pluralistic societies, must never be accepted by men who worked for political or social change in predominantly Roman Catholic ones. It could too easily become an instrument by which the Church fought the secularization of society, thus effectively blocking its modernization.[40] Not surprisingly, Proudhon's *De la Justice* was seized by the authorities upon publication for its content offensive to religion. Rather than face another prison term, the author fled to Belgium. Ferrari looked after his wife and children until they too were able to leave Paris. In November 1858, he wrote: "You have great courage, too much courage. . . . I admire you without being able to imitate you; accuse me of selfishness, if you will, but a bitter experience has shown me that revolutionary crowds are no better than reactionary ones; and the classic platitudes of my fellow republicans have disgusted me to a point that in all probability I shall never again be able to leave the sanctuary of science."[41] There were several reasons behind Ferrari's stated intention to remain "within the sanctuary of science." For one thing, after twenty years in French intellectual circles, the recent publication of his *Histoire des révolutions d'Italie* was earning him substantial recognition as a philosopher of history. Although usually modest, he could hardly refrain from basking a little in the sunlight of success. Besides, he was deeply disillusioned with the policies of Napoleon III, and especially with the outcome of the Crimean War.

After the proclamation of the Second Empire, Ferrari and Proudhon had lost hope in a democratic reorientation of Bonaparte's domestic policies. But Proudhon had argued that an international crisis, by pitting France against the conservative powers of Europe, might produce those domestic changes that did not otherwise seem possible. Thus the outbreak of the Near Eastern crisis of 1853 filled his breast with excitement. Eager to return to political activity, he petitioned the imperial government for permission to launch a newspaper. Ferrari pleaded with him to weigh carefully the perils of political journalism. In a ferocious satire of Second Empire politics, he voiced the imaginary objections of the Minister of the Interior, Persigny, to Proudhon's proposed undertaking:

And so—say I/Persigny—you wish to launch a journal? For what purpose? To attack me? Thanks. To defend me? But I don't want to be defended by the likes of you. Surely you know what have been the circumstances of the coup d'état; given that the clubs are unreasonable, given that freedom of the press is an incitement to rebellion, given that the national assembly is a stage for civil war, we have suppressed the clubs, the press, and the assembly. Such has been our achievement, and you are asking us to reopen the doors to debates in the press, to let your voice echo amidst the conversations of club members, and to take us back to the days of the assembly? Suppose that I let you defend me . . . you would expose my affairs to the whirlwind of discussion, you would forbid me to be Legitimist, Orleanist, liberal, democrat, pacifist, bellicose, reactionary, socialist, Catholic, or atheist depending upon the circumstances. . . . [42]

But although he preached aloofness from politics, Ferrari confessed that he was fascinated and thrilled by the prospect of a Bonapartist war against the conservative powers of Europe. He welcomed any war that might alter the status quo in Italy.[43] At the beginning of the Crimean War, Ferrari assumed that Austria, and possibly Prussia also, would side with Russia against the liberal monarchies of the West. If Austria became involved in the war, he argued, France might then be able to strike at her position in Italy and resume the task of consolidation and modernization that had been undertaken by Napoleon I.[44] But his hopes were dashed by the international developments of 1854–55. The war affected Italy only in a marginal way, when Britain and France solicited manpower from the Kingdom of Sardinia.[45]

At any rate, as Proudhon was first to realize, the unpopularity of the war among the French people, and its adverse effect upon the Paris Bourse, ruled out a Bonapartist campaign in Italy.[46] Ferrari acknowledged that Proudhon's reading of French public opinion was probably accurate. But he was convinced that this first international adventure of the Bonapartist regime was only a portent of things to come. He wrote:

What is certain is that France has wanted war, that she has voted for it, that Bonaparte provoked it, that he wants to be Napoleon reborn, the Napoleon of 1848. The issue now is to find out which war this new Napoleon will fight. You see—my imaginary Persigny tells me—we are in a curious dilemma; the French are war-horses; if you leave them in the stables, they get rusty, they take up metaphysics, they lapse into antinomies. Thanks to the Holy Places (about which, like you, I don't give a damn), I have stirred up warlike feelings everywhere. . . . But we have to move beyond that.[47]

When Napoleon III's war materialized, in 1859, it wrecked Ferrari's determination to remain "within the sanctuary of science"; the temptation to take part in the Italian Revolution proved irresistible. At first Proudhon criticized Ferrari's decision to return to his native homeland, because he disapproved of the Italian state brought about by the Bonapartist intervention.[48] In support of his critical view of Italian unification, he cited what Ferrari himself had told him, "that the immense majority of the Italian people [were] committed to federalism; that they regarded unity as little more than a revolutionary machination."[49] Ferrari was embarrassed by Proudhon's statement, because he had decided to come to terms, after all, with the movement for unification. But he could not deny that the statement flowed logically from the federalist position that Proudhon had developed under his influence.

As all interpreters of his thought agree, Proudhon throughout his life displayed a visceral distrust of the power of the modern state, in particular of the French tradition of *étatisme*. Thus, he was receptive to any political theory that promised to safeguard the rights of the individual citizen and the rights of free associations of citizens, without turning into an anarchist utopia à la Fourier or Cabet. In the 1850s he was attracted to federalism both as a means of weakening the *étatiste* tradition at home and of preventing wars abroad. That Proudhon was familiar with Ferrari's *La Federazione repubblicana* and *Histoire des révolutions d'Italie* is quite apparent in his main work on the subject.[50] But in some respects his application of federalist theory to contemporary domestic and international issues went far beyond that of his Italian friend.

Ferrari's federalist position had evolved primarily from his study of Italy's political traditions. These had been shaped, he thought, by the universalist principles of the papacy and the empire. He had never argued that federalist principles were universally applicable to the realm of politics. His only claim was that they were applicable, for quite peculiar historical reasons, to the Italian case. By contrast, Proudhon in his *Du principe fédératif* argued for the universal applicability of federalism. Indeed, he went so far as to propose the political decentralization of the French state, which Ferrari had cited again and again as the example par excellence of a unitary historical tradition. Proudhon also believed that the existence of major European powers with strong central governments had been the cause of all major wars in modern times. If the existing major powers could not be broken up, it seemed to him imperative at least to prevent the formation of new ones. Like Ferrari, he regarded the creation of a united Italy as incompatible with that country's historical traditions. But even an Italian federation under the wings of France seemed to him undesirable, because it might add luster to the Bonapartist eagle and because it was bound to weaken Austria, the only federal state among the major powers.

These Proudhonian arguments were, of course, anathema to all European nationalists of his generation. Even Ferrari, although less sensitive than most Risorgimento intellectuals to nationalist sentiments, found them hard to swallow, for he had never denied the possibility of an independent Italian state.[51] At any rate, in the late 1850s, just as Proudhon was carrying federalist theory to its most extreme conclusions, the Italian nationalist movement was rejecting those federalist and democratic strains that had survived the Revolution of 1848. Soon Ferrari faced a difficult choice: either to remain loyal, as Proudhon urged, to his federalist and radical principles, and therefore to reject the Italian settlement of 1859–60, or to accept that settlement, and therefore to revise his ideological position. This dilemma was not his alone. Between the Crimean War and the Plombières Conference of 1858 all the leading figures of Italian democracy had to make similar political choices.[52]

The outbreak of the Crimean War brought together for a brief moment Italian nationalists of every region and every political hue in a climate of messianic expectation. Their naive hopes for revision of the treaties of 1815 in a sense favorable to their cause were evidence of their mounting frustration. Ever since the 1840s they had debated among themselves how to break the Habsburg stranglehold over their country and what to do about the papacy. Those debates had produced no concrete results. Gradually Cattaneo, Montanelli, Manin, and other democratic leaders of 1848 had concluded that the status quo in Italy could not be altered without the aid of some exogenous event that might weaken the Habsburg Empire.[53]

Giuseppe Mazzini was one exception to the rule. He was spared disappointment with the outcome of Bonaparte's Russian adventure because he had never believed that Italy would benefit from it. The failures of 1848 had not shaken his conviction that Italy could free herself without the help of foreign powers. He still believed that, given proper indoctrination and sufficient financial means and weapons, the Italian people were strong enough to overthrow the existing governments, free their country of foreign troops, and establish a united, democratic republic. In his view, episodes like the Milanese insurrection of February 1853, even when they failed, served a useful function. The repressive measures that usually followed such attempts widened the gap between the Italian governments and the people, and therefore hastened the day of reckoning. Abortive revolutions, as

Lenin was to say much later, were necessary dress rehearsals for successful ones.[54]

While Mazzini's writings and letters hardly justify the portrait of bloodthirsty, irresponsible fanaticism sometimes painted by his conservative opponents, it is clear that he made grave personal sacrifices, and demanded the same of his followers, in the name of Italy's emancipation. Ferrari was completely impervious to this psychological dimension so typical of the professional revolutionary of modern times. He doubted more than ever that an abstract program of independence, unification, and political rights could mobilize the illiterate and impoverished masses.[55]

But until the Franco-Sardinian alliance of 1859, Ferrari's criticisms of the Party of Action were confined to private conversations with close friends. He seemed eager to avoid the polemics and confrontations that had occurred in 1850 between his friends in Capolago and the followers of Mazzini. Thus, when Cattaneo asked him to write a memoir on their interview with Mazzini in April 1848, Ferrari complied with a vivid account that was quite critical of Mazzini, but he pleaded successfully with Cattaneo not to publish it in the *Archivio triennale*.[56]

The Paris Peace Conference of 1856 paved the way for a rapprochement between Napoleon III and Cavour and for the alignment of prominent Italians in the moderate liberal camp with the anti-Habsburg policy of the Sardinian government. The Party of Action responded to these developments with renewed attempts to arouse the masses and to force a revolutionary solution of the Italian question. With a handful of companions, Pisacane attempted to set off a popular uprising against Bourbon rule in southern Italy. His untimely death on the sun-scorched plain at Sapri left an irreplaceable gap in the already thin ranks of the Italian revolutionaries, who had counted on his military expertise in a future war of national liberation.[57]

Ferrari had barely recovered from his sorrow over "the loss of yet another brother and a probable asset to the cause" when, in January 1858, Felice Orsini and his accomplices brought their revolutionary protest to the very heart of the French capital. The attempted assassination of Napoleon III as a means of dramatizing Italy's plight resulted in stricter police surveillance over the Italian exiles in Paris and in more rigorous censorship of their political writings.[58] In the latter part of 1858, Ferrari was so absorbed in the writing of a new book, the *Histoire de la raison d'état*, and so busy helping the Proudhons and other victims of political repression that he paid little attention to the development of Franco-Sardinian relations. Orsini's desperate act stirred up the French Emperor's latent sympathy for Italian nationalism and set the stage for the secret negotiations with Cavour at Plombières.[59]

In 1859 news of the Franco-Sardinian alliance that resulted from those negotiations brought to the fore new conflicts within the Italian nationalist movement. As in 1848, Mazzini and his followers stood ready to subordinate their democratic and republican preferences to the cause of Italian independence and unification. But they also remained true to their principles of 1848 in rejecting French intervention in Italy. And so they found themselves in a paradoxical position: on the one hand, they wished Cavour well; on the other, they wanted him to renounce the one diplomatic weapon most important to the success of his foreign policy.[60]

In contrast to the Party of Action, Cattaneo welcomed the prospect of Napoleon III's intervention in Italy. He thought that the direct participation of France in a war against Austria would curb both the expansionist ambitions of the Sardinian government and the "fusionist" zeal of Cavour's ally, the Italian National Society.[61] Inevitably, by making these views public, he opened himself up to charges of being a Bonapartist agent. His political enemies attempted to substantiate these charges by pointing out, among other things, that he was the brother-in-law of the French minister in Naples, Anatole Brénier, and a close friend of that notorious Francophile, the expatriate Ferrari.[62]

In the 1850s Ferrari was accused by Italian exiles close to Mazzini not only of having Bonapartist sympathies but also of working for a restoration of the Murat dynasty in the Kingdom of the Two Sicilies.[63] Plans were indeed afoot in those days among French and Italian supporters of prince Lucien Murat, King Joachim's son, to promote a Murat candidacy in the event of a French military intervention in Italy. For various reasons nothing ever came of these plans. Murat's partisans found it difficult to make contacts with opposition groups in Naples, and they received no encouragement from Napoleon III. But perhaps their greatest liability was the candidate himself, an amiable, lethargic, dull man who had inherited none of his father's dashing qualities.[64] Ferrari regarded the reign of King Joachim, on balance, as a progressive moment in the otherwise dismal recent history of the Two Sicilies. However, far from being part of a Muratist cabal, before the unification of Italy he was not even acquainted with Lucien Murat.[65] His flirtations with Muratism, if such they were, came later, in the chaotic and troubled years that followed the annexation of southern Italy to the kingdom of Victor Emmanuel II.

Il piccolo corriere, the official mouthpiece of the Italian National Society, was especially persistent in searching for evidence of Ferrari's fondness for French imperialism and of his disdain for his native homeland. Ferrari did not intend to make apologies for what he had said long ago, particularly during his bitter feud with Gioberti. But he reacted very sharply to charges that he was anti-Italian.[66] Convinced that the Italian Revolution which he had advocated for twenty years was at last imminent, he was anxious to establish his right to speak on the subject, despite his French citizenship and his long absence from Italy. Indeed, he was eager to play a role in that revolution; and he hoped that the course of events would bear out the theories about Italy's past that he had formulated in the *Histoire des révolutions d'Italie*. Before discussing the Italian war of 1859 and Ferrari's subsequent return to his native land, we must now turn to an examination of those theories.

Sharing with Carlo Tenca his first reaction to Ferrari's *Histoire des révolutions d'Italie*, Cattaneo complained: "What a heavy, indigestible book! I can barely recognize the author."[67] The contemporary reader cannot help but sympathize with Cattaneo.

The *Révolutions d'Italie* lacks both the elegance of Ferrari's political and philosophical essays of the 1840s and the incisiveness of polemical works like *La Federazione repubblicana*. Its four massive volumes, replete with obscure, bizarre episodes from Italy's medieval past, try the patience of even the most tenacious reader. But the length of the work and a certain awkwardness of style do not explain why it is virtually unknown today even among specialists in nineteenth-century European historiography and why it must still be consulted in its original edition.

When the *Révolutions d'Italie* was published, in April 1858, it sparked a lively controversy among French intellectuals who knew its author. It was reviewed by such respected figures as Renan, Quinet, Brisset of the *Revue des deux Mondes*, and Zeller of the *Journal général de l'instruction publique*.[68] It received less attention (and far less praise) in Italy, but it was reviewed in Tenca's *Il Crepuscolo* and in the *Archivio storico italiano*. On balance, Ferrari's contemporaries judged it to be an original and interesting work. In the last fifty years, however, all of Ferrari's historical writings, the *Révolutions d'Italie* in particular, have suffered from the harsh indictment pronounced against them by Benedetto Croce, Italy's leading philosopher of history of the early twentieth century. He dismissed Ferrari as an antihistorical mind whose work had no sound intellectual precedents and who left no disciples.[69] One important reason for Croce's negative judgment was Ferrari's openly stated intention to interpret Italy's past freely, in order to understand her political and intellectual condition at mid-nineteenth century. For Croce, this was the quintessence of an antihistorical position. But it seems likely that Croce's historiographical judgment was also influenced by factors such as Ferrari's reputation for radical politics and his persistent habit of relating the emergence of new political ideas to "social movements," that is, to changes initiated by the masses. Whatever the motives behind it, Croce's critical assessment was hasty and superficial, and it should be revised.

That Ferrari's work lacks respectable intellectual precedents can be said only if we overlook the fact that it was written in France, not in Italy, by a man who was thoroughly familiar with the writings of such eminently "antihistorical minds" as Guizot, Thiers, Michelet, and Quinet. In the lecture halls of the Collège de France Ferrari had learned to appreciate the political uses of history.[70] That he did not initiate a new historiographical school is true in a literal sense. Since his death, only one Italian intellectual of mediocre gifts, Alfredo Oriani, has ever attempted to interpret Italy's political history in a similar vein.[71] But because his attention was focused exclusively upon history and historians, Croce overlooked the broader implications of Ferrari's work for other disciplines, most notably for political theory. The *Révolutions d'Italie* and its sequel, the *Histoire de la raison d'état*, prepared the ground for a generational theory of historical change of which Ferrari was one of the foremost nineteenth-century proponents.

After the Bonapartist coup, an involuntary absence from public life left Ferrari free to continue his philosophical and historical studies. In the libraries of Paris, Turin, and Florence he consulted the rare pamphlets and manuscripts pertaining to Italy's political history that provided the backbone for the *Révolutions d'Italie*. He was searching for answers to a crucial question in Italian historiography: why had Italy, at the end of her glorious Renaissance, failed to develop into a centralized modern state? The question, of course, was not new. Witness to the twilight of the Renaissance, Machiavelli had blamed his countrymen for leaving Italy exposed to foreign invasions and for failing to protect her independence. Historians of Ferrari's own generation often bemoaned (without explaining) Italy's inability to produce political leaders capable of combining daring invention, versatility, grace, and strength as her best artists had done. The *Révolutions d'Italie* reexamined the popular and persistent notion of Italy's "failure" and subjected it to close scrutiny. Since today it is still fashionable to talk about Italy's "failed transition to political modernization" in the seventeenth century, Ferrari's ideas on this subject should be of more than marginal interest to contemporary historians.[72]

In search of an explanation for Italy's "failed transition," Ferrari examined the entire span of her history from the fall of the Western Roman Empire to the early sixteenth century. His reading of the medieval chronicles made him realize that, at first glance, Italy's history lacked a sense of logical development. It read like an endless catalog of what he called "mutations" or "convulsions"—that is, small upheavals in which class was pitted against class, faction against faction, town against town, and village against village. The overall picture was one of perennial chaos and instability marked by frequent "revolutions"—that is, changes in political leadership. As he saw it, "Now somber, now splendid, Italy's history unfolds in innumerable episodes spawned by the inexhaustible vitality of her soil, in a labyrinth of unreal scenes in which reason is lost and all the laws of the human mind seem suspended. . . . How many times have we searched for a principle that might tame this disorder? Discovering anomalies everywhere, I resolved at least to make a note of those traits that set [the history of our] peninsula apart from that of other nations."[73]

In his writings of 1847–48 on the Italian question, he had already discussed one trait that he regarded as unique to Italian history, that is, the heavy and enduring influence of the papal and imperial traditions.[74] In his essays for the *Revue indépendante* and in the *Machiavel*, he had argued that in early sixteenth-century Italy "an imperial and papal restoration" had stifled the emerging independent and secular governments. But he had not explained why the Italian people had supported or tolerated such a restoration.[75] The more thorough study of Italy's past undertaken in preparation for the *Révolutions d'Italie* convinced him of the need to revise somewhat his previous interpretations of Italian history.[76]

First of all, he came to believe that the period ca. 500 to 1500 A.D. had been shaped by not two but three major traditions. The papal and imperial ones, both universal in their claims and federal in character, had been challenged at various times by what Ferrari called "the royal tradition." By this he meant a trend toward centralized governments under rulers whose power derived neither from the Church nor from the Empire, such as the Lombard invaders, the Franks before Charlemagne's pact with the Church, and the most powerful Signorie of the Renaissance.[77] But Ferrari did not associate the royal tradition with a monarchial form of government. Venice, for example, was part of the royal tradition—that is, a tradition of secular and independent government—although she had developed along the lines of a republican oligarchy.

Decade after decade, century after century, he wrote, the royal tradition had attempted to put down roots in Italian soil. But each time it had asserted itself, a papal or an imperial reaction had been able to crush it. A few exceptions, like Venice, confirmed the rule. What explained the seemingly inevitable victories of two leaders, one more often than not unarmed and the other more often than not absent from Italy? Having examined thousands of episodes in Italy's history, Ferrari concluded that the papal and imperial interventions (or "reactions," as he called them) had succeeded because the politically important segments of the population had wanted them to succeed. He wrote: "But, you might say, the pope is unarmed, the emperor is absent; where, then, do I find the enigmatic greatness of the Italian nation? Contrary to your prejudices I find it precisely in the absence of the emperor, in the military weakness of the pope, in the freedom they represent."[78]

Ferrari argued that the Italian people, to a greater extent than other western Europeans, had perceived the growth of independent, centralized governments as a threat to local rights, to individual liberties, and, at times, to their economic well-being.[79] Perhaps, he speculated, their attitude stemmed from the experience of tyranny in the last days of imperial Rome, or from the fact that they had identified royal government with the traditions of Italy's barbarian invaders. At any rate, the record showed that in the face of extreme chaos and insecurity the Italians had often tolerated despotism. But, with very few exceptions, they had refused to legitimize the royal tradition. In his words, "revolutionary Italy . . . spurns the false unity of the political arts and offers the extraordinary sight of a nation without boundaries, of progress without government, of a supremacy achieved without the benefit of imported theories about independence, force, or the

greatness of the state."[80] By rejecting strong centralized governments in favor of the weakest of leaders and by playing the
papacy and the empire against each other (the real meaning, he
thought, of the feuds between Guelphs and Ghibellines), the Italians had not only maintained control over their civic and individual destiny, but they had also kept the door open to a wider
range of opportunities for social change than existed under the
military monarchies of other countries. If historians were dwell-
ing upon Italy's "failed transition" in the sixteenth and seventeenth centuries, Ferrari suggested, it was because they paid too
much attention to political developments and not enough to
social trends.[81] By shifting the focus of historical investigation
away from the emergence of the modern state, it became easier to
appreciate Italy's outstanding achievements in other areas. She
had led Europe, for instance, in the development of a powerful
mercantile bourgeoisie. She had also pioneered in certain forms
of democracy, as reflected in the struggles of the Florentine *popolo minuto* against the privileged merchants and artisans, the
popolo grasso, or in the challenge of Cola di Rienzo to the
Roman patriciate. Anticipating the criticism that no comparable
claims could be made for Italy in the area of economic growth
and innovation after the early sixteenth century, Ferrari observed
that shifting trade routes and a scarcity of good land had posed
greater obstacles to economic progress than the lack of a centralized government.[82]

It should be clear from this brief summary that, read on one
level, the *Histoire des révolutions d'Italie* is a political statement.
Certain that Italy was on the verge of yet another great upheaval,
Ferrari warned the leaders of the revolutionary movement that
they would fail if they continued to focus exclusively upon political or diplomatic objectives. Italy's successful revolutions, he
wrote, had always been *social*, not political or diplomatic, ones:
"Progress was achieved within each historical period by the actions of ordinary men. There is not a single year in Italy's history
that does not bristle with comical, trivial, bloody episodes. . . .
Her social movements are always impressive, her political movements always insignificant."[83]

The *Révolutions d'Italie* is a political statement also in the sense that it places the Italian masses at center stage in the complex drama of their country's history. In Ferrari's work, the collective actions of obscure men and women, peasants, townsfolk, monks, and mercenaries receive greater attention than the deeds of famous personages or the history of important institutions. In this respect, the work certainly reflects what he had learned over the years from other scholars of Romantic and democratic inclination, especially Fauriel and Michelet.

Finally, the *Révolutions d'Italie* is noteworthy for the feeling of warm patriotic pride that shines throughout its erudite volumes. Ferrari had often scoffed at the Giobertian idea of the moral supremacy of Italian civilization and at the Mazzinian vision of a united Italy as the focal point of a democratic and nationalist Europe. But now he too made sweeping claims on behalf of his native homeland. With the publication of this work he took his place among the nationalist writers of his generation. Although he had never expressed a desire to return to Italy on a permanent basis, it is obvious that he wanted to be better known among fellow Italians. For that reason, he was unhappy when publishers in Genoa and Florence refused the manuscript of the *Révolutions d'Italie*, which was clearly addressed to an Italian audience.[84]

Read on a different level, the *Révolutions d'Italie* and the *Raison d'état* mark an important watershed in the evolution of Ferrari's philosophical outlook. Ever since the beginning of his training under Romagnosi, he had shown an interest in the problem of historical change.[85] In the *Essai sur le principe*, he had wavered between the belief that historical transitions resulted from the application of enlightened human reason to the problems of society and the Hegelian conception of inevitable metaphysical stages, open to rational exploration, yet beyond the scope of individual human actions. In the late 1840s, when he had been most closely associated with the Leroux-Sand circle, he had leaned more heavily in the direction of the Enlightenment view, probably because faith in the power of human reason and an optimistic view of human nature were necessary preconditions for the brand of humanitarian socialism that his friends preached.

But the failure of the Revolution of 1848 led him to rethink the whole question; and in the 1850s he began to articulate a new theory of historical change. Because Ferrari's theory was fully developed only toward the end of his life, it will be discussed in the last chapter of this work. A first tentative formulation of that theory appeared in the fourth volume of the *Révolutions d'Italie* and in the *Raison d'état*.

Studies of Italian history from 500 to 1500 A.D., he wrote, at first created the false impression that the innumerable mutations or convulsions had happened by accident, without any inner logic or pattern. The medieval chroniclers, unable to establish connections among thousands of seemingly unrelated episodes, had attempted to find specific explanations for each change.[86] But Ferrari, returning to a major theme of his *Essai sur le principe*, argued that it was possible (and indeed necessary for the sake of historical accuracy) to find patterns amidst the apparent chaos of the Italian revolutions. In the first volume of the *Révolutions d'Italie*, he discussed the methodology that distinguished the modern philosopher of history from the chroniclers of old. The philosopher of history must begin with a broad hypothesis and he must not be reluctant to extract connections, comparisons, and generalizations from a mass of seemingly disparate elements.[87] Having identified some patterns in the history of medieval Italy, such as the perennial struggle between federal and royal traditions, he suggested that his findings could perhaps be generalized into universally applicable historical laws. In order to test this hypothesis he began an ambitious study of other European nations and of non-Western cultures, especially ancient China. Eventually he became convinced that universally valid laws did in fact exist.[88]

The history of medieval Italy suggested to him that changes in political leadership (revolutions) brought about by changes in the social structure (mutations or convulsions) had occurred at intervals of approximately 120 to 125 years. Between revolutions, he wrote, the thousands of episodes and events immortalized by the chroniclers could be arranged in four phases, each one lasting approximately one generation. During the first phase (subversion), new ideas produced by social mutations arose to challenge the established political principles and leaders; but the challenge was covert and indirect—for example, through theology, philosophy, or the arts. A direct challenge occurred during the second phase (solution); it brought about a confrontation (combat) between the old principles and the new. When the new principles became established (victory), the cycle began all over again.[89]

In contrast to Ferrari's earlier writings, which reflect the influence of the Enlightenment, these works convey little sense of progress in the unfolding of successive historical phases. On the immense stage of the *Révolutions d'Italie* the gods, kings, and heroes of ancient epics give up their places under the spotlight to the Italian masses. In this sense, Ferrari's work certainly has a contemporary flavor. But his actors are not free to choose their roles or to improvise their lines. Their collective actions, which initiate each new phase, do not result from conscious choices, but seem to be determined by an unfathomable fate. "It is not justice that establishes kingdoms nor virtue that distributes crowns," Ferrari wrote; "a crime may usher in the birth of an empire, imposture at times creates popular religions, and glaring iniquity is often responsible for the rise and fall of states, as if good and evil were equally necessary. Only a natural law equally indifferent to God and Satan can account for liberties, servitudes, parties, wars, revolutions, for the factions that initiate revolutions and for those that resolve them."[90] This mechanistic and fatalistic view of history, which Ferrari held for the rest of his life, set him apart from the radical and socialist friends whose ideas and goals he had shared in his younger years. Above all, it set him clearly apart from the Marxist intellectual and political tradition.

In 1848–50 Ferrari's analysis of contemporary events from the perspective of a class struggle had been substantially close to that of Marx. Because he did not believe that the class struggle of 1848 in France had been inevitable and because he favored, like Proudhon, the preservation within certain limits of noninherited private capital, it is unlikely that he could ever have followed Marx's brand of revolutionary socialism. But by adopting this position of historical fatalism in the late 1850s, he made it extremely difficult for himself to maintain a radical or socialist political outlook.

When he began a new career in Italian politics, he stuck to his political views of the 1840s. But he did so only at the price of a glaring contradiction with his own philosophical outlook. This contradiction made him vulnerable to attack by his adversaries and it allowed contemporary and later critics to make light of either his historical theories or his commitment to radical politics, or both. On this point, it is interesting to note that Italian Marxist scholars, who in the last fifteen years have done much to illuminate Ferrari's contribution to Italian history, have virtually ignored the works under discussion, as well as *La Chine et l'Europe* of 1867 and the *Teoria dei periodi politici* of 1874. They have chosen to focus upon Ferrari's political views and upon his relationship with other radical or socialist intellectuals, and they have brushed aside the embarrassing contradiction between Ferrari the politician of the Left and Ferrari the theorist of generational change.[91]

And yet, without underestimating the weakness of his ideological position as he entered the politically active phase of his life, it is possible from the perspective of the late twentieth century to sympathize with Ferrari as his own contemporaries perhaps could not. Even if man believes that God is dead (a contemporary phrase that is most applicable to Ferrari), even if he suspects that human events are controlled by irrational forces and that the progress of mankind is, at best, a doubtful proposition, he must still continue to use his reason to make this the best of all possible worlds. This was, briefly stated, Ferrari's philosophical outlook from the late 1850s to the end of his life. His was basically an existentialist position, closer to the twentieth century than to the attitude of such famous contemporaries of his as Marx, Comte, or Mill. Perhaps his position was more attuned than theirs to the increasingly cynical atmosphere of the 1850s and 1860s, when the political and intellectual heirs to the French Revolution were giving way to a new breed of leaders and the ideals of European liberalism to the exigencies of *Realpolitik*.

PART TWO

THE POLITICIAN

[5]

Return to the Roots

EARLY IN 1859 the prospect of a French intervention in Italy once again highlighted the difference between Ferrari, who looked forward for ideological and historical reasons to such an intervention, and the Mazzinian radicals, who opposed it as a threat to Italian liberty. The Franco-Sardinian alliance also created a serious rift between Ferrari and his friends in France. Quinet, Renan, and, above all, Proudhon were adamantly opposed to any Bonapartist adventure in Italy.[1]

But in March and April 1859 Ferrari's expectations and the misgivings of Bonaparte's adversaries seemed equally unfounded. In view of differences between France and Sardinia and of an Anglo-Prussian initiative to stave off a European crisis by means of an international conference, the preservation of the status quo or a diplomatic solution to the Italian Question seemed more likely than a forthcoming military intervention by Napoleon III in Italy.[2] Like Cavour and his supporters, although for quite different reasons, Ferrari was disappointed by this turn of events.

We do not know how he reacted to the ultimatum of 23 April 1859, by which the Habsburg government demanded the demobilization of Sardinian troops deployed along the Ticino River and therefore precipitated the outbreak of war. But we can assume, in view of his previous statements, that the Austrian move was as welcome to him as it was to Cavour. He was excited about the war in Lombardy and delighted with the brilliant, if costly, French victories. Although he had been suffering for some time from muscular cramps, he wasted no time in applying for a passport when he heard of the liberation of Lombardy from Habsburg rule. By mid-July 1859 he was already back in Milan. "How could I resist"—he wrote—"the temptation . . . to verify with my own eyes the great historical laws of Italy?"[3]

The homecoming was a joyous one. The festive mood that had seized the people of Milan upon the departure of their Austrian overlords had not yet given way to the bleak realities of political and administrative unification with Sardinia. With wry amusement, Ferrari noted that the popular enthusiasm for the French emperor and for the gallant *zouaves* far exceeded his own. But his customary skepticism was for once overcome by the sheer pleasure of revisiting the familiar places of his youth and greeting relatives and old friends, many of whom were returning from political exile. At last he met his brother's second wife, Maria Cristina Arpagans, the handsome, dark-haired daughter of a peasant proprietor from the Canton Grigioni. Cristina, as everyone called her, was a simple woman of limited education, very different from the sophisticated ladies found within Ferrari's circle of friends. Nonetheless, he became fond of her and looked after her, especially after Carlo's death in 1869. Perhaps he sensed that she could not be completely happy in her marriage to a staid civil servant who was one generation older than herself and whose only surviving son, Cristoforo, despised her.[4] But ultimately, the pleasure of revisiting familiar places was spoiled by the disappointing outcome of the war. Having expected a French conquest of Venetia, Ferrari was shocked by the Villafranca armistice between Napoleon III and Francis Joseph of Austria.[5]

Napoleon III did not claim one inch of Lombard soil. Thus, Ferrari argued, the French victories became in effect the victories of King Victor Emmanuel and of his father's old allies, the Lombard patricians. As in 1848, the patricians saw in the unification of Lombardy with Piedmont-Sardinia a means of attaining liberal institutions while avoiding the dangers of radical popular movements. Ferrari still hoped, however, that this unexpected success of "the royal tradition" in his native region might be thwarted by a mass movement of the type that he had discovered in the history of medieval Italy: "The true Caesar in Vienna has sown the seeds of socialism throughout the Lombard countryside; his generals have shown the peasants at swordpoint the lands of the wealthy to be divided up; the peasants despise this war, which they call the war of the rich, of the nobles, of the Lombard warriors in the service of the king; and the democratic side may have the opportunity to reverse the current trend."[6]

Ferrari was by no means the only repatriated Lombard to sense the unpopularity among the peasantry of the war in general and the Sardinian intervention in particular.[7] But he was the only one to argue that Cavour's radical adversaries should exploit any existing social and economic grievances among the masses to prevent the annexation of Lombardy by Sardinia and the political victory of the moderate liberals. Even after the Villafranca armistice, he hoped that his native region, under radical leadership, might initiate the long-awaited Italian Revolution. His hopes stemmed from the political ideology that he had formulated in *La Federazione repubblicana* and other writings. As he admitted upon his return to Paris in September 1859, they were unfortunately based upon an unrealistic assessment of the current situation in Italy. Reluctantly, he concluded that the conditions for a radical political and social revolution did not yet exist. To the ever-inquisitive Proudhon, who invited him to philosophize upon the prospects of federalism and socialism in Italy, he wrote:

The essential point is that in Italy all *political* questions boil down to *diplomatic* questions. Those who want to drive out the Austrians rely upon France; those who want to drive out the French invoke Austria, the pope, their allies. . . . Left to her own devices, Italy is nothing. . . . Her state of decadence is such that it frightens me; she is so corrupt that the preaching of sermons (through the press) seems utterly futile. Do you accuse Cavour of being a rogue? But he brags about his lies! Do you tell Mazzini that he is an absolutist? But he is proud of it! Coups d'état, conspiracies, duplicity, false rumors and slander are the typically Italian weapons of the war of independence. . . . The Italian revolutionaries have a cut-and-dry view of the revolution. *Grosso modo*, they think that it consists of driving out the Austrians. . . .[8]

Toward the end of September 1859 Proudhon believed that Tuscany and the Duchies would resist annexation by the Kingdom of Sardinia. But what about Lombardy, he inquired. Were the Lombards happy about the double diplomatic exchange that had brought them under the Cross of Savoy? Was it true, as he read in the French and Belgian newspapers, that the two emperors had pledged to prevent the establishment of republican regimes in Italy? Did the Italian republican movement show any vital signs? Was there a Savonarola, a Machiavelli, a Cola di Rienzo on the scene?[9]

In his answer Ferrari emphasized again that the Italian war that he had so eagerly awaited had turned out to be a war of independence, and not in any sense a revolutionary war. For the time being, the Lombards were cheering King Victor Emmanuel, because his arrival had marked the end of Habsburg rule. As for the Italian republicans, they could be said to be "the foremost enemies of republicanism, of philosophy, of socialism. . . . They say with Manin and Mazzini: I am a republican, but first of all the war against Austria; I am a socialist, but first of all independence; I fight God with P.-J. [Proudhon], but first of all the king, Cavour, the monarchy."[10]

A few weeks later, a very disgruntled Proudhon reflected upon the recent triumphs of the moderate liberals in central Italy. The real tragedy, he complained, was not the absence of revolutionaries in Italy, but the presence of the wrong kind of revolutionaries, those "atheistic bourgeois, businessmen and brokers hungry for the powers and the estates of the Church, . . . exploiters and cannibals, whose hegemony in the nineteenth century would ruin mankind, unless they were stopped by the men of the social revolution." It could be said that capitalist greed was the only modern idea to have taken root on Italian soil.[11] Ferrari agreed with this assessment. But he regarded "the false revolution" of which the propertied classes were the obvious beneficiaries as a less vexing problem, for the moment at any rate, than the Italian obsession with the war of independence.[12]

Despite his obvious disappointment with the outcome of the Bonapartist intervention in Italy, Ferrari was completely fascinated by the fluid political situation that he found upon his arrival in Milan. To his chagrin, at the end of August a personal matter required his presence in Paris. But before leaving he urged Carozzi, who had returned to Milan at the same time, to stay on and to keep his eyes open for whatever opportunities the situation might offer. After all, he wrote, they were not getting any younger.[13]

There can be no doubt of Ferrari's desire to become better known in the political and intellectual circles of his native city. In the summer of 1859 and during a subsequent visit in October, he missed no opportunity to renew old friendships and to seek out new ones. He was seen regularly at the fashionable Caffè Cova, and he looked for an apartment in the elegant district between the Teatro alla Scala, Piazza San Babila and the Duomo. Moreover, he made plans for the future publication in Milan of his political works, heretofore little known in Italy.[14] But in his initial contacts with former members of the Romagnosi circle, with the editor Carlo Tenca, with repatriated radicals like Macchi and Daelli, and with members of political clubs in and around Milan, he was shy, almost secretive, as if he feared a rebuff. After all, except for two brief visits he had been absent from Milan for over twenty years, he had become a French citizen, and he had played only a minor role in the Lombard Revolution of 1848. Besides, he knew that his views on the Italian Revolution were regarded as extremist by most of his contemporaries, even those within the radical camp.

He was delighted to find that his presence in Milan was welcome; indeed, his friends there wanted him to become the editor of a new anti-Cavourian newspaper. In November 1859 he declined that invitation, primarily because he wished to be free to travel back and forth to Paris. "To leave France," he wrote, "would be like losing one arm." But he confessed to Proudhon:

My trip to Milan has disclosed a thousand opportunities that I lack in Paris, a much greater number of personal friends than I had expected, a very different situation from that of February 1848, and an easy way to make an impact. . . . As long as I remain at Impasse Mazagran [his Parisian residence], I am a foreigner, an expatriate, a man alone; in Milan it is different, so very different that I was myself surprised, touched, and deeply moved. There is a Ferrari whom you do not know and whose existence I had not suspected myself; his polemics of long ago have left their mark; people remember them, and my arrows are still embedded in the flesh of my opponents.[15]

The opportunities that Ferrari had discovered in Milan and that were unavailable in Bonapartist France were above all political ones.[16] Although deeply attached to his adoptive homeland and proud of the success of his most recent books, he was restless and disenchanted with the policies of Napoleon III. The political campaign that followed the transfer of Lombardy from the Habsburg Empire to the Kingdom of Sardinia offered him the chance of a new beginning. And he felt ready to take that chance. The encouragement that he received from personal friends certainly played a part in his decision to seek elective office in Italy. So did his own conviction that he had something worthwhile to contribute to the intellectual progress of the new Italian state. But there were also strong psychological motives behind his decision. As his letters to Proudhon and Carozzi indicate, he was acutely conscious of the passing of time and eager to test his mental and physical energies outside the cozy but confining haven of the Impasse Mazagran. In approaching his new career Ferrari needed all the energy, self-confidence, and enthusiasm he could muster, for the path leading to Turin was long and steep.

The campaign that preceded the parliamentary elections of March 1860 in northern Italy was a complicated affair for all political factions and for all candidates, but especially for the repatriated exiles. In a few months they had to rebuild political bases that had been destroyed over the years by persecution or neglect, or they had to build new ones where none had existed before. With the return of Cavour to power in January 1860, the moderate candidates could count on the support of the Sardinian government. Further, they had access to the substantial organizational and financial resources of the Italian National Society. But the radical candidates, divided since 1848 into small competing groups, lacked comparable resources.[17] For Ferrari these common difficulties were compounded by the particularly controversial nature of his ideas, by his unusually long absence from Italy, by his lack of organizational experience, and, last but not least, by the attitude of his friend Cattaneo.

Returning to Paris in February 1860 from a political tour of some Lombard districts, Ferrari reported to Proudhon that four nominations were all but certain in Milan: Cavour and Luigi Carlo Farini for the moderate party, Cattaneo and himself for the opposition. He was wondering whether or not to accept the forthcoming nomination, which "threatened to change the entire course of [his] life." Although the lure of politics was strong indeed, he hesitated to take the final steps. He knew that, if elected, he would be one of a small minority of deputies detested by the moderate majority. He confessed to Proudhon that he was worried and even a bit frightened.[18]

Proudhon had argued earlier that the mere editorship of an anti-Cavourian newspaper was not important enough to warrant Ferrari's return to Italy. But now he urged his friend to accept the forthcoming nomination. His very presence in the Chamber of Deputies would serve as a reminder to other politicians and to public opinion that the ideals of federalism, secularism, and social revolution were alive and well.[19]

Ferrari had every reason to expect a difficult race. From the press clippings which his friends had sent him in 1858, he already knew that his Francophile attitude and his ideological battle cry, "*irreligione e legge agraria*," made him vulnerable, particularly in a country where Roman Catholicism was a powerful force and where the propertied classes had complete control of the electoral process. To make matters worse, he could not expect help from the followers of Mazzini, with whom he had been feuding for years.

Ferrari made the best of the few political assets he did have: his reputation as a philosopher and political theorist, his oratorical ability, the assistance of a few devoted friends like Carozzi, and the financial help of Enrico Cernuschi. A graduate of the anti-Habsburg barricades of 1848, Cernuschi had fled to France in 1850 and had settled down to a career in banking. His fortunes had risen with those of the Crédit Mobilier, and by 1860 he was a very wealthy man. Although he did not wish to return to Italy himself, he was willing to help his fellow radicals of 1848, especially Ferrari, who had assisted him generously in the early 1850s.[20]

But a scholarly reputation and the assistance of a few friends were clearly not enough to win the election. In March, with only two or three weeks' time, Ferrari doubled his efforts to canvass support within the anti-Cavourian Associazione Elettorale Milanese and to enlist the help of his fellow candidate Cattaneo. Ferrari did not expect much help from the Associazione Elettorale, because he knew of strong Mazzinian sympathies among its members. Two of them, the lawyer Michele Cavaleri and the insurance executive Francesco Cardani, sympathized with his federalist ideas and became, in time, his trusted friends and his allies in Lombard politics. But it is clear that Ferrari counted more heavily upon Cattaneo's support, and that he was confused and angered by his friend's behavior during the campaign.[21]

Cattaneo had accepted the nomination in Milan as much to annoy his moderate and Mazzinian critics as to humor his few but zealous disciples. Tired and ailing, content with his quiet life in the Swiss countryside, he had no intention of returning to Italy and beginning a new career. He was, after all, ten years older and much less wealthy than Ferrari. He felt that, if elected, he would not be able to afford the expenses of parliamentary life. Thus, to the chagrin of his supporters, he flatly refused to campaign on his own behalf.[22] There is no doubt, however, that he could have helped Ferrari's candidacy had he wished to do so. He might have withdrawn from the race and asked his supporters to vote for Ferrari. If this did not seem advisable (in view of Ferrari's controversial ideas), he might at least have agreed to make joint appearances at political meetings in Milan or to write one of the customary campaign pamphlets endorsing his friend's candidacy. That Cattaneo refused to do any of these things was due only in part to the pressure of other commitments or to the torments of ill health. There is evidence that he was less than pleased with Ferrari's candidacy for Parliament.[23] A certain tension between the two men had already developed, as we have seen, after the publication of Ferrari's *La Federazione repubblicana*, when Cattaneo had expressed strong reservations about the concept of *legge agraria*. But their personal relationship had remained cordial. Only in March 1860 did Ferrari, who had deferred to Cattaneo in all matters of political strategy, begin to suspect that his old friend had turned against him. In fact, he held Cattaneo responsible for the failure of his own candidacy in Milan.[24]

But fortunately for his political future, Ferrari was careful not to place all his eggs in one basket. While he wished to be elected in Milan, he also accepted the nomination in the district of Gavirate-Luino. The notables of that picturesque, mostly rural district in northwestern Lombardy had approached him, it seems, not because they agreed with his ideology but simply because they wished to be represented in Parliament by a fellow Lombard of distinguished intellectual accomplishments. Ironically, Ferrari observed, the fact that many distinguished Lombards were already serving in the Sardinian government or in the bureaucracy, while others were temporarily in disgrace for having served the Habsburgs, was working in his favor. There were only so many distinguished Lombards to go around, and the worthy electors of Gavirate-Luino had settled for him.[25]

When he learned that he had won only in Gavirate-Luino, he reconsidered the whole question of a political career. He might try again in Milan, but a different outcome seemed unlikely so long as both Cavourians and Mazzinians were against him while Cattaneo remained aloof. And what kind of future could he have as the representative of Gavirate-Luino? What if the notables of that district came up with a distinguished native son whose political ideology they found more palatable? Further complications arose while he was trying to decide whether or not to accept the mandate from Gavirate-Luino.[26] He learned that, if he accepted it, his right to a seat in Parliament would be challenged because, having opted for French citizenship voluntarily in 1842, he was not covered by the Sardinian Law of Naturalization. As usual, he shared his troubles with Proudhon.

"Should I accept [the mandate]? Should I swear allegiance to a kingdom which I have opposed, to a dominant religion that proscribes my books, to a Chamber of Deputies who serve without stipend, one chock-full of counts and marquises? Should I sacrifice to Victor Emmanuel my French citizenship, which is my life, my academic credentials, which may be valuable some day, my scholarly work, which gives me such a splendid introduction to the world of French letters?"[27] Proudhon, other friends in Milan, and, of course, the electors of Gavirate-Luino all urged Ferrari to accept the mandate and to take his chances on the matter of citizenship. His case was unusual but not unique, and it seemed probable that the Chamber would rule in favor of letting him take his seat. This did in fact happen in May 1860.[28]

Having accepted the mandate, Ferrari urged Cattaneo, who had been elected in Milan, to do likewise and to go to Turin for the opening of the new Parliament. To make his point more strongly, he actually visited Cattaneo in Castagnola. But that visit marked the rapid deterioration of a friendship that had lasted for more than thirty years.[29] Already piqued about Cattaneo's behavior during the electoral campaign, Ferrari was incensed by his cavalier attitude toward the mandate. He rejected as a lame excuse Cattaneo's contention that the radical viewpoint on the current Italian situation could be expressed as effectively in the pages of Il Politecnico as in Parliament. Borrowing an argument or two from Proudhon, Ferrari pointed out that books and journals could never have the same impact as "the legitimate, solemn, sovereign acts of sitting, speaking, and voting in Parliament."[30]

We cannot but agree with him that Cattaneo's decision to accept the mandate without taking his seat was unwise, indeed irresponsible. And perhaps we can also agree with him on the symbolic importance of a token radical presence in the new Parliament. But his own position in the spring of 1860 was no less open to criticism than Cattaneo's. Political adversaries were only too happy to point out, for instance, that Ferrari the socialist was also Ferrari the Parisian *rentier* and that he had spent generously of his own and of Cernuschi's money in the Milanese campaign. They also noted that Ferrari the republican was willing to swallow an oath of loyalty to Victor Emmanuel in order to take his seat and that he had long talks with Urbano Rattazzi, the King's friend and favorite minister.[31]

In general, Ferrari's activities between July 1859 and May 1860 created the impression that he was an unscrupulous, ambitious trimmer, ready to cast aside his political and philosophical convictions for the sake of fame and power. The same could be said, of course, of other Risorgimento radicals who entered Parliament in 1860. Yet on both personal and ideological grounds Ferrari was perhaps more vulnerable to charges of opportunism and inconsistency than any of the others. Obviously, he did not regard himself as a trimmer or his presence in Parliament as a betrayal of revolutionary ideals. But he was aware of the criticism of his conduct during and after the Lombard campaign.[32] In the next several years he tried hard to prove that his motives in returning to Italy had been honorable and that he could work effectively within the existing political framework on behalf of his electors, even while remaining loyal to his secular, federalist, and socialist principles. He was no less eager to prove that he could serve Italy well while continuing his love affair with France. In the 1860s, however, the interests of his two homelands diverged more often than not, and painful choices were required of him. The first of these presented itself just after he had taken his seat in Parliament.

When Ferrari arrived in Turin, the new Parliament was in the throes of its first major debate, concerning the proposed cession of the Duchy of Savoy and of the city of Nice to France. The reason behind Cavour's proposal was clear enough to the King, the moderate majority, and the opposition: there was a price to be paid for Napoleon III's help in Lombardy and, perhaps more important, for his acquiescence to the annexation of Tuscany, the Duchies, and the Papal Legations. The cession, to be legitimized by plebiscites, of two border areas where French dialects were spoken seemed a logical, if not an ideal, way to settle the account with France. But although it was acceptable in Paris,

Cavour's proposal ran into a storm of criticism in Turin. Understandably, Victor Emmanuel balked at the idea of losing the rugged mountain region that had given his ancestors strength in times of growth and expansion and protection in times of crisis and retreat. With equally strong emotions, Giuseppe Garibaldi, the popular guerrilla leader of 1848 and 1859, denounced the proposed cession of his native Nice.[33]

But Cavour's plan raised difficult questions even for leaders whose personal feelings were not at stake. As Cattaneo pointed out in a perceptive article, the deputies who sat in the majestic Palazzo Carignano (or at least those who subscribed to the *programma unitario*) claimed to represent the Italian nation. Actually they represented only two-fifths of Italy. How could they expect the Italian people and the governments of Europe to take them seriously, he asked, if they inaugurated the new era by giving up territories to which the Kingdom of Northern Italy had historic claims and which were necessary to the defense of its capital?[34] Speech after speech on the floor of the Chamber, from the moderate side, from the radical opposition, and from Rattazzi's so-called third party, suggested that Cattaneo had indeed put his finger squarely on the spot.

If the question of Nice and Savoy was a difficult one for all Italian leaders, Cavour included, it was especially so for Ferrari. As a new face in the Chamber and an as yet unknown quantity within the thin ranks of the radical opposition, he was not expected to take active part in this debate; the decision to make his maiden speech on this particular issue was entirely his own, and it surprised his closest friends.[35] He wanted to make his oratorical debut in the Chamber before the VII Legislature adjourned, as it was expected to do after the vote on Cavour's proposal. But political vanity aside, Ferrari had been challenged to speak out on this issue, and he felt that he must answer the challenge. During their political quarrel in April, Cattaneo had taunted him about his Francophile outlook and had suggested, in a malicious vein, that the forthcoming debate on Nice and Savoy was certain to put him on the spot.[36]

Like Cattaneo and Montanelli, Ferrari had disapproved of

the plebiscites and subsequent annexations in central Italy. He regarded them not as a political victory for the Italian people but as a barely camouflaged conquest by the Kingdom of Sardinia. He had argued that a federation in central Italy under native leaders was more consistent with Italy's historical traditions, less threatening to France, and therefore less likely to require territorial sacrifices elsewhere. But the annexations were now a fait accompli, and a price clearly had to be paid. The real issue now was whether or not Italy could afford the bill which "the conspirators of Plombières" had presented to her.[37]

Ferrari thought that she could not. To give up Savoy, he said, meant "to sacrifice Piedmont to France after Italy had been sacrificed to Piedmont." The proposed cession, in fact, would leave Turin exposed to attack and would make a mockery of the "great and mighty kingdom" of which Victor Emmanuel and Cavour were boasting. To the argument that the French-speaking people of Nice and Savoy had to be given the option to become French citizens, Ferrari replied that it made sense only if the Italian-speaking people of Corsica were given the same option. At any rate, he added, France had never shown much concern for the national rights, for instance, of the Germans in Alsace and the Arabs in Algeria. And so there was no need to take seriously the argument of Cavour and Napoleon III that her claims to Nice and Savoy were based on nationality. He suggested that a new round of negotiations with Paris or, if that could not be achieved, amendments to Cavour's proposal and other delaying tactics were to be preferred to a hasty vote on the matter. Garibaldi's recent departure for Sicily was very much on his mind as he proposed this strategy of delay.[38] But the very same consideration made Cavour double his efforts to secure the speedy passage of his bill. And once again Cavour had his way.

If the purpose of Ferrari's maiden speech was to show that his admiration for France did not preclude his appreciation of and loyalty to Italian interests, he succeeded admirably. His intervention was well received by his Lombard supporters; it made his reputation, confirmed by many subsequent speeches, as one of the most gifted orators in the Chamber; and, more important, it facilitated a rapprochement with anti-Cavourian deputies from Piedmont and other regions who had been wary of his close ties with France.[39] But neither the June sunshine nor the praise earned in Italy could warm the chilly reception that awaited his return to Paris, where he planned to spend the summer recess. His friends there, and Proudhon in Brussels, clearly regarded his speech on Nice and Savoy as an insult to France. On the defensive once again, Ferrari explained: "Listen! Take Nice and Savoy, if you like . . . but don't expect me, a deputy, a simple mandatory, bound by concrete interests, unable to give away any gift whatever, to vote a gift of territory without compensation, as a gesture of gratitude that has no legal justification, only a moral one. Such a gesture would have been a very bad start of my new career."[40] But his French critics were not appeased. And he began to realize how dangerous it was to have divided loyalties in an age of nationalism.

His embarrassing position in Paris compounded his sadness over the poor showing of the radical group in the March elections and over Cavour's lopsided victory in the matter of Nice and Savoy. However, like other men of the Left, in the summer of 1860 he was given new hope by the spectacular progress of Garibaldi's revolutionary war in the Two Sicilies.[41] Because he believed that Garibaldi's success offered the last chance for a democratic and federalist revolution, he decided to join other men of the Left who were already in the South. Their purpose was to thwart, if they could, the annexationist aims of the moderate party. Before departing for Naples he had to prepare himself for the opening of the new legislative session. Having left his belongings in a Turin hotel, he rushed off to a tour of his district and a visit with political friends in Milan. Exhausted, complaining to Proudhon that he was "condemned to the forced labor of Italian politics," he arrived in Naples around 10 September, accompanied by Cavaleri.

This was his first encounter with a part of Italy that, he later admitted, seemed more foreign to him than France had seemed in the 1830s. On this first trip he did not have the time to visit much more than the historic monuments of Naples and the enchanting Gulf of Posillipo. His only excursion outside the capital, on 24–25 September, took him to Garibaldi's headquarters in Caserta. Most of his time was spent in closed meetings with other men of the Left. Like him, they had come to observe the situation and to counteract the influence of Cavour's and the King's agents upon Garibaldi, now the dictator of the conquered Two Sicilies.[42]

Nearly all the important names of Italian radicalism were present in Naples as that fateful summer of 1860 came to an end: Crispi; Agostino Bertani and Alberto Mario, Garibaldi's lieutenants in the daring Expedition of the Thousand; Aurelio Saffi, survivor of the Roman Republic of 1849; Filippo De Boni from Venetia; Cattaneo; and even the proscribed Mazzini, who had travelled back to Italy from London at grave personal risk. In some twenty years of political struggles, these men had never been more united on one issue—the need to delay, if not prevent, further annexations to the Sardinian Kingdom. Even Mazzini at this point agreed with Ferrari that the unification of Italy already resembled "a royal conquest" much more than the spontaneous and democratic process for which he had struggled so hard and so long.

To the extent that a common radical strategy existed in September 1860 (the old personal and ideological differences had not disappeared and there had not been much time for planning), it consisted of driving a wedge between Garibaldi and the royal government in Turin. It was no easy task, since the Two Sicilies had been conquered in the name of "Italy and Victor Emmanuel." But the basis for a rift existed in Garibaldi's bitterness toward Cavour, whom he blamed for the sacrifice of his beloved Nice and whom he regarded, correctly, as the chief obstacle to his plans for the future conquest of Rome. When they learned that Victor Emmanuel had refused to dismiss Cavour at Garibaldi's request, the radicals doubled their efforts to persuade the General not to give up the political power that was his both by right of conquest and by popular acclaim. Cattaneo and Ferrari urged him to hold elections for constituent assemblies in Naples and in Palermo, in order to counteract the moderate propaganda in favor of immediate and unconditional union with the North.[43]

In Naples the two old friends became temporarily reconciled.

They certainly discussed Lombard as well as southern politics, because at the end of the year, when Cattaneo decided not to run again for Parliament, he endorsed Ferrari's candidacy in his own district.[44] But this was the only positive outcome of their trip to Naples. Garibaldi's personal loyalty to the King, the ability of Cavour's agents, the invasion of the Papal States by the royal army (ostensibly to prevent a revolutionary attack upon Rome), and the mounting fear of the propertied classes in the face of peasant unrest—everything suggested that the dreaded annexations were not far away.

On 2 October 1860, Cavour inaugurated the legislative session with a speech in favor of immediate annexations, legitimized, as elsewhere, by plebiscites. There was no time, he warned, for prolonged debates in the various regions whose fate hung in the balance. With every hour the threat of anarchy in those regions became greater, and with it grew the danger of foreign intervention. But annexation could give the unfortunate people of the South the peaceful, liberal government for which they yearned. At the same time, it could reassure the European powers of Italy's ability to keep her own house in order. With the annexation of the South, he concluded, the goal of national unity for which many Italians had suffered and died would be attained. As for Rome and Venice, the political realities of 1860 put them beyond reach. Their liberation would have to wait for more propitious times.[45]

The parliamentary Left reacted feebly to Cavour's statement. Even his most tenacious opponents recognized that his arguments, right or wrong, drew strength from the recent shift of public opinion away from the earlier enthusiasm for Garibaldi to the more limited, less dangerous goals of the moderate party. But one voice did ring out loud and clear from the Left: the Cassandra-like voice of Giuseppe Ferrari.

While conceding victory to Cavour and his party, he felt the need to go on record against the annexations. First of all, he predicted, they would harm the economy of the South, by forcing it to compete with more advanced regions for markets and capital. Second, they would dilute the strength of the North Italian

Kingdom and diminish its ability to defend itself from future attacks by Austria or France. And finally, they would compel the Habsburg government to tighten its grip on Venetia and Napoleon III, the agnostic and former revolutionary, to become more than ever the protector of the temporal power. To these political objections Ferrari added an appeal on behalf of all the Italian revolutionaries, whose sacrifices seemed about to be forgotten in the rush to bring yet another part of Italy under the government of Victor Emmanuel:

The revolutionary says: what? I rebelled against Austria, against the dukes, against the pope; I spent long years in prison, I gave my blood for the fatherland, I gave my fortune; and now I am cast aside . . . by whom? By strangers, by government agents, by military men . . . I am persecuted by the very men who only yesterday clasped my hand and urged me on to the battlefield. . . . I am called a subversive, even a republican, by those who feigned brotherhood and who claimed to hold views similar to mine. . . . Perhaps this revolutionary is wrong, but this is how he feels and how he speaks. . . . [46]

His speech was interrupted several times; when he left the rostrum there was a stony silence on the Left of the Chamber, while a chorus of lusty boos rose from the Right and Center. Only one other deputy, Riccardo Sineo, voted with Ferrari against Cavour's proposal; but Sineo's support meant little, because he was known to be something of a Piedmontese isolationist. His reasons for opposing the annexations did not have much in common with Ferrari's. The reaction of the press to Ferrari's speech was as negative as that of the Chamber.[47] Indeed, the only comforting news in those days came from Gavirate-Luino, where there had been, it seems, no complaints about this antiannexationist speech.[48]

Although he did not lack courage and poise, Ferrari was badly shaken by this experience; clearly he did not cherish his new role as the Don Quixote of the Italian Parliament. Several weeks later, he wrote to Montanelli: "Some words that you told me long ago on the boulevards of Paris have flashed through my mind again. Gioberti, you said, went into exile because his own friends in Turin made his life utterly miserable. I understand now how "consensus," may God deliver us from it, is arrived at in Italy; and if I am not completely desperate, it is only because I know that my poor bed at Impasse Mazagran is always awaiting me."[49] But if Ferrari was sad and angry, he was also ambitious. Moreover, he was absolutely convinced that any hope of effective opposition to the moderate hegemony lay within Parliament.[50] He ignored, in fact, the proliferation of short-lived political associations that characterized the extraparliamentary Left in the 1860s. On 18 February 1861 he returned to the Chamber after a narrow victory over two opponents.

He acknowledged that the new Italy, which had taken her place among the liberal states of Europe, was more advanced than the previous regimes. But she was a far cry from the secular and egalitarian state that he advocated, and that could only be brought about by an intellectual and social revolution. As he saw it, there had been no Italian Revolution in 1859–60, only a war of independence followed by a change of government. The victorious moderates, he noted, obviously agreed with his assessment; indeed they seemed eager to impress upon the Italian people and upon foreign governments the fact that there had been no revolution. Those who believed otherwise, he argued, were well advised to look at the institutions of the new Italy. Her constitution was the Sardinian *Charte octroyée* of 1848, which at that time had brought Italy up to the level of Restoration France, and was now becoming an anachronism. Italy's first national Parliament was called the VIII Legislature, again following the constitutional history of Sardinia. Italy's new capital was Turin, historically and geographically less central to the life of the nation than other major cities, but the city of Cavour and Victor Emmanuel. Perhaps the most telling illustration of what had really occurred in Italy, Ferrari complained, was the legislation that enabled the King of Italy to keep the name Victor Emmanuel II, according not to logic or justice but to the traditions of his house.[51]

According to Ferrari, the unification of Italy had not brought the Italian people significantly closer to the reign of science and equality. From his point of view, the Church enjoyed entirely too much power and too much freedom in this new state. To make matters worse, a French government that had reneged on its revolutionary origins assured the continued existence of the temporal power. As for the reign of equality, in the new state Ferrari saw an emerging parallel between regional inequality, expressed by the cultural and economic predominance of advanced regions over backward ones, and societal inequality, expressed by the power of the wealthy over the poor. He thought that the political unification had brought about the former kind of inequality and that it had perhaps strengthened the latter.

From 1861 until his death, in his activities as a deputy, a publicist, and a teacher, he strove to make his contemporaries aware of these inequalities. He was not the only member of the Italian Parliament to oppose the new order from a secular and a radical or socialist point of view, but he was certainly among a small minority. Of the 443 deputies elected in January 1861, only about 80 could be classified as anti-Cavourians, although the lack of a modern party structure and of well-defined groups within the Chamber precludes a truly accurate estimate. And among those 80 "opposition" deputies were also the members of the Rattazzi and Mordini factions, which were absorbed into the moderate majority between the death of Cavour in 1861 and the "parliamentary revolution" of 1876. In 1861 Ferrari himself counted about 30 deputies whose views were compatible with his own on the most important national issues.[52] The number of his actual or potential allies varied over the years, of course, but it never added up to more than a small fraction of the Chamber of Deputies. In view of Ferrari's usually isolated situation in Parliament, of his frankness, respected even by his adversaries, and of his consistent refusal to be coopted by the moderate majority, it is surprising that he had a political career at all.

[6]

The Art of Political Survival

AN OVERALL VIEW of Ferrari's career in the Italian Parliament suggests that there were several reasons for his political survival over a period of sixteen years. Some of these reasons were of a personal nature; they will be discussed only briefly in this chapter. But other explanations must be sought in the political culture within which he worked, particularly in his relationship with his district, with other leaders of the Left, and with the moderate governments of the 1860s. An exploration of these broader reasons offers us important clues about nineteenth-century Italian politics and about the problems that confronted an elected official before the advent of mass political parties.

If politics did not upset completely the pattern of Ferrari's life (as he had feared during his first electoral campaign), it did require adjustments on his part. The first of these was the need to give up his French citizenship, to establish his official residence in Italy, and to transfer some assets from Paris, so as to pay the minimum forty lire per annum in direct taxes that was required of all candidates for Parliament.[1] But he did not give up his apartment in Paris, where he usually spent the summer recess and where he often returned between legislative sessions or during the winter holidays. Even though he was disillusioned with French politics, he continued to find Paris as enchanting as it had appeared to him in 1838. The freedom to return there at regular intervals represented for him a psychological lifeline, a deep well from which year after year he seemed to draw emotional strength and intellectual vigor.[2]

But the constant traveling back and forth took its toll in a number of ways. It was, of course, expensive to travel so much and to maintain two residences, no matter how modest, one in the French and one in the Italian capital. As a result, over the years Ferrari's financial resources dwindled; toward the end of his life he had to do without the amenities of spacious quarters, a servant, and fashionable clothes to which he had been accustomed as a young man.[3] But even in reduced circumstances he enjoyed a degree of economic independence that was unusual among his colleagues in the Italian Parliament.

During the 1840s and 1850s Ferrari had spent most of his time on scholarly research and writing. Political responsibilities curtailed the amount of time that he could devote to scholarship. He made the necessary adjustments, but with obvious reluctance. Whenever possible, he wrote during his summer sojourns in Paris; but it was also not unusual for him to be seen scribbling away in the library of the Chamber of Deputies between roll calls or caucus meetings.[4] Occasionally he complained about the too hectic pace of his new life and about the slow progress of his scholarly work.[5] His schedule became even more demanding when he accepted part-time academic assignments. He enjoyed teaching, but these assignments meant more work and, at times, additional travel. As a consequence, his health suffered.

During his last years in Paris he had complained about stiff joints and muscular spasms; this condition became more bothersome during his sojourn in Turin in the early 1860s. He blamed it on the unpleasantly damp and cold subalpine winter, on inadequate heating in his apartment, and on the aggravations of political life.[6] He was spared really serious health problems, however, until 1864–65, when he was embroiled in a political battle over the transfer of the capital to Florence and was trying at the same time to finish a book, *La Chine et l'Europe*. In those days, he complained frequently of aching joints, fatigue, and insomnia. In the last few years of his life, and especially after the move to Rome, he was often too sick to attend the parliamentary debates and to travel. The symptoms of ill health that had been building up over the years were then aggravated by occasional spells of dizziness. His letters to Cardani and to Cristina Arpagans suggest that he may have suffered from hypertension, which indeed seemed to have caused his unexpected death years later.[7]

In the first decades following Italy's unification, the new political leaders were faced with the herculean task of molding eight political entities at various stages of development into one modern state. Their work was made none the easier by two transfers of the Italian capital in ten years, from Turin to Florence in 1865 and from Florence to Rome in 1871. Like most of his colleagues, Ferrari was inconvenienced by these moves. Although he approved of transferring the capital to Florence, he lamented that accommodations in that lovely but small city were difficult to come by and expensive.[8] He was even less happy about the move to Rome, which he opposed in any event for political and ideological reasons. The Eternal City, he wrote, was a dirty, parasitic, corrupt place that showed the disfiguring scars of many centuries of papal misrule.[9] Practical difficulties aside, these moves had an adverse emotional impact on Ferrari. The furnished rooms which he rented in Turin, Florence, and Rome seemed cold and inhospitable when compared with his quarters on the Impasse Mazagran, which contained much of his private library and the furnishings and mementos of twenty years in France. Other deputies, no doubt, also missed the comforts of their permanent residences; but many of them enjoyed the company of their families, while Ferrari was quite alone. In Paris and Milan there were old friends with whom to share joys and sorrows; it was never quite the same in Turin, Florence, and Rome. In a particularly dark moment of his political life, he wrote to Cardani: "You are envious of my independence; but I am envious of your family life, your daughters, your directorship of the insurance company; I envy you everything. If you had seen me here quite alone on Christmas Day, with not even a dog to comfort me with his affection, you would certainly have pitied me."[10]

In his youth Ferrari had not been very close to his family,

with the possible exception of his mother. But he had shown affection for his brother's children. Returning to Italy in 1859, he was delighted to embrace his surviving nephew, Cristoforo, now a grown man with a family of his own.[11] But over the next ten years the family relationship became strained, initially because Cristoforo, an unemployed lawyer, badgered his uncle the deputy with requests for patronage, and later on because of a quarrel over Carlo Ferrari's inheritance. Like most Lombard civil servants, after the unification Carlo Ferrari had been integrated into the Italian bureaucracy, and he had continued in his post until his seventieth birthday in 1865. His death in the summer of 1869 left his second wife the beneficiary of his government pension and the heir to most of his assets.[12] Cristoforo, who was in bad financial straits, decided to challenge the paternal will. His claim to a larger share of the estate was based upon the dowry by which his late mother, Marietta Caimi, had increased the fortune of the Ferrari family. In a vengeful mood, he accused his stepmother, who was approximately his own age, of having tricked her elderly husband into changing his will to her advantage. Inexperienced and frightened, Cristina turned to her brother-in-law for protection. He did in fact intervene, and with the help of his lawyers the matter was eventually settled out of court.

We do not know whether Cristina Arpagans was guilty or even capable of the machinations of which her stepson accused her. What we do know is that Giuseppe Ferrari without hesitation took her side in the family dispute and thereafter broke off all relations with Cristoforo.[13] In the years that followed, Cristina showed her gratitude and her affection for Ferrari by providing the only sense of home and family that he had known in all the years since his departure for France. That she looked forward to his visits is indicated by the elaborate preparations she made in his honor and by her distress on the one occasion when illness prevented her from giving him an appropriate welcome.[14]

If Ferrari found his life-style as a carefree bachelor less appealing with advancing age, he may have found comfort in the knowledge that a measure of financial independence and the lack of family responsibilities were valuable political assets. He was never a very wealthy man. In his last years he knew that his capital was dwindling; but because he had no family to provide for, he could afford not to worry about the situation. Although his life as a politician and a scholar was a bit hectic, it could not compare with that of less fortunate colleagues forced by economic necessity to make compromises between their political interests and a teaching position, a legal or medical practice, or other occupations. The defrocked priest Giorgio Asproni, for instance, born in Sardinia of very poor parents, supported himself by tutoring and teaching at various levels.[15] Middle-class lawyers like Francesco Crispi or Giuseppe Zanardelli, at least in the early part of their political lives, had to devote much time and energy to their law practice; even so they barely managed to support their families.[16] Their colleague Angelo Bargoni of Cremona could manage by holding down two jobs, one as a lawyer and one as the editor of the newspaper *Il Diritto*.[17] Even as important a politician as Agostino Depretis, who managed a large estate, had to schedule his political engagements around the perennially revolving cycle of plowing, sowing, and harvesting.[18]

But a certain amount of leisure was not the only advantage of economic independence. A man like Ferrari, unless he happened to be greedy (as Ferrari clearly was not), could more easily resist the temptations of corruption and graft and the pressure of special interests. And in the fluid situation of the 1860s such temptations and pressures surrounded the Italian Parliament like the lush undergrowth of a tropical forest. Independent wealth per se was surely no guarantee of a deputy's integrity, just as the lack of it did not ensure his corruption. But economic independence made it easier to resist temptations. On at least two occasions during his parliamentary career Ferrari was, in fact, tempted. In the early 1860s he was extremely interested in the southern question and was feuding with various southern deputies. He went along with the attempt by a southern admirer, Giuseppe Dassi, to engineer a Ferrari candidacy in Naples. But at some point he discovered that Dassi, in order to pay himself back for his political labors, was trying to use their friendship on behalf of a North Italian firm which had monopolistic designs on the lumber resources of the South.[19] A few years later an old Parisian friend and business associate, Euryale Cazeaux, proposed to use him as a conduit for the purchase and speculative resale of expropriated Church lands.[20] These experiences strengthened Ferrari's conviction that elected officials should receive a salary from the state. He could certainly sympathize with the difficult moral choices to which his poorer or more greedy colleagues were subjected year after year.[21]

During his sojourn in Florence and in Rome, Ferrari at times experienced an acute loneliness, relieved only in part by the affection of his sister-in-law and of old friends. But from the standpoint of his political career, the lack of family responsibilities may well have been an asset. In contrast to the situation in other countries, the Italian politician of the 1860s and 1870s who projected the image of the responsible and respectable paterfamilias enjoyed, it seems, no particular advantage over a colleague who did not. Ferrari's electors, in any event, seem to have liked his carefree, cosmopolitan, somewhat nonconformist lifestyle.

To economic independence and the lack of family responsibilities we should add, among the personal qualities that helped Ferrari's career, a natural grace and charm, mellowed rather than diminished by advancing age. Charm was surely not the only quality which the electors of Gavirate-Luino expected of their representative in Parliament, but it was an important one. Ferrari knew the secret of winning the confidence of the notables who decided nominations and elections, and that of their womenfolk as well.[22] The ladies could not vote; but it was they who often arranged the social occasions so important to the transaction of politics in the small, provincial world of nineteenth-century Lombardy.

Beyond doubt, an important reason for Ferrari's political survival in the national Parliament was the nature of his electoral district. He had settled for Gavirate-Luino after twice suffering defeat at the polls in his native Milan. But in the long run, he came to regard the electoral results of 1860 and 1861 as a blessing in disguise. His district stretched from the eastern shore of the Lago Maggiore in the west to the Olona River in the east and from the Swiss border in the north to the town of Varese in the south. It was, and still is, one of the most beautiful corners of Lombardy, but not one of the most prosperous or politically significant. It was a district of small towns and villages, with no urban center of more than ten thousand inhabitants. The two most important towns, Gavirate and Luino, approximately equal in size and wealth, competed fiercely for the privilege of being regarded as the true capital of the district.[23]

The economy of Gavirate-Luino was primarily agricultural. The lakes and streams, steep valleys, and thickly wooded mountain ranges that crisscrossed the region, especially in its northern part, were the reason for its enchanting scenery but also for its relative poverty. Rich, flat land suitable for the large-scale cultivation of cereals, legumes, and fodder crops was in short supply there, by comparison with other areas of Lombardy. Typically, the most productive fields in the lowlands were farmed by the tenants of aristocratic or middle-class landowners, while the small terraced plots that clung tenaciously to the surrounding slopes bore witness to the patient labor of generations of peasant proprietors. Aristocratic and middle-class landownership was widespread, but the large-scale absentee landlord was a rare exception. Most proprietors, if they did not actually reside on their lands lived close enough for direct supervision of their managers and tenants. Only an estimated one-fourth of the holdings in this region produced for outside markets; the rest produced for local consumption. Most of the mountain farms yielded barely enough to sustain their owners. Quite apart from the scarcity of good land, the more prosperous landowners were handicapped in their efforts to reach wider markets by the lack of good transportation ties with the rest of Lombardy and with Switzerland. As the representative of Gavirate-Luino in the 1860s and 1870s, Ferrari spent much time working on this problem.

Small-scale manufacturing was the second most important economic activity in the district. The domestic manufacture of wool and silk cloth supplemented the income of many peasant families, while modest entrepreneurial opportunities were available to village and town artisans in the lumber and mining industries. Finally, tourism provided some investment opportunities for the middle class and employment opportunities for the poorer families in the area. The sheltered coves and picturesque islands of the Lago Maggiore attracted foreign visitors throughout the year and summer residents from Milan and other cities.[24]

The relative economic backwardness of Ferrari's district had important political implications. For all practical purposes, only the aristocratic and middle-class landowners and a handful of civil servants, professional men, and entrepreneurs paid enough direct taxes to qualify for the vote. Some peasant proprietors who met the financial requirements may well have failed to meet the literacy test. In fact, although the rate of illiteracy at the time of Italy's unification was estimated at roughly 50 percent for Lombardy as a whole, it was probably much higher than that in remote rural districts like Gavirate-Luino.[25] Economic and cultural factors combined to produce an electorate that was small in number and fairly homogeneous in character. It is obvious that the deputy who stood for such a district enjoyed an advantage over colleagues chosen by larger and more heterogeneous groups.

In order to understand the relationship between Ferrari and his district, we must bear in mind, first of all, the small size of the electorate. During his sixteen years in Parliament, the number of eligible voters in Gavirate-Luino fluctuated between 685 and 800, and of these only about 40 to 60 percent actually turned out on election day. In effect, Ferrari's future was determined by 300 to 400 men at any given election.[26] Under these circumstances, issues were raised and discussed, contacts made, and alliances sealed through an informal yet intricate and fragile network of interpersonal relationships. The setting for such activities was sometimes a political banquet or the local town hall or clubhouse, but more often the drawing room, office, or summer cottage of this or that local notable. In such situations, grace, charm, and tact were perhaps more useful qualities than expertise in a particular legislative area, oratorical gifts, or even important connections in the national Parliament.

To the democratic politician of our time, besieged by the strident claims of competing interests, watched by the media, and subject to the constraints of party ideology and discipline, the small world of rural politics in nineteenth-century Lombardy may appear idyllic indeed. But in fact it was not so. The nineteenth-century politician did enjoy some advantages over his counterpart today, but he also lacked many resources that our own contemporaries take for granted.

The very nature of politics in Gavirate-Luino required frequent personal visits on Ferrari's part.[27] But just getting to the district was a complicated, time-consuming affair. The transfer of the Italian capital to Florence and then to Rome did not make things any easier for him. Even in the 1870s, with rail links completed, the trip from Rome to Milan took twenty-two hours; then it took another half day to reach Gavirate. Whenever possible, Ferrari scheduled his visits in consultation with his chief contact in the district, about whom more will be said later. Adequate notice and meticulous planning (neither of which were Ferrari's forte) were especially important in a district like Gavirate-Luino, where the electors lived scattered throughout dozens of towns, villages, and isolated farms.

If he came for an extended visit, as was generally the case around election time, he was expected to tour several towns and villages and to accept the hospitality of the local mayor or other notables. Those prominent families who supported his candidacy in each locality vied for the privilege of entertaining him in their homes, and they invited potential supporters to meet with him. Food and drink, sometimes even overnight accommodations, had to be provided for scores of people. The willingness of these families to foot the bills for such political gatherings was invaluable to the candidate, particularly so if he was of modest means. But for each occasion careful records had to be kept of the communities that he had visited and the notables whose hospitality he had accepted. For to be less than even-handed in such matters over a period of time was to court political disaster.[28] It was in these situations, when the exclusively male domain of politics impinged and became almost dependent upon the female preserve of household management, that many upper- and middle-class ladies played an unofficial but important role. The fact that Ferrari regarded the move of one such lady to a different district and the death of another as political defeats suggests that they did something more than pour tea or serve hors-d'oeuvres at gatherings sponsored by their husbands or fathers.[29]

An altogether different procedure was used if Ferrari's visit was limited to one or two days, as was frequently the case between elections. Instead of touring his district, he stopped at one of the larger towns and invited his electors to meet him there. Although this arrangement allowed him to keep in touch with the district with a minimum expenditure of energy, time, and money, Ferrari much preferred the more informal and convivial atmosphere of the private homes that he visited during his tours.[30]

But the problems of keeping in touch with the district were only the tip of the iceberg for the deputy seeking reelection. In Ferrari's district a very effective organizational effort was necessary to make sure that his supporters went to the polls on election day. Some of them, especially if they were getting on in years and if the weather was bad, were reluctant to make the trip to the polling place unless transportation and refreshments were provided for them—so on the appointed day coaches and drivers had to stand ready. Couriers and poll-watchers were no less necessary to make sure that all went smoothly in the various parts of the district. Success did not come easily. Indeed, Ferrari's campaign workers sometimes complained that the apathy of his supporters, poor roads, and erratic weather gave them bigger headaches than the candidacy of his opponents.[31]

Today, these humble yet essential political functions are the responsibility of professional organizers in the European party system and of ward leaders in the American system. But in nineteenth-century Italy the organizational responsibility fell upon the candidate himself and upon such a political machine as he was able to assemble. By today's standards, the Ferrari machine was an unsophisticated shoestring operation, which lacked the expert assistance of a central party organization or a Madison Avenue executive suite; but it worked well enough to secure his reelection in 1861, 1865, 1867, 1870, and 1874.

By his own admission, Ferrari had no organizational talent.

He was absent-minded, especially when he was immersed in the writing of a book, and woefully prone to misplace important papers, to neglect correspondence, or to miss scheduled appointments.[32] But if he did not have the qualities necessary to create and to run a smooth political machine, he obviously knew how to work with men who did have such qualities. His political alter ego in the district was Achille Longhi, a middle-class landowner and lawyer from Laveno. In 1860 Longhi had been among those electors who had invited Ferrari to run in their district. In their invitation they had emphasized their desire to be represented in Parliament by a man of distinguished intellectual achievements. But actually, by nominating Ferrari several notables hoped to reduce the political influence of an insider, Count Guido Borromeo, the scion of one of Lombardy's most distinguished families.[33] This political game plan worked very well. After his defeat by Ferrari in 1861, Borromeo chose to run in another district. But if the electors of Gavirate-Luino thought that they had found a docile candidate, they were certainly disappointed. Ferrari had a definite view of the parliamentary mandate, and his willingness to stand for Gavirate-Luino depended, in part, upon the willingness of his electors to accept that view.

As the deputy from Gavirate-Luino, he knew that he had a clear obligation to handle swiftly and conscientiously all matters pertaining to the well-being of his district. If, for instance, the district needed a rail link, or if one of his constituents needed his recommendation for a job or an exemption from military service, it was his duty to use whatever influence he had with the prefect or with the appropriate ministries to see that such matters were taken care of. But in all matters that transcended the specific interests of Gavirate-Luino, Ferrari reserved the right to express views and to cast votes that might or might not reflect the opinions of his constituents, or even those of just his electors. In matters that affected the entire nation, he viewed himself not as the representative of a particular geographical area, political faction, or social class, but as the proponent of his own secular and radical-socialist ideology.[34] Achille Longhi accepted Ferrari's view of the parliamentary mandate. To him Ferrari entrusted not only the organization of a political machine but also the more delicate task of persuading other notables that a deputy had the right to express his own views on national issues, no matter how controversial or unpopular, so long as he "delivered" in matters of local concern.[35]

If this political network based upon close interpersonal relationships worked well, it was also as vulnerable as a spider's web. Ferrari experienced this in a dramatic way just before the national election of 1874. Although, as in 1870, he won reelection by a wide margin, in the summer of 1874 he was worried about the vociferous opposition to his candidacy by the young editors of *Il Convegno*. His critics pointed out that ever since the transfer of the capital to Rome he had visited the district infrequently (while traveling to Paris as often as he could) and that he was known to be in bad health.[36]

With the electoral campaign in full swing, tragedy struck the family of Achille Longhi. In July 1874 his beloved only child died at the age of twenty while giving birth to twins. The infants survived only a few days. These crushing blows were more than his wife's delicate health could take, and she died in August.[37] In vain Longhi tried to carry on, which was particularly important since Ferrari had gone back to Paris and was not planning to campaign in the district until mid-September. But Longhi was so distraught and gloomy that his friends feared he might lose his mind; with Ferrari's blessing they prevailed upon him to take a leisurely trip abroad. The Ferrari machine came dangerously close to a halt with his departure. Only the timely arrival of the candidate himself and the efforts of two younger supporters, Giulio Adamoli and Giuseppe Parietti, saved the day.[38]

But to emphasize the importance of Longhi's role and of the political network that he established is not to imply that Ferrari's continued success at the polls was simply the automatic output of a well-oiled machine. Longhi could succeed only so long as the local notables, or at least a majority of them, were satisfied with Ferrari's performance on local issues. There is in fact ample evidence of Ferrari's efforts on behalf of his district during the decade 1861–71. Economic and social problems were of paramount concern to the communes of his corner of Lombardy. He was asked to help, for instance, with the appropriation of funds for better roads and rail spurs from the Lago Maggiore to Milan and Switzerland, for flood and erosion control programs, and for schools and orphanages. The chambers of commerce of Gavirate, Varese, and other towns constantly impressed upon him the importance of stimulating the economy of the district. Other groups wrote of the need to improve vocational education and to open more lay schools for girls' education. In addition, there were scores of petitions from individual constituents seeking his help in cutting through the red tape of governmental bureaucracy.[39] Many such petitions were forwarded to him through Longhi or Cardani, who handled whatever cases they could. But the bulk of the petitions became his direct responsibility, and he had to handle them without the aid of a staff. For many years he was obviously able to please his constituents.[40]

Ferrari realized the importance of working closely with his Lombard colleagues on issues, such as transportation, that transcended the limits of his own district. For that reason, long after he had given up any hope of representing a Milanese district, he followed closely the activities of the major political groups and the shifting moods of public opinion in the Lombard capital. And here again, the assistance of a politically knowledgeable and trustworthy friend was invaluable. Ferrari found an able agent in Francesco Cardani. Director of an insurance company, Cardani was a busy man; yet he liked to keep up with politics and he had enough free time, it seems, to read regularly the three or four important Milanese newspapers and to visit the favorite watering holes of the local politicians and intellectuals.[41] For years he sent to Ferrari almost daily summaries of what was happening in the Lombard capital. At least once a week he forwarded a package of press clippings and other items of interest. He was also responsible for arranging Ferrari's public appearances in Milan and for screening his mail during his sojourns in Paris, in the event that some urgent matter came up.[42] There is no doubt that this kind of assistance enhanced Ferrari's effectiveness as a member of the Lombard delegation in the Chamber of Deputies. But, as in the case of Longhi, the informal political liaison between the deputy and his unofficial agent could easily be disrupted by personal conflicts or problems. This happened, for instance, in 1874, when Cardani suffered from a prolonged illness.[43]

But even the assistance of Longhi and Cardani could not prevent a deterioration of Ferrari's performance on behalf of his district during his last four or five years in the Chamber of Deputies. Indeed, despite his victory in 1874, his electors were probably pleased when he resigned his seat in May 1876. *Il Convegno's* critical editorials of 1874 had mentioned his failing health and his preoccupation with France as reasons for his less than sparkling performance on behalf of Gavirate-Luino. But his opponents overlooked the two most important reasons for his diminished ability in the 1870s to meet the needs of his constituents. Those reasons, very closely related, were his consistent refusal over the years to be coopted by the moderate majority and his increasing alienation from the political attitudes and practices of the Left.

Whether his constituents realized it or not, the effectiveness of their deputy depended in large part upon the network of relationships that he was able to establish in the national capital. In the 1860s Ferrari had been able to establish such relationships, primarily because the leaders of both major alignments in Parliament valued his intelligence and sought his support. But in the 1870s, with the issues of the Risorgimento for better or for worse resolved, they could afford to ignore him—and they did. Ferrari's acceptance of a senatorial appointment at the end of his life was due, in part, to the realization that if he clung much longer to his parliamentary mandate the district of Gavirate-Luino would be lost next time around to a candidate of the Right. By going to the Senate he could continue to speak out on major national issues (and to antagonize powerful figures if he must) without endangering the interests of his district.

Without either joining a moderate government or becoming the leader of a major opposition group, Ferrari for over ten years of his political life managed to be an active, outspoken member of the Chamber of Deputies and an effective representative for his district. This was no small achievement for a man who had returned to his native homeland after a very long absence with few political friends and little experience. Personal factors and the type of district that he represented accounted in part for his success. Yet if he survived politically long enough to make his mark upon the history of united Italy, it was also because he was able to move deftly amidst the opportunities and the dangers that beckoned every Italian politician in the last decade of the Risorgimento. His success in Parliament depended upon his ability, on the one hand, to become integrated within the leadership of the Left and, on the other, to maintain a working relationship with the governments of the Right.

Reflecting upon his first year in Italian politics while the Chamber of Deputies debated the issue of the King's title, Ferrari remarked to Proudhon: "What would you say if I told you that Cavour is closer to my point of view on the issue of a federation than are my own friends on the Left? But then, do you really believe that there is a Left in our Parliament? Do you realize that the style of the Italian Left is to thunder against the government, and then give it votes of confidence?"[44] There was, of course, a parliamentary Left in 1861, even though it was small. But, as this letter suggests, Ferrari was not very comfortable with it. In part this was due to the fact that his colleagues distrusted him. His republican preference was shared by Bertani, Crispi, Mordini, and other revolutionaries of 1848 and 1860. But the federalist and socialist principles of his *La Federazione repubblicana* (which he had never repudiated) were anathema to them no less than to Cavour. Moreover, his record as a Francophile and his close friendship with foreign revolutionaries like Proudhon aroused suspicion. But quite apart from this, Ferrari found it difficult to establish a rapport with his most likely allies in the Chamber because in the early years of the Kingdom of Italy the Left was beset by grave dissensions and by a lack of clear common goals.[45]

The weakness of the parliamentary Left in the 1860s was not surprising, since its members came from different currents of the Risorgimento. Their movement had enjoyed moments of glory in 1848–49 and of heroism in the 1850s, and it could boast an impressive intellectual heritage. But it had always been small and divided. The unification of Italy did not put an end to these differences. A few intellectuals, like Cattaneo, rejected the new political order, and as a sign of their rejection they declined either to run for political office or to take the required oath of loyalty to the King. But most of the prominent figures in the movement, from socially conservative republicans like Crispi to democratic republicans like De Boni and colorful mavericks like Garibaldi and Ricciardi, ran for Parliament in 1860–61 and took their seats. Like Ferrari, they decided that in a new and politically backward country such as Italy the national Parliament could provide an important forum from which to voice their opposition to the moderate liberal hegemony. But there was an important difference between Ferrari's attitude toward the parliamentary mandate and that of other men of the Left.

As his letters of 1860 to Cattaneo and Proudhon suggest, the only role that Ferrari regarded as meaningful, realistic, and legitimate for himself and his colleagues on the Left was one of loyal opposition to the King's government.[46] This implied a willingness to work within the framework of the Sardinian monarchy, of the *Statuto*, and of a very narrow franchise. It meant recognizing the events of 1859–60 for what they had been, a change of government without the transformation of the social order, but a necessary change. Admittedly, the unification of Italy had created a less than satisfactory situation for the long-time advocates of republicanism, of constituent assemblies, and of political democracy. It was least satisfactory, in fact, for Ferrari himself, the extremist who favored not only a federal republic but also an intellectual and social revolution in Italy. But he believed that no other framework was possible, at least until such time as the European revolutionary tradition knocked again at Italy's door.[47]

Unfortunately, most of his colleagues did not have an equally clear view of their role in Parliament. Their inability to agree upon the proper function of the opposition diminished their individual and collective effectiveness.[48] In fairness to them, however, it must be said that a resigned acceptance of the new political framework was not as easy for them as it apparently was for Ferrari. Despite his controversial writings on the Italian question, Ferrari had played only a minor role in the making of Italy. Although in France he had experienced briefly the torments of political harassment, censorship, and exile, he had sacrificed little to the cause of Italian liberty, while his colleagues had sacrificed a great deal. He had never approved of terrorist or conspiratorial tactics to achieve political ends; but men like Crispi, Bertani, De Boni and others had lived through the whole gamut of revolutionary experiences, from membership in secret societies to gun running for insurrections and guerrilla warfare. The psychological transition from the tranquillity of the Impasse Mazagran to the public forum of the Palazzo Carignano was difficult, but surely not as difficult as the transition experienced by long-time revolutionary activitists. Finally, if Ferrari's colleagues found it difficult to play the role of a loyal opposition, it was also because, unlike him, they saw in the future liberation of Venetia and Rome the opportunity to complete the territorial unification of Italy through a revolutionary war, and thus to turn the tables on Cavour and his successors. From 1861 to 1864, Ferrari spent much time persuading his colleagues on the Left to concentrate their energies upon the monumental internal problems of the new state. And they attempted, now and then, to make a revolutionary activist out of him. During this tug-of-war, memorable clashes occurred, sometimes behind the scenes at the Palazzo Carignano and sometimes on the very floor of the Chamber.

In the summer of 1860 Ferrari and the leading Risorgimento radicals had found a brief and rare moment of unity in their attempt to delay the annexation of the South. But in October of that year he was shocked to find himself almost alone in refuting Cavour's argument that prompt annexations were advisable in order to safeguard the peace, stability, and prosperity of Naples and Sicily. What were the reasons, he asked, for the sudden and disgraceful silence of the opposition? He began to suspect that his colleagues of the Left, no less than Cavour, dreaded the potential for a social revolution that seemed to exist in the rural South. Some southern deputies (especially the republican Crispi) reminded him, he wrote, of Mazzini's conduct during the war of 1848 in northern Italy and of the supporters of the French *repubblica formale* in 1849–51.[49] The rift between him and Crispi became public the following year. Spurred by a šense of responsibility as a deputy and by personal curiosity, Ferrari toured the South; he returned to Parliament to denounce both the government's policies toward the annexed provinces and the collusion of the southern delegation with those policies.[50]

While he argued that the fear of social revolution was quickly turning self-styled southern radicals like Crispi into supporters of the government, Ferrari also expressed reservations about deputies of Mazzinian or Garibaldian stripe. Mario, Bertani, Giuseppe Guerzoni, and others seemed ready at any moment to neglect their parliamentary responsibilities in order to pursue the elusive revolutionary conquest of Venetia and Rome. Ferrari clashed with them on at least two occasions, in 1862 and early 1863, before the major showdown that split the caucus of the parliamentary Left in December 1863.

In the summer of 1862, Garibaldi attempted to carry out that invasion of the Papal States from the south that had been forestalled two years earlier by the move of the royal army from the north into Umbria and the Marches. His attempt to resume a revolutionary war for the liberation of Rome was crushed by the regular army at Aspromonte, in the mountains of Calabria. On the floor of the Chamber Ferrari used the Aspromonte incident as a starting point for a broad critique of the equivocal conduct of Rattazzi and the King. But privately he blamed his colleagues of the Left no less than the government for this tragic event. And he lashed out against those deputies who had neglected their responsibilities toward their own electors to follow Garibaldi. Once again, he urged them to reassess the national priorities and their own role within the Italian political system.[51]

He launched his second attack upon "the disease of Garibaldism" (to be distinguished, he wrote, from Garibaldi himself, whose courage and integrity commanded respect) early in 1863. The occasion was a mass rally in Como in support of the Polish rebellion against Russian rule.[52] As his audience expected, Ferrari began his speech with a warm declaration of solidarity with the Polish rebels and a denunciation of Russian autocracy. But he also issued a stern warning against Italian involvement in the struggles for national independence that were under way in the Romanov and Habsburg Empires. The new Italy, he argued, had to reach maturity before she could presume to guide the first steps of even younger nations.[53] The speech stunned the organizers of the rally, whose Garibaldian sentiments were obviously offended.[54] But it also provoked lively discussions at the Palazzo Carignano. Although he did not mention any colleagues by name, Ferrari knew that Bertani, Mordini, Benedetto Cairoli, and possibly others were hatching plans in conjunction with Garibaldi and with Polish and Hungarian emigrés for subversion and insurrections in central and eastern Europe.[55] The Como speech put these activists on notice that he intended to denounce any such plans no less vehemently than he had denounced his southern colleagues' supine acceptance of misgovernment and repression in their region.

If it clarified the differences between Ferrari and the revolutionary activists in the Chamber, this speech also produced much speculation about his relationship with the Minghetti government. Was he making an overture to the government, his friends asked, noting that the influential moderate newspaper *La Perseveranza* for the first time ever had praised his political conduct.[56] The same question had come up in 1860–61, when his long talks with Rattazzi had kept Turin and Milan buzzing with rumors of his participation in a future government headed by the Piedmontese politician. In August 1862 his speech on Aspromonte had made it quite clear that he intended to remain a member of the opposition.[57] But after the Como speech he found it necessary to make that point even more emphatically.

While feuding with important figures of the Left, Ferrari was careful to avoid an excessive isolation in Turin that might be tantamount to political suicide. Because in the election of 1861 he had been rejected by the voters in Milan and had won by only a narrow margin in Gavirate-Luino, he needed time to establish deeper political roots in his district. In his dealings with the Ricasoli, Rattazzi, and Farini-Minghetti governments, he exploited to the advantage of his district the desire of successive ministers of public education to secure his assistance for a massive reorganization of Italian higher education. But in 1861–63 he was also very active within the caucus of the parliamentary Left. Revealing a quiet patience and a tactful skill that contrasted oddly with the flamboyant, provocative style of his speeches and with the witty sarcasm of his private letters, Ferrari cultivated political alliances with fellow members of the Lombard delegation like Bargoni and Giovanni Cadolini, with Piedmontese deputies like Sineo, and with independent southerners like Floriano Del Zio and Francesco De Luca. Thus, he was not alone in December 1863 when he faced Bertani and his cohorts in the battle over a proposed resignation en masse of the parliamentary Left.

Toward the end of 1862, the leaders of the parliamentary Left devoted most of their energies to hounding Rattazzi out of office, because they held him responsible for the Aspromonte incident and for the unconstitutional repression of radical associations and newspapers that had followed it. With the assistance of Rattazzi's enemies on the Right, they achieved their objective in November. But the formation of a new moderate government under Farini and later under Minghetti again raised the question that had haunted the parliamentary Left since 1860: what was the proper role of the opposition? The debates that took place behind the scenes at the Palazzo Carignano on the question of a vote of confidence for the new government were echoed by polemics in the press.[58] Bargoni's *Il Diritto* reemphasized the concept of loyal oppostion, while calling upon the new government to restore full civil liberties. The Mazzinian *Il Dovere* urged the parliamentary Left to make its support of the new government contingent upon a firm commitment to the liberation of Rome and Venetia. In the last issues of *La nuova Europa* (one of several radical newspapers of the decade to die of financial starvation), Mario cried out against the futility of parliamentary games, called for a complete break with the monarchy, and announced his forthcoming resignation from the Chamber. The opinion expressed by Bargoni prevailed, and a majority of the parliamentary Left gave the new government a vote of confidence. But the debate continued.

One example will suffice to illustrate the uncertainty and confusion that reigned as late as 1863 among the leaders of the parliamentary Left. The new moderate government agreed to conduct an investigation of southern banditry and appointed a commission that included four men of the Left, Nino Bixio, Aurelio Saffi, Stefano Romeo, and Giuseppe Sirtori. The commission reported to the Chamber in May and proposed new legislation for a more severe crackdown on the bands.[59] Since the report described banditry quite clearly as a product of a deep socioeconomic malaise, Mordini suggested to the caucus of the Left that support for any additional repressive measures in the South be made contingent upon the appropriation of special funds for public works. He could not get the support of the caucus for this very moderate proposal. Incredibly, of the four men who had served on the commission, only two—Saffi and Sirtori—bothered to attend the caucus at all, and only the former voiced support for Mordini's proposal. When the new repressive measures came to a vote in the Chamber, only one deputy of the Left, Luigi Miceli, spoke against it, while others offered a series of uncoordinated, easily defeated amendments.[60]

Toward the end of 1863, the members of the caucus could agree on one point: ever since the downfall of Rattazzi they had been lamentably ineffective in the Chamber. But the success of various mass rallies during that same year indicated that they enjoyed a following outside the Chamber. Mario, Bertani, and others began to argue that they could work more effectively for the completion of Italy's unification and for the democratization of Italian society if they withdrew from Parliament and devoted themselves entirely to extraparliamentary political agitation. While Mario pursued this course of action on his own, Bertani urged a more dramatic resignation en masse.[61]

Within the caucus, Bargoni took the responsibility for presenting arguments against the proposed resignation. But he was working hand in hand with Ferrari. At a strategically opportune moment, the latter introduced a historic motion—"The Left shall not desert its post." The motion carried; and it marked a major step forward for the advocates of the concept of loyal opposition. Bertani withdrew from Parliament and so did Garibaldi, followed by men who were more loyal to him than to the political institutions of the new state. But other former revolutionaries, including Mordini, reexamined their role and decided, in deference to their electors and in the interest of the nation, that they must continue to man their posts at the Palazzo Carignano.[62]

Ferrari came out of this confrontation with an enhanced reputation and with a more solid base in his district, where his political conduct earned high praise.[63] His new self-confidence became obvious about a year later, when he supported the Minghetti government in the matter of the September Convention with France. At that time he found it possible to differ radically from most of his colleagues of the Left without having to fear for his political future, as he had during the debates on the annexation of the South. The election of 1865 proved that his self-confidence was justified—he was reelected by a comfortable margin.

In the late 1860s Ferrari devoted his political energies to attempts, mostly unsuccessful, to formulate within the caucus of the Left a set of coherent alternatives to the economic and foreign policies of the La Marmora, Menabrea, and Lanza governments. From the Garibaldian attack of 1867 upon the Papal States until the transfer of the capital to Rome, he was always in the front ranks of the opposition, speaking on issues of foreign policy, economic policy, and civil liberties. Although he regarded the *Statuto* of 1848 as an anachronism, he was forced by the increasingly authoritarian tendencies of the moderate governments to insist again and again upon the strict observance of constitutional liberties. This role of persistent, trenchant criticism was expected of him on the Left of the Chamber, and it was in keeping with his own feelings and ideology. But it was a role that exacted a heavy price. Gradually, it eroded the network of relationships that he had established with the moderate leadership in the early 1860s through his interest in teaching and in educational reform. Under the Menabrea and Lanza governments, he found it increasingly difficult to gain favors for his constituents, and this in turn affected his relationship with his district.[64] Then in 1871 his opposition to the transfer of the capital to Rome isolated him from most of the parliamentary Left. But this time, in contrast to the situation of 1864–65, he did not earn his way back into the fold. Ironically, his rapid political decline after 1872 coincided with the deterioration of the moderate leadership that brought the Left to power only months before his death.

As a young man, Ferrari was attracted to an academic career by the examples of scholars like Romagnosi, Michelet, Fauriel, and Thierry. The unification of Italy offered him new opportunities to play a role in higher education. And he was quick to seize them, for they meant almost as much to him as the opportunity to run for Parliament. On the whole, his experience in the Italian world of higher education was happier and more productive than his experience in France. He quickly learned that in his native country, too, political issues impinged constantly and inevitably upon the life of the academy. But he was spared personal debacles like those of the 1840s. Indeed, at times he was able to turn to his own advantage the intimate relationship between national politics and higher education.

Among the many demanding tasks that confronted the leaders of united Italy in the 1860s was the need to establish uniform standards for primary and secondary education and to modernize and coordinate the existing institutions of higher learning. Italy's new leaders, whether moderate liberal or radical, understood very well the importance of education for the vast project of modernization which they had undertaken. In 1860–63, the controversy over educational policy centered primarily around the Casati Law of November 1859, which had been promulgated in Sardinia by royal decree and had later been extended to the annexed provinces. Named after the Milanese emigré Gabrio Casati, the minister of public education in the first La Marmora government (July 1859–November 1860), the law established a centralized administrative structure at all levels of public education and provided for almost exclusive ministerial control over

educational policy and personnel selection. Under the Casati
Law, educational policy was reviewed by the Consiglio Superiore
della Pubblica Istruzione (High Council on Public Education).
But its twenty-one members (seven of whom served without stipend) were appointed by the king upon the recommendation of
the Minister of Public Education; moreover, its decisions were
not binding upon the minister.[65]

In the hasty process of Italian unification, the Casati Law
became the educational law of the entire Kingdom. But even its
supporters realized that there was much opposition to it, and
that it would have to be revised. In Lombardy and in Tuscany, the
opponents of the law objected most of all to the highly centralized features of the new educational system. In parts of central
Italy and in much of the South there was widespread discontent
with the provisions that made the communes responsible for
establishing and financing local primary schools. Knowing how
much work had to be done at all levels of the educational system,
the moderate leadership was eager to recruit all the talent available in this area. But those called upon to help had to meet two
minimum requirements: a genuine interest in secular education
and a willingness to accept the legitimacy of the new political
order. These requirements, although consistent with the ethos
and the interests of the liberal leadership, restricted the pool of
available talent. This was particularly true of the country's universities, academies, and normal schools, where a purge of clerical and reactionary personnel occurred in 1860–61. Given the
relative dearth of academic talent, the moderate governments of
the early 1860s turned to members of the parliamentary opposition such as Ferrari, who were interested in educational policies,
but who could also give guarantees of anticlericalism and of
loyalty to the institutions of the liberal state.

The Italian Kingdom's first ministers of public education—
Terenzio Mamiani, Francesco De Sanctis, and Pasquale Stanislao
Mancini—knew of Ferrari's interest in higher education and of
his desire to teach. Because the Casati Law in its sections on
higher education provided for the establishment of an academy
of letters and sciences in Milan, they regarded him as a logical

recruit to the faculty of that institution. Pressures in this sense also came from his friends in Milan.[66] Ferrari was attracted by the prospect of devoting the last years of his life to the education of Milanese youth. But he suspected that the desire of the moderates to see him among the leading lights of a Milanese academy was motivated by other than educational considerations. By law, in fact, a salaried post as either a *professore ordinario* or a *dottore aggregato* was incompatible with the parliamentary mandate. Because he did not wish to choose between Parliament and an academic appointment, Ferrari rebuffed the ministry's overtures about a possible appointment to the Milanese academy, and he requested instead permission to lecture on a part-time basis and without stipend at the University of Turin. His course on Italian political theorists from the thirteenth to the nineteenth century was so successful that he was asked to repeat it twice in Turin and later on in Milan and Rome. As part of his deal with the ministry, he also agreed to serve on a ministerial commission that screened candidates for academic appointments.[67]

The success of his courses and his willingness to perform other duties earned him the gratitude of the ministry. He was quick to capitalize on that, in order to obtain patronage appointments for his constituents and the government's attention for a pet project of his, a national institute for the advancement of science. Another sign of appreciation for his talents came in February 1862, when he was named an honorary professor at the University of Naples. This was also an appointment which he could accept without resigning his seat. Subsequently, he was offered a chair of the philosophy of history at the Milanese academy. This offer, which far exceeded anything he had expected from his previous negotiations with the government, raised much speculation. Was the ministry trying to lure him away from the Chamber with an offer too flattering to resist? Or was this offer a cover for negotiations over his possible replacement of Mancini, who was about to resign? Only in June 1862, when he turned down an unsolicited royal decoration with a caustic statement about the proper role of an opposition deputy, were his friends and adversaries convinced at last that he did not intend to leave Parliament for the sake of an academic career, much less join the Rattazzi government.[68]

By his conduct in the early part of 1862, Ferrari made it clear to all the leading moderate politicians that if they wished to secure his cooperation on educational or other issues they could only do so on his own terms. Carlo Matteucci and Michele Amari were generally willing to respect his wishes. Thus, during their tenure (1862–65) he was able to work closely with the Ministry of Public Education while maintaining his cherished independence.

A physicist by training, Matteucci devoted most of his attention as Minister of Public Education to the vexing question of university reform. His predecessors had extended the Casati Law to the system of higher education. But a systematic survey of the universities, academies, institutes, and normal schools that had existed in Italy prior to 1860 convinced him that the Italian system of higher education needed profound structural reforms, not just a centralized administration. He noted that many of the traditional faculties, such as theology, philosophy, and letters, which attracted few students, were overstaffed and offered identical programs at different institutions, while the faculties of law, medicine, and natural science lagged behind those of Germany, France, and England, with inadequate personnel and laboratories. In order to modernize the system and to conserve Italy's scarce intellectual and financial resources, he proposed a reduction in the total number of institutions of higher learning. The remaining ones were to be limited to the two or three faculties that could offer really strong programs. Matteucci's purpose was to give Italy, in his words, "few but outstanding universities." His plans, however, proved much too controversial to implement. Municipal governments and deputies objected to the proposed closing of some institutions; rectors and professors balked at the prospect of early retirements, dismissals, or involuntary transfers; and student groups protested the proposed elimination and consolidation of faculties, which would have forced many more of them to commute or to live away from home.[69]

But Ferrari found much merit in Matteucci's proposals, particularly in his emphasis upon scientific education. Toward the end of April 1862, when student leaders approached him and asked him to denounce Matteucci's policy of centralization, he did the opposite. Privately and in a letter to the editor of *Il Diritto* he argued that the upgrading of academic standards, not bureaucratic centralism, was at the heart of Matteucci's proposals. He did criticize the rigid and pervasive practice of ministerial control at all levels of the educational system, but he pointed out that this was not the work of Matteucci. It was the inevitable result of the political centralization that most Italians had accepted willingly enough in 1860.

Ferrari's intervention in this polemic over university reform earned him the friendship of Matteucci and some tangible rewards as well.[70] In 1864 royal decrees made him a permanent member of the Lombard Institute of Sciences and Letters and a *professore ordinario* at the University of Turin. The latter decree raised a few eyebrows within the academic community, because it allowed Ferrari to hold the position without stipend so that he could remain in Parliament.[71] But the high point of his good relations with the Ministry of Public Education was reached in 1864–65, when he was appointed to the High Council on Public Education.

Although its recommendations and decisions were subject to ministerial approval, the Council was the most prestigious policy-making body in the area of public education. It acted as the liaison between the government and the local school and university administrations, it supervised the competitive examinations for academic positions, and it heard appeals by university professors whenever issues of academic freedom were involved. Its twenty-one members were an intellectual elite that commanded respect in political and academic circles. But although the members of the Council enjoyed prestige and influence, they were also expected to perform a variety of demanding tasks. During the hectic year that preceded the transfer of the capital to Florence, Ferrari had many opportunities to discover just how onerous his new duties were.[72]

The election of 1865 and the subsequent move to Florence added a new burden to his already busy schedule as a deputy, a professor at the University of Turin, and a member of the Council. After the move, he complained of fatigue, and he fretted over the lack of time to finish his comparative history of China and Europe. He was obviously proud of the recognition that he had earned since his return to Italy; and he acknowledged that a close relationship with an important ministry had political advantages for himself and his district. But he was tired, and he began to reassess his commitments. In order to reduce the amount of necessary travel, he requested the transfer of his unpaid professorial appointment from the University of Turin to the Istituto di Studi Superiori in Florence. But his request could not be acted upon immediately, because the Istituto was undergoing a complete review of programs and personnel.[73]

We do not know which of his various roles Ferrari intended to give up, if any. Early in 1866, at any rate, the newly elected legislature forced him to make a choice, by ruling that unpaid as well as paid service in any branch of the state bureaucracy was incompatible with the parliamentary mandate. The ruling affected Ferrari both as a member of the Council on Public Education and as a professor. He protested its retroactive application, but he could not avoid complying with it. In February 1866 he decided to resign his seat and to continue his teaching and administrative duties. But his resignation did not mean a farewell to politics; his letters to friends who inquired about his future plans make it clear that he intended to return to Parliament before long. He was confident that he could be reelected in Gavirate-Luino, or find another district if his old electors did not want him back.[74]

His absence from Parliament was actually very brief, from February 1866 to March 1867. In the latter part of 1866, a serious financial crisis following the war against Austria, major riots in Palermo, and strong parliamentary opposition to a proposed settlement with the Holy See led to the downfall of the second Ricasoli government and to the dissolution of the Chamber. The results of the election showed that Ferrari's resignation from Parliament had cost him some support in the district; but a few months of political fence mending made his position stronger than ever.[75]

Before his return to the Chamber, however, Ferrari had a major disagreement with Domenico Berti, the Minister of Public Education in the second Ricasoli government, concerning the reorganization of the Florentine Istituto di Studi Superiori. He accused Berti of dragging his feet on the matter of academic appointments to the Istituto. And he complained about Berti's failure to press for a clarification of the legislative ruling of 1866 concerning the incompatibility of unpaid public service with the parliamentary mandate. For his part, Berti accused Ferrari of intriguing within the High Council on Public Education to obtain a chair for himself and other appointments for his friends.[76]

There was some truth to the accusations on both sides. Ferrari was indeed eager for an appointment to the Istituto, and he was not averse to assist, if he could, the academic aspirations of his political allies on the Left of the Chamber.[77] But it is also true that Berti and his staff had neglected to act upon an issue that affected several deputies. When Berti did act, in December 1866, he restructured the Council in such a way that only paid, full-time members could serve. Ferrari then resigned from the Council because he did not intend to abandon his political and academic ambitions, but he denounced Berti's failure to obtain parliamentary approval before implementing such a major policy change.[78] Although Ferrari worked with Berti's successors, his assignments were of lesser importance. Except for a brief period during the tenure of his friend Cesare Correnti (February–April 1867), he no longer enjoyed the direct access to the Ministry of Public Education that had proved very useful in the early 1860s as a conduit to other branches of government. Correnti again served as Minister of Public Education in December 1869; but by that time Ferrari's relationship with the governments of the Right had become badly strained, to the point that access to one man no longer made much difference.

Intellectual gifts, negotiating skills, financial independence, and a fair amount of good luck all contributed to the political survival of Giuseppe Ferrari in the first Italian Parliament. We must now turn from an analysis of the general factors that helped his career to an evaluation of his political role in the history of united Italy. This can best be accomplished by analyzing how Ferrari applied some aspects of his ideology to the three most important issues of the 1860s: the southern question, the Roman question, and economic policy.

[7]

Gadfly of the Chamber

WITH THE POSSIBLE exception of state-church relations, no issue in modern Italian history has loomed larger than the southern question.[1] In the decade after the unification, Ferrari was among those political leaders and intellectuals who investigated the conditions of the Italian South and who brought those conditions to the attention of Parliament, of the press, and of public opinion in other regions. Indeed, by the mid-1860s his special concern for the problems of the South was well known among southern intellectuals, politicians, students, and labor leaders.

There was irony in all this. Before 1860 Ferrari had never traveled south of the Po Valley, a fact that did not keep him from making derogatory remarks about the Kingdom of the Two Sicilies and its people. In the late 1830s, for instance, he wrote to Cattaneo that among the Italian exiles in Paris he found the Southerners especially difficult and unpleasant to deal with. He added that for him "the South" really began at Bologna.[2] During his long sojourn abroad only two southern exiles, the gifted historian Amari and the Romantic hero Pisacane, ever became his friends. In 1860 he complained bitterly that a housing shortage in Turin had forced him to rent rooms from "a filthy Neapolitan" who combed her hair in the kitchen and whose maid was always forgetting to clean the chamber pots.[3] Indeed, Ferrari's prejudice was so obvious that it may have affected his political views at the time of Italy's unification. His opposition to the annexation of

Naples and Sicily was certainly consistent with his federalist convictions. But perhaps it also reflected a certain fear that as a result of the annexation the focal point of Italian politics and culture might be shifted away from the Po Valley.[4] Ferrari's trips to the South in the 1860s did not quite erase from his mind the stereotyped image, quite common even then in Lombardy, of Neapolitans and Sicilians as lazy, untrustworthy, backward people corrupted by Bourbon despotism. He never really learned to like the South and its people. But he did try to understand them. Firsthand knowledge of the region revealed to him the dismal economic and social realities in which its people were trapped, and his sensitive nature made it impossible for him to ignore those realities. Indeed, he felt a strong obligation to make sure that his colleagues in Parliament also faced up to them.

His first trip to the South, as we have seen, took place in September 1860, while Garibaldi was still dictator in Sicily and Naples. Given the brevity of his sojourn in Naples and the numerous political meetings that he attended there, Ferrari did not have the opportunity to travel into the interior of Campania or to visit Sicily. But he became acquainted with Neapolitan politicians such as the powerful Liborio Romano, with influential magnates like the brothers Savarese, with newspaper editors, and even with student leaders at the University of Naples. After losing to Cavour the political battle over the annexations, he wanted to turn away from the South and its problems. But in February and March 1861 his interest was aroused again by a flood of complaints and petitions addressed to him and other members of Parliament suggesting widespread discontent with the new regime among the people of the South. Ferrari's colleagues seemed inclined to dismiss them as signs of temporary dislocations brought about by the great upheaval of 1860. But he decided to take a closer look into such issues as the treatment of Garibaldi's former comrades-in-arms, the impact of the new fiscal system upon the economy of the South, and the conditions of the peasantry. Not content with whatever information he received from his southern colleagues, he requested reports and materials on the southern provinces from Giuseppe Dassi, Giacomo Savarese, and Gennaro Riccio, men well acquainted with Neapolitan politics, and from several Sicilian correspondents. These included Giovanni Raffaele, editor of the ultraradical newspaper *La valle di Giosafat,* but also two respected intellectuals of more moderate inclination, Gabriele Carnazza and Giuseppe Costantini.[5]

In April 1861 he was drawn more deeply into a study of the southern question by the first round of parliamentary debates concerning the causes of banditry and the most effective ways of dealing with it.[6] Ever since the collapse of the Bourbon dynasty, the southern provinces had been plagued by marauding bands of armed men. They were most numerous in the interior of Campania, Calabria, and Basilicata and in parts of Sicily, where rugged mountain chains, forests, and poor roads offered ideal sanctuary and enabled small groups of mounted men to keep superior forces at bay. In those areas, banditry was by no means a new phenomenon. It had appeared in the second half of the eighteenth century and during the Restoration in response to every major change in the political or economic structure of the Bourbon Kingdom. But in the early 1860s the bands were more threatening than at any time in the recent past. And their criminal activities had ominous political implications, because the exiled Bourbon monarch, Pope Pius IX, and the French Legitimists regarded them as a possible instrument for a counterrevolution that might spread from the countryside to the cities.

Thus, for the Italian governments of the early 1860s, banditry represented not only a constant threat to the lives and property of southern citizens but also a potential danger to the security of the state. The rapid elimination of the marauding bands seemed necessary, whatever the cost. The unsavory task of seeking out and punishing the outlaws fell upon the brand-new Italian army, created by a merger of Sardinian, Tuscan, and Neapolitan cadres. But repression could not be effective unless the army knew who the enemy was, where he was, and, above all, why he was fighting. By the spring of 1861 this problem was uppermost in the minds of Italy's political leaders. Although large forces had been deployed for what contemporary strategists might call "search-and-destroy operations," the bands were growing in numbers and audacity, and they held most of the roads and mountain passes that connected the interior of Campania in the west with Apulia in the east. The dismal reports of violence and destruction prompted deputies from every part of Italy to ask with an ever-increasing sense of urgency what was really happening in the South and why the Italian army, despite superior discipline, organization, and weapons, seemed unable to crush the outlaws.

Ferrari's first intervention in the debate on the southern question took place on 4 April 1861. A barrage of questions concerning the conditions of the southern provinces had been addressed during the preceding sessions to the Minister of the Interior, Minghetti, and to the Minister of Justice, Cassinis. Both had given rather lame answers. Pointing to a major reorganization of the office of the lieutenant general that was then in progress in Naples, they had suggested that discontent and lawlessness in the South would gradually disappear as the ongoing task of administrative unification and rationalization was completed. Until then, the government's main responsibility was to protect the southern population from the counterrevolutionary terrorism of the bands. In short, the policy of Cavour's colleagues was guided by two assumptions. One was that the emerging southern question was primarily an administrative issue, not a political one. The other was that banditry, although rooted in the ancient peasant culture of the South, was an exogenous phenomenon, kept alive by counterrevolutionary elements.[7]

Ferrari was prepared to challenge both assumptions. Although the South and its people were as alien to him as they were to Cavour or Minghetti, he had made some effort to gather information about the causes of discontent and lawlessness. With sardonic pleasure he reminded the Chamber of the debates of October 1860. At that time, Cavour had stated that the prompt annexation of Naples and Sicily was necessary in order to avoid violence and civil disorders. Almost everyone had believed him. Yet it could not be said that the moderate government had put its political triumph to good use:

Shall we talk about the municipal governments? They are still pretty much what they were under Garibaldi. Shall we mention the National

Guard? . . . By your own admission, it is still unarmed and disorganized. Let us talk about the people. Have you earned their affection? . . . The very fact that your men are always on the move is a sign of the resentment they inspire. . . . I need not mention the bandits, the robbers; I know very well that crime should have nothing to do with politics. Nonetheless, whose fault is it that in the streets of Naples the bandits open fire on the National Guard . . . that public safety is in danger . . . that banditry has become an independent power within the state? Is it Garibaldi's fault?[8]

All indications were that the hasty annexations had not given the southern provinces a more appropriate and more respected government than the Garibaldian dictatorship. If anything, the contrary seemed true. Admonished by the president of the Chamber that the territorial integrity of the Kingdom of Italy was no longer subject to discussion, Ferrari denied any intention of encouraging southern separatism. But he confessed to be deeply troubled by the strained relationship between the government and the people of the South.

Every state that had not been completely corrupted by misgovernment, he continued, was usually able to police its own territory and to deal with the few individuals who engaged in criminal activities. Before sending more policemen and soldiers, was it not necessary to ask *why* thousands of citizens were engaging in violent crimes? Amidst stern warnings from the chair, he suggested that the Italian government was doing battle not so much against outlaws as against the ancient traditions of the Southern Kingdom. Recognizing that the annexations could not be undone, he pleaded with the government to establish which political, social, and economic traditions of the southern provinces had been upset in 1860, before tightening the screws of military repression.[9] At the very least, he hoped that the government and the Chamber would establish a special parliamentary commission to investigate the southern question. Such a commission, he thought, "might dispel many misgivings, assist the government, further the education of the North Italians, and carry a message of loving concern to the people of the South." But when his proposal was put to a vote, only one of his colleagues supported it. Evidently, at this point most deputies accepted the government's argument that unrest and banditry would cease as soon as the administration of the southern provinces had been reorganized and the agents of Bourbon reaction had been eliminated. Only later, in the wake of the Aspromonte affair of 1862 and of the Palermo rebellion of 1866, did they recognize the wisdom of his suggestion and move belatedly to implement it.

Among the most controversial passages in Ferrari's speech was a reference to the reign of King Joachim Murat in Naples. To those colleagues who saw a Bourbon agent behind every bandit, every tax-evading peasant, and every opposition newspaper, he pointed out that the chivalric Murat and the revolutionary legislation of the early 1800s were as much a part of the southern political heritage as the paternalistic despotism of the Bourbons. He made this reference to underscore his point that in the South the introduction of Piedmontese laws and administrative practices had clashed with the local traditions even more violently than in the annexed regions of northern Italy. His flattering remarks about King Joachim's reign, gratefully acknowledged by prince Lucien Murat, rekindled the suspicions of those former exiles in France who had once suspected him of Muratist leanings.

There is no solid evidence that in the early 1850s Ferrari had supported a Murat candidacy in southern Italy. At that time, he was not acquainted with the Murat pretender, and he had no plans to return to Italy on a permanent basis. There are indications, however, that in 1861–62 he may have flirted briefly with separatist elements in Naples, some of whom were attempting to revive the Muratist tradition. We do know that he followed with interest the activities of Lucien Murat and his supporters in Paris and he kept in touch with Giacomo Savarese, an influential and outspoken critic of the Italian government.[10]

Was Ferrari playing a political double game? Was he encouraging southern separatism, perhaps even a Murat candidacy in Naples, while preaching the ideal of loyal opposition to his revolution-minded colleagues of the Left? The suspicions that had been aroused in Parliament by his reference to King Joachim were strengthened by his tour of the southern provinces in November 1861. Upon his return he realized that any flirtation with southern separatism could do irreparable damage to his position within the parliamentary Left and to his political career in Lombardy. Thus, in 1862 he began to rebuff tactfully but firmly Savarese's attempts to get him involved in Neapolitan politics.[11]

Although Ferrari extricated himself easily and gracefully from the equivocal machinations of Neapolitan separatists, he found it rather more difficult to resist the overtures of radical friends. A Ferrari candidacy in Naples was the brainchild of Giuseppe Dassi, who canvassed support for it in intellectual circles, at the university, and among skilled artisans. Dassi must have painted a glowing picture of the opportunities that beckoned in Naples, for we know that Ferrari gave serious thought to the matter. At the end of 1861 he was still smarting from the electoral defeats in Milan; and he did not know whether Gavirate-Luino would continue to support him. He was unquestionably flattered and captivated by the prospect of representing a major city.[12] But within a few months, he began to suspect that Dassi's efforts on his behalf were motivated more by an interest in lucrative deals with North Italian speculators than by genuine political convictions. This was reason enough to proceed with extreme caution in pursuit of political opportunities in the South. Another factor to be weighed carefully was the attitude of the southern delegation in Parliament toward his prospective candidacy in Naples.[13]

Ferrari's southern colleagues were not particularly grateful for his efforts to understand the plight of their region. On the contrary, they suspected him of exploiting the southern question for demagogical purposes. By the summer of 1862, the tension between him and the most prominent southern deputies of the Left became so great that it could not be contained within their own caucus. It erupted on the floor of the Chamber, during debates over the proclamation of the state of siege in the South that followed the Aspromonte incident.[14] Given the attitude of powerful men like Crispi, Ferrari came to realize that his continued involvement in southern politics would cause grave dissension within the already divided ranks of the parliamentary Left. Thus, he chose to abandon the idea of a Neapolitan candidacy, and he toned down his criticism of the southern delegation. But he never forgot the poverty and the despair that he had seen in the rural South. Indeed, during the debate on the grist tax in the late 1860s he defended the interests of the southern peasantry with greater compassion and conviction than most southern deputies.[15]

It is clear from Ferrari's correspondence with Dassi, Savarese, Riccio, and others that during his second trip to the South late in 1861 he spent a certain amount of time discussing the political situation in general and his own prospects in particular. But this was not the primary purpose of the trip; it was above all a fact-finding tour. After the Chamber had rejected his proposal for a special commission to investigate the conditions of the South, Ferrari began his own independent survey. During the summer and early fall of 1861, he familiarized himself with the geography and the economic structure of Campania and Sicily, and he read reports from the mayors of several towns and villages, particularly on the subject of banditry.[16] But for all the vivid and eloquent descriptions that he read in those reports, he was not prepared for the cultural shock of his first visit to the rural South.

His impression of small-town Sicily was, quite simply, that he had arrived on another planet. In a historic town like Agrigento, he was particularly struck by the heartbreaking contrast between the grandeur of the ancient monuments and the grinding poverty of the present. Above all, he was taken aback, almost offended, by the sullen, distrustful attitude of the ordinary Sicilians with whom he came in contact.[17] But the one episode that most affected him was a visit to Pontelandolfo, a town of some five thousand people in the interior of Campania. Like other towns in that region, Pontelandolfo had recently been held by one of the major bands. Rightly or wrongly, the military authorities believed that the occupation had taken place with the consent of the townspeople, who had welcomed the opportunity to get rid of unpopular officials and to stop paying taxes to the government. Thus, the army had wanted to teach the people of Pontelandolfo a lesson. On his way back from the South aboard the S.S. *Venezia,* Ferrari reminisced:

On 3 November I set out for Pontelandolfo with an escort of three *carabinieri*; Dassi had a revolver; the mayor of Solopaca and his brothers were loaded with shotguns and pistols; as for myself, I was given a sword to use in the event that the worst happened.

What a heart-breaking spectacle awaited us in Pontelandolfo! This town of some 5,000 people had been burned to the ground; only three houses had been spared. The swarthy people stared at us sullenly at first; then, having understood the purpose of our visit, they showed us the ruins of their town. The mayor and other survivors told us every detail of this great atrocity, which was repeated at Gioja, at Casalduni, in some twenty other towns, not to mention the innumerable executions in yet other localities. . . .

You would not believe how much hatred all this bloodshed has sown. Among my fellow passengers is a captain of the *carabinieri* who has suffered a nervous breakdown; in some localities the mere sight of soldiers is so frightening that the people approach them in religious procession, holding up the Holy Eucharist and pleading for their lives. . . .[18]

With these harrowing memories fresh in his mind, a few weeks later Ferrari again addressed the Chamber on the subject of southern banditry. In 1860 the enthusiasm for Garibaldi and the results of the plebiscites had shown how little the people of the South cared about their Bourbon rulers. Why, then, was there so much talk of a Bourbon counterrevolution only a few months after the annexations? What, if anything, made the people of the South nostalgic for a dynasty that had clearly failed to keep pace with the overall progress of European society? These were questions that he had asked himself ever since the first outbreaks of unrest in the South. His observations in a number of southern towns and villages suggested some answers, which he was eager to share with his colleagues.[19]

True to its liberal origins, the Italian government had introduced economic freedom throughout the kingdom. But, Ferrari pointed out, many people in the South missed the paternalistic Bourbon policy of "bread and work," that is, of artificially low bread prices and of public works projects for the unemployed. The new economic freedom meant nothing to the impoverished southern peasants, who had neither capital to invest nor skills or intellectual resources that could be employed for productive enterprises. Clearly, some sort of compromise was necessary between the paternalistic policies of the old government and the liberal policies of the new.

An even more important insight that Ferrari gained from his trip to Campania and Sicily was that the southern question was essentially a land question. In village after village he had heard pleas for the quick and equitable distribution of state lands (*beni demaniali*) to peasant families. This was a long-term project that the Bourbons had initiated and that the new government had pledged to continue.[20] But—the peasants complained—the distribution was proceeding much too slowly and widespread corruption in the administration of the project allowed already wealthy proprietors and speculators to benefit the most. It was obvious, Ferrari stated, that an effort to eliminate delays and corruption in this area of great concern to the rural masses of the South would pay handsome political dividends.

Returning to the issue of banditry, he concluded that it was a primitive form of social protest by poor peasants and unemployed former soldiers much more than the arm of a reactionary political movement. Therefore, it could not be solved without regard to the social and economic grievances of which it was an expression. The Pontelandolfo tragedy had convinced him that the present policy of repression and retaliation did more harm to the villages and towns of the affected areas than to the highly mobile, loosely organized bands. He suggested a change of tactics, and he urged that Garibaldi be sent to Naples in the name of the King.

Finally, Ferrari spoke about the Italian army. He predicted that in the long run the policy of repression and retaliation in the rural South would produce as much alienation among the troops charged with implementing it as it did among the civilian population. How could the soldiers tell friend from foe? The southern bandit could at any time hide his shotgun behind a hedge, pick up a hoe, and look for all the world like the peasant that he was or had once been. In such a situation, more atrocities seemed likely to occur, and the army would bear the scars of this war against fellow Italians for a long time to come.

In Parliament, the immediate impact of this memorable

speech was very small; it certainly did not produce any significant change in the government's policy toward the South. But
the response of public opinion in Naples, in Palermo, and in
many smaller communities was overwhelmingly favorable. For
many years thereafter, individuals and political groups in the
South regarded Ferrari as a friend. Their gratitude was his only
reward for his efforts to understand and to publicize the southern
question. During his lifetime, he had to be content with that. But
later on, the analysis that he had undertaken on his own, with
limited means and in a very brief period of time, bore fruit in the
more thorough investigations by Giustino Fortunato, Leopoldo
Franchetti, Sidney Sonnino, and Gaetano Salvemini.

The southern question attracted Ferrari's attention in the 1860s
because it seemed to confirm his earlier critique of the unification
from a federalist perspective. Moreover, the plight of the southern populations struck a sympathetic chord in the humanitarian
socialist aspect of his character. But the one national issue that
most fascinated him was the question of church-state relations.
This is not surprising, in view of the central importance of secularism in his ideology.

It has often been said that the Italian national revolution of
the nineteenth century was inevitably anti-Catholic because it entailed the destruction of the temporal power, but that it was not
basically antireligious.[21] In fact, religious strains are found in
the thought of several Risorgimento leaders, and above all in
Mazzini. But Ferrari wanted Italy's Risorgimento, her second
Renaissance, to be a thoroughly secular movement. In 1860, the
annexation of the Papal Legations and the subsequent occupation of Umbria and the Marches by the army of Victor Emanuel
II brought about a breakdown of relations between the Italian
government and the Holy See.[22] Ferrari would have preferred to
see Garibaldi's Red Shirts, rather than the royal army, march
into papal territory. Nonetheless, he rejoiced over the fact that
the new state and the Roman Catholic Church had officially
become enemies. Indeed, this was the only aspect of the settlement of 1860 that he contemplated with unabashed satisfac-

tion.[23] In the early 1860s he waged a war on two fronts: on the one hand, he led the parliamentary opposition to Cavour's and Ricasoli's attempts to negotiate a settlement with the Holy See; on the other hand, he worked against those revolutionary activists on the Left who were committed to the liberation of Rome by armed intervention at the earliest possible time.

Ferrari found the Cavourian formula "A free church in a free state" wholly inappropriate to the Italian situation. In the language of his *Filosofia della Rivoluzione*, he wrote:

A free state is one that does not subscribe to the dogma of any religion, one that respects all of them, provided they abide by its laws; one that allows all sectarian differences, which it regards as intellectual errors or as matters for the individual conscience. A free state is one that does not pay the clergy, that does not confiscate the property of any church, that does not request Te Deums, or religious funerals, or blessings from the clergy of the various religions. A free state is that of North America, and it is such an ideal, such an exception, that even France and England have not dared go so far. A free religion is one that does not kneel in the sight of any worldly power, that is not subject to the laws, the advice, or the conditions imposed by a people or by a king; a free religion is either one that exists inviolate in the conscience of the individual or else one that permeates the whole society. And here again, a free church on this earth is such an ideal, such an exception . . . that we find it only in the medieval papacy or, within the sphere of the individual conscience, across the Atlantic in America.[24]

Returning to a major theme of his secular ideology, he argued that the concept of freedom of worship was only acceptable in pluralistic societies, where no single religious group or institution could claim a dominant influence. But this was clearly not the case in Italy. Given the influence of the Roman Catholic Church on Italian culture, the Cavourian formula assured the survival within the liberal state of a powerful and insidious enemy. The pope had shown himself to be a more obstinate foe of political modernization than the Austrians. Why, then, enter negotiations with the Holy See that threatened the freedom of the state without even assuring the freedom of the Church?

If he distrusted Cavour's formula for reconciliation with Rome, Ferrari was dismayed by Ricasoli's attempts to combine it with proposals for that *renovatio Ecclesiae* ardently desired by many Italian Catholics. How, he asked, could the head of the Italian government preach the ideal of "a free church in a free state" and at the same time presume to tell the pope what to do in the religious sphere? In short, he urged Italy's leaders to drop their efforts (rebuffed, in any event, by the papal secretary of State, Cardinal Antonelli) to make peace with the pope, and to concentrate instead on other pressing problems of the new nation.[25]

Many criticisms of Cavour's ecclesiastical policy had been heard from the Left of the Chamber; but one aspect of that policy had received almost universal approval: the idea that some day Rome would become the capital of Italy. Ferrari hated the very words *"Roma capitale,"* whether they were uttered by Cavour or by the revolutionary activists of the Left. As he saw it, those words were a convenient excuse to avoid coping with more important national issues. He made this point in especially strong terms in a speech of November 1862, when memories of Aspromonte still haunted the Chamber:

As a question of domestic politics, what is the Roman question, as formulated by Cavour, as proclaimed by this Chamber, as accepted by the people? It is nothing less than the key to all other questions; whether true or false, good or bad, it does not matter. It is a profoundly popular, mythical, ritualistic solution. . . . If we are burdened by taxes, let us go to Rome; if we are weak, to Rome; if we are bankrupt, to Rome; if the people clamor for autonomy, to Rome; if banditry is flourishing, to Rome; if seditious elements threaten us, to Rome; if a war against Austria over Venetia is too much to handle, to Rome. . . . [26]

The feeling that the Roman question was a pretext for avoiding other issues was one important reason why Ferrari objected both to peaceful negotiations with the Holy See and to armed interventions à la Garibaldi. But there were other reasons as well. An uncompromising atheist, he was completely impervious to the moral dilemma that prompted devout men like Ricasoli to seek a reconciliation with the Church. Moreover, he opposed negotiations because the very word implied some sort of give-and-take between the liberal state and the Church. To put it briefly, he wanted the state to concede nothing and to take as much as possible. Thus, he argued for complete state control over the educational system, for the outright confiscation of Church properties, for the gradual suppression of cloistered religious orders, and for the proclamation of the equality of all religious denominations before the law.[27] These drastic measures were certainly consistent with his secular ideology. But were they attuned to the political realities of his generation? Were they not likely to exacerbate the hostility of the Catholic powers toward Italy and to aggravate the problem of Catholic abstentionism?

Ferrari was aware of these problems, but he took them less seriously than most Italian politicians of the 1860s. With regard to the Catholic powers, he pointed out that only one of them, France, was really in a position to make trouble. And she was already in Rome.[28] There were two reasons behind his relative indifference to the problem of Catholic abstentionism. First of all, unlike other leaders of the Left, he did not believe that a clerico-conservative coalition posed a serious threat to the liberal state, except possibly in the former Kingdom of the Two Sicilies. The collapse of the old Italian governments, he argued, had been so rapid and so complete that a third Restoration was simply impossible, despite the obvious weaknesses of the Kingdom of Italy. Second, he did not think that the Catholic loyalties of the Italian people ran very deep. The failure of the neo-guelph movement pointed in this direction. Moreover, the historical record showed that in the past Italy's rulers, cities, and states had often made alliances with the emperor or with foreign powers against the papacy. It also showed that her leading thinkers had been heretics more often than not. He was confident, in short, that the descendants of Campanella, Galileo, Machiavelli, Bruno, and Giannone were basically willing to accept a secular state.[29] In part, his interpretation of Italian history also accounted for his hostility to the slogan "*Roma capitale*." Historically, Rome had been the city of emperors and popes, the keeper par excellence of Italy's federal traditions. What major city, he asked, was *less* suited than her to become the capital of a centralized nation-state? He looked forward with unmatched eagerness to the end of the temporal power, but he opposed any special efforts to obtain Rome. She would join the Kingdom of Italy in due time, he thought, when the pope's remaining subjects saw the happiness of their fellow Italians under liberal rule and when the inevitable revival of the French Left freed Bonaparte from the absurd role of protector of the papacy.[30]

Given his attitude on church-state relations, Ferrari was delighted with the failure of Cavour's and Ricasoli's negotiations with the Holy See.[31] A major turning point in the Roman question came in 1863–64. The Farini-Minghetti government, which had succeeded the discredited Rattazzi, knew that the intransigence of the Holy See was likely to thwart further attempts at reconciliation. But it saw an opportunity to negotiate the withdrawal of French troops from Rome, in exchange for a pledge to transfer the Italian capital to Florence, to assume a major part of the public debt in the annexed papal territories, and to stop any future attacks upon Rome. The time was right for such a move because Napoleon III, beset by domestic and international problems, was eager to reduce his military commitment to Rome. The result of these Franco-Italian negotiations was the Convention of September 1864.[32]

Ferrari was jubilant. Although the convention had not actually stifled the obnoxious cry of "*Roma capitale*," it was certainly a step in the right direction. The withdrawal of French forces from Rome meant, he thought, that the papal government would collapse like a house of cards as soon as the Romans decided that they had had enough of it. Moreover, the transfer of the capital to Florence put an end to the era of Piedmontese hegemony in Italian politics. His Lombard friends and constituents were as pleased about that as he was.[33] But the proposed Convention ran into a storm of criticism. The King and the leading Piedmontese moderates had not been told that the proposed agreement with France was contingent upon the transfer of the capital to Florence. Their angry reaction was shared by the people of Turin, who rioted for several days. But even politicians from other regions, who had often railed against the "Piedmontization" of Italy, had serious misgivings about Minghetti's initiative.

From all sides of the political spectrum he was accused of repudiating the Cavourian pledge, endorsed by the Chamber in March 1861, that someday Rome would be the capital of Italy.[34]

Although the treaty with France was ultimately ratified by Parliament, the opposition to Minghetti's diplomacy was strong enough to force his resignation. The task of steering the controversial proposals through the Chamber was left, appropriately enough, to General Alfonso Ferrero de La Marmora, a Piedmontese moderate very close to the court. Rather unexpectedly, he found support among a small group of deputies who sat on the extreme Left in the Chamber. Their spokesman was Ferrari, who made one of the most dazzling speeches of his career on behalf of the proposed move to Florence. For once, he was fighting on the government's side. In his district and in Milan there was again speculation about his possible drifting into the moderate camp.[35] But actually, his speech was less a defense of Minghetti's diplomacy than an attempt to change the views of fellow opposition deputies with regard to the Roman question. It should be read in the context of his previous efforts to rearrange the political priorities of the parliamentary Left.[36] From the end of 1864 to the early part of 1867, Ferrari had reason to be pleased with the impact of his speech. With the ratification of the September Convention, the Roman question became more or less dormant. Then, in 1866, the war against Austria diverted the attention of the revolutionary activists to the conquest of Venetia, which had seemed utterly impossible only two years earlier.[37]

Ironically, the acquisition of Venetia, the penultimate step in the completion of Italy's territorial unity, threw the country into the deepest crisis since the unification. The circumstances of the acquisition dealt a severe blow to the morale of the young nation: there was no denying that her army and navy had failed their first test against a foreign enemy. As always, Garibaldi and his volunteers had fought well, but their feats could not offset the humiliations of Custoza and Lissa. The La Marmora ministry, interrupted by the outbreak of war, and the second Ricasoli ministry labored under the shadow of this strange turn of events. But questions of national morale aside, the war of 1866 aggravated the budget deficit, which every government since the unification had tried to eliminate. As a partial solution to the financial crisis of 1866–67, Ricasoli's Minister of Finance, Antonio Scialoja, proposed the definitive disposition of ecclesiastical properties, partly by expropriation and partly by public auctioning. Under his plan, a Belgian financier was to make an immediate payment of 600 million lire to the Italian government in exchange for the right to administer the auctions and to keep 10 percent of all profits. Ricasoli was receptive to this plan but was unwilling to implement it unilaterally. He instructed Scialoja and the Minister of Justice, Francesco Borgatti, to draw up a proposal to be presented to the Chamber. At the same time, he reopened negotiations with the Holy See for that broader settlement of all outstanding issues which had eluded him during his first ministry. His envoy, Michelangelo Tonello, was fairly successful. Thus, in January 1867 Ricasoli was able to present to the Chamber a plan that combined the Borgatti-Scialoja economic proposal with a tentative agreement with the Holy See.[38]

The opposition to this plan was so strong that in February Ricasoli received a vote of no confidence, and the King agreed to dissolve the Chamber. The general elections of March 1867 brought Ferrari back to his seat, after the brief interruption discussed earlier. Unable to put together a ministry acceptable to the king, Ricasoli was once again replaced by Rattazzi. Like others on the Left of the Chamber, Ferrari hoped that the Piedmontese leader, not known for his piety, would turn his back upon the policy of reconciliation with the Church. But such was not the case.[39]

Ferrari's turn to speak against the proposed settlement came in July 1867. According to the Borgatti-Scialoja plan, Church lands and other real property in the annexed territories were to be sold against a down payment of 10 percent and an eighteen-year mortgage at 6 percent. Moreover, the government was authorized to issue bonds at 5 percent for an amount of up to 400 million lire and to accept such bonds as payments for Church properties. Ferrari was unhappy with these financial arrangements. They favored, he thought, Italian and foreign bourgeois investors who were already tied to the liberal regime by other economic interests or by ideological preference; they did nothing for millions of poor peasants who had no capital for a down payment or for the purchase of redeemable state bonds. He would have much preferred the distribution of some former Church properties among landless families.[40] But he set the economic issue aside, and focused instead upon the political implications of the proposed settlement. His choice reflected both ideological considerations and political expediency.

He knew, of course, that most of his colleagues in Parliament, including the advocates of political democracy, looked askance at any plans for radical social and economic reform. He also realized that the primary purpose of the proposed liquidation of ecclesiastical properties was to reduce the budget deficit—hence the need to sell those properties, instead of giving them away, and to make the sale as attractive as possible to investors with readily available capital. Given the acute crisis of state finances and the socially conservative mood of the Chamber, Ferrari sensed that the Borgatti-Scialoja plan would be approved. But he also sensed, correctly, that there was a chance of defeating a political settlement with the Holy See.

As part of the proposed settlement, the state was to waive the right to approve the appointment of Italian bishops by the pope. Before 1860 the Italian states had exercised this right in various forms. But on behalf of the government, Tonello had tentatively agreed not to challenge the nomination of twenty Italian bishops recently made by the pope without state approval. Ferrari used this controversial issue as a convenient platform for a renewed attack upon the Cavourian concept of freedom of worship. He told his colleagues:

You have witnessed the negotiations between the [Italian] government and the Roman court. I have tried hard to find some lofty justification for them. Perhaps, I told myself, caught up in a vision of unbounded liberty, the government dreamed that Italy could be as great, free, and audacious as America. But what similarity is there between Italy, the home of the papacy, and the American Union, the child of Protestant liberty? There every believer is free, every industry is left alone, the government is republican; a Roman Catholic counts the same as a Protestant, as any sectarian. Free from the nightmare of the papacy, why should the American government seek to control Catholic bishops, who are as powerless as Protestant ministers are here?[41]

But perhaps, he continued, it was too charitable to think that Ricasoli and his successor had been led astray by the glorious, and totally irrelevant, American example. The formula "A free church in a free state," borrowed by Cavour from Charles de Monta-lembert, suggested that the Italian moderates had found inspiration not across the ocean, but across the Alps in France, "and not even in the France of Bossuet, of Louis XIV, of the Republic, or of Napoleon I . . . but in a sinister and crazy France . . . the France of *Le Monde,* of *L'Univers* of *L'Union catholique,* of the fanatical and libelous newspapers that railed against the publicists, against the Université, against the most distinguished professors, accused of spreading immorality and corruption."[42] For the spokesmen of this "sinister and crazy France," he added, freedom of worship was simply a code word for clerical control over the intellectual life of the nation. Italy could not afford to follow such an example. With fine irony, Ferrari offered his sympathy to those politicians who wanted freedom for the Church (after having just robbed her of her property). Theirs was indeed a difficult dilemma. Italy lacked the political culture necessary to the successful adaptation of the American model, while the concordats in force elsewhere restricted the freedom of the Church.[43]

His intervention in the parliamentary debate contributed to the defeat of the proposed settlement; but he had little time to rejoice over his victory. In the autumn of 1867, the Mentana crisis ushered in a new phase of the Roman question. In December 1866, the beginning of Ricasoli's negotiations with the Holy See had coincided with the end of the French occupation of Rome, as stipulated by the Convention of September 1864. But French soldiers and officers, organized in the so-called Legion d'Antibes, had remained behind to serve in the papal army. Italian public opinion had reacted negatively to the presence of the legion in Rome. The newspapers of the Left had called upon the government to repudiate the treaty with France, as a prelude to the Italian occupation of the Papal States. And plans were afoot in

Rome for an insurrection against the papal government. Instead of repudiating the September Convention, Rattazzi opened new negotiations with Paris; but he also kept in touch with the Roman revolutionaries. As in 1862, his ambiguous policy encouraged an already impatient Garibaldi to try another revolutionary coup de main. In open defiance of the September Convention, he began to organize volunteer cadres and to gather arms. At the end of October 1867 he led his followers into papal territory.[44]

The General and his volunteers had expected their intervention to set off a major insurrection in Rome itself, if not in the countryside. In fact, only small groups of conspirators were ready for action, and they were easily overcome by the papal army. Garibaldi's expedition was already doomed to failure when, on 3 December 1867, regular units of the French army arrived once again in the Papal States. Outnumbered and demoralized by the apathy of the Roman populace and by the superior firepower of the French, the *Garibaldini* were stopped at Mentana. The crisis that had begun with a French violation of the spirit, if not the letter, of the September Convention ended with a renewed French commitment to the defense of the temporal power. Rattazzi, who had wished to preserve the Convention and to liberate Rome at the same time, suffered the inevitable fate of the politician who plays an unsuccessful double game. The revolutionaries criticized him for not repudiating the Convention; the conservatives berated him for not having disbanded Garibaldi's troops before they had entered papal territory. And everyone realized that the cause of "*Roma capitale*" had suffered a major setback.

Ferrari spoke on these events in December 1867, after Rattazzi had already been replaced by the more conservative Luigi Federico Menabrea. As he saw it, Mentana was the bitter fruit of "the politics of despair," which he had denounced so many times. He had harsh words for Rattazzi. If France had violated the Convention, he argued, a government that was committed to "*Roma capitale*" should have seized the opportunity to repudiate that document and to march immediately into the Papal States. If, on the contrary, Rattazzi had not wanted to break with France and to take Rome, he should have calmed public opinion and acted more decisively against Garibaldi.[45] But recriminations were useless. The important question was the future of Rome. The Menabrea government intended to resume negotiations with France and, possibly, to submit the Roman question to the arbitration of a European congress. Where, Ferrari asked, did that leave Italian independence? To the surprise of his fellow deputies, he argued that 1867 was much too late to tolerate the presence of French troops in Rome. The military conquest of the city was not feasible and, in his view, was not even worth attempting. But especially after Mentana, it was the government's duty to uphold the national honor. Hence, he urged Menabrea to demand the evacuation of Rome by the French army and by the Legion d'Antibes, and to break off diplomatic relations, if France refused to comply.

Ferrari the Francophile had obviously faced up to two unpleasant facts. First of all, the liberalization of the Second Empire had not reduced Legitimist and clerical influences over the foreign policy of Napoleon III. Second, the interests of his two homelands had diverged quite a bit since 1859. As an elected official, he felt a clear obligation to choose Italian over French interests. With regard to the Roman question, he was resigned to see an unpleasant deadlock between Italy and France. It had resulted, he thought, from Bonaparte's betrayal of the French revolutionary tradition, but also from the Italian obsession with "*Roma capitale.*" The errors of 1862 and 1867 could not be reversed. But the Italian government, he thought, could at least atone for its shabby role in the recent crisis. He urged it to show clemency toward the *Garibaldini*; and later on he sponsored legislation to grant a government pension to the families of two workers sentenced to death by a papal court for their role in the abortive Roman insurrection.[46] Nothing more could be done until such time as a republican movement in France or a major international crisis deprived the pope of military protection and thus hastened the fall of the imperial power.

As a young disciple of Romagnosi and a friend of Cattaneo, Ferrari had learned quite early in his career to appreciate the importance of economics in the development of modern society. Later on, his awareness of economic issues had been much strengthened by his contacts with Proudhon and with Cernuschi, an expert on bimetallism and other monetary questions. But he was too much the philosopher to become immersed in the planning of new economic institutions that fascinated Proudhon or in the intricacies of international finance that were Cernuschi's forte. His own interest focused primarily upon a more general, but very important, question—the relationship between economics and politics. He did not bring to the Italian Parliament the financial expertise of Sella or Cambray-Digny, nor did he have the practical managerial experience of Depretis. And yet, in his numerous speeches on economic and fiscal policies, he made a distinct contribution.

First of all, he had few rivals in the art of exposing, discussing, and dissecting the political and social values upon which the economic policies of the Right were built. Like some Marxist deputies in the postwar Italian Parliament, Ferrari never looked at a piece of economic legislation without asking himself how it related to the overall strategy of the bourgeois ruling elites. Second, he felt a special responsibility to protect the interests of those citizens whose lives were affected by the economic policies of the Right, but who by virtue of their illiteracy or poverty were denied a voice in the national Parliament. And third, having sworn loyalty to the unitary national state despite earlier misgivings, he spoke against those economic policies that, in his view, weakened the country's control over its own destiny. His speeches, in fact, reflect the same tension between the exigencies of rapid economic development and the desire to protect the nation's independence that troubles the leaders of new states in our time.

The parliamentary records of the 1860s offer numerous examples of Ferrari's ability to relate specific items of economic legislation to the broader context of national policy. The first such example was a speech of 26 June 1861 on a proposed bill authorizing the government to borrow 500 million lire. The Minister of Finance, Pietro Bastogi, acknowledged that the loan was necessary in order to close a budget gap of unprecedented proportions in the history of the Italian states. But he assured the Chamber that this was an extraordinary measure due to the unusual expenses of war and unification and not to be repeated in the future.[47]

Ferrari questioned Bastogi's pledge that the state would never again resort to such measures to balance the budget. This promise of fiscal responsibility, he pointed out, did not square with the commitments recently made by the moderate leadership to the completion of Italy's territorial unity. The liberation of Venetia was not possible without another war against Austria. The acquisition of "*Roma capitale*" entailed a conflict with France, and possibly with other Catholic powers as well. As long as these goals remained at the top of the political agenda, it made little sense to talk about balanced budgets. Italy's ambiguous policies, conceived in a limbo "between fiscal conservatism and revolutionary activism," were making investors unnecessarily nervous. Clearly, then, her political leaders were well advised to make a choice. In the short run, he argued, an Italian Kingdom of twenty-two million people that was solvent and relatively secure was much to be preferred to a larger one that was likely to be bankrupt and to have France as an enemy.[48]

The ever-growing deficits of the following years showed that his warnings had been justified. To the enormous but inevitable expense of administrative unification was added the cost of suppressing banditry in the South and of building a larger army and a navy. In order to increase revenues, the governments of the 1860s relied less upon new taxes than upon the sale of ecclesiastical and state properties, including the existing railroad lines and the tobacco monopoly. But these sources of revenue proved woefully inadequate, and the financial health of the Italian Kingdom grew progressively worse. By 1864 appeals for financial reform were heard from all sides of the political spectrum. During a major parliamentary debate in July of that year, many items in the government's proposed budget were specifically challenged for the first time since Cavour's death. And Ferrari introduced a resolution calling for a parliamentary investigation of existing budgetary practices.[49]

Leaving the analysis of specific budget items to more technically competent critics, he focused on the amount that was being spent to service the public debt. A major share (about 55 percent) of Italy's public debt, he observed, came from expenditures that the Sardinian government had incurred during the drive for unification. The consolidation of the public debt of the former Italian states meant that now the taxpayers of every region were called upon to pay off debts incurred by the Sardinian government. His correspondents suggested that the discontent of the southern population was due in part to this state of affairs. It was not very useful to remind reluctant taxpayers in the South or elsewhere that the Sardinian public debt had been the inevitable price of unification. It made more sense, he argued, to see how the current budget could be reduced. Ironically, in calling for reduced expenditures he was on the same side as the leading fiscal conservatives, Sella and Cambray-Digny, with whom he clashed a few years later over the issue of the grist tax. Once again he singled out "the national obsession with Venetia and Rome" as a source of financial difficulties. A mistaken sense of national priorities, he thought, had produced a military budget larger than was necessary to defend the settlement of 1860.[50]

Ferrari may have been naive to insist that the completion of Italy's territorial unity could be put off to a distant future. But there was no gainsaying his prediction that a race for Venetia and Rome might bankrupt the new state. The war of 1866 against Austria and the Mentana crisis of 1867 had extremely severe repercussions upon Italy's financial situation. Even the introduction of the unprecedented *corso forzoso* (the inconvertibility of bank notes into gold or silver) and the sale of Church properties and railroad concessions could not shore up the value of Italian government bonds on the international money markets. By early 1868, the Italian Parliament was in the midst of a stormy debate over new taxes proposed by Cambray-Digny, the Minister of Finance in the three Menabrea governments (27 October 1867–14 December 1869). The most controversial of the proposed new taxes was the grist tax (*tassa sul macinato*).

Levied on all ground cereals, the proposed tax affected every Italian consumer. But it fell far more heavily upon the rural poor, whose diet consisted mainly of cereals, than upon other social classes. Moreover, the proposed tax was higher on high-grade cereals like wheat than on low-grade cereals like maize or rye. Thus, it was evident that the southern peasants would be the hardest hit, because they consumed more wheat flour per capita than their counterparts in other regions, whose diet also included maize, potatoes, or rice.[51] The grist tax, long forgotten in the northern regions, had been completely abolished in the South only at the time of Italy's unification. The reintroduction of this tax was certain to create resentment among the peasantry, especially in the South. But Cambray-Digny defended the proposed tax as an equitable one, because it would be paid by every consumer; and he warned that the state might have to default on its obligations if it was not passed by the Chamber of Deputies. In March 1868 the caucus of the parliamentary Left designated Ferrari, Crispi, and Depretis among many willing candidates to be the keynote speakers against Cambray-Digny's bill.[52]

Ferrari's speech against the grist tax illustrates his ability to use a specific piece of legislation to question the entire value system of Italy's political leaders. But it also offers moving evidence of his social conscience. As he saw it, the grist tax was the economic aspect of "the politics of despair," which he had lamented for several years. Only despair, he argued, could have induced the Italian government to propose a tax that was "condemned by nearly all economists, outdated, borrowed from the ruins of medieval society, listed in the register of those taxes most emphatically rejected by modern civilization."[53] He went on to discuss the probable impact of the proposed tax upon poor peasants. For this very serious topic he chose the ironic mode, of which he was an acknowledged master. He conjured up an imaginary character, Giannastasio, southern peasant son of peasants. Rain or shine, Ferrari said, Giannastasio worked in the fields fourteen hours a day to produce his only treasure, a sackful of wheat. One day, tired of thrashing his wheat by hand, the resourceful Giannastasio had invented the grindstone. The tax collector had smiled benignly and had congratulated him on the invention. The naive Giannastasio had expected a reward from the state for his efforts; instead, he had received a tax bill. Then one day, Ferrari continued, some smartly dressed young men had visited Giannastasio's village. They had told him that he was now a free citizen, that he would have a government of his own choice, and that he would only pay those taxes of which he approved. Beside himself with joy, Giannastasio had promptly joined those who shouted "Long live Italy!" On election day, he had cheerfully gone to the nearest polling place. But the tax collector, now bedecked in the tricolor, had appeared once again and had turned him away at the door: "You are not qualified, you are not an elector, you are illiterate, you do not pay [property] taxes." Giannastasio had been disappointed, of course, but at least he was now free to enjoy his sackful of wheat without having to worry about the hated grist tax.[54]

If that tax was reintroduced, Ferrari pointed out, the government would have to persuade millions of peasants like his imaginary Giannastasio that the tax was, in Cambray-Digny's words, both unavoidable and equitable. Perhaps it would not be too difficult to convince Giannastasio that the grist tax was equitable. Sensible man that he was, he could surely understand that the tax affected both the price of his own hard bread and the price of the pastries that the wealthy had to have as the proper accompaniment to their dinners of chicken, turkey, and pheasant. But it would be rather more difficult to convince Giannastasio that the reintroduction of the grist tax was necessary in order to save the state from bankruptcy. In the first place, Ferrari noted, the government had not demonstrated that all other means for increasing revenues had been adequately explored before resorting to this desperate measure. Second, how could the Giannastasios of Italian society be made to feel responsible for the current financial crisis? They had never been consulted by the advocates of hasty annexations, territorial expansion, and inflated military budgets. An appeal to the patriotism of the Italian peasants would sound hollow, particularly in the South, where the people had so recently been deceived by false promises. But there was a way to make Giannastasio and his fellow peasants put up with the proposed grist tax, if the government could demonstrate that it was truly unavoidable. While making them members of the community of taxpayers, the Chamber of Deputies could also make them members of the polity. It could extend to them the right to participate in the governing of the state that had been vaguely promised in 1860.

Because the government was not holding forth any political quid pro quo and because it knew the grist tax to be especially unpopular, one could only assume that it was prepared to collect the new tax by force. Quite apart from the probability of riots, the need to police literally every mill in the country would significantly reduce the amount of revenue predicted by Cambray-Digny. Moreover, the collection of taxes at gunpoint would make a mockery of the economic and political freedom which the moderate liberals claimed as their greatest gift to Italy. And it would jeopardize the future of the liberal state no less than a default on its financial obligations. The reintroduction of the grist tax did in fact produce widespread riots, protests by the beleaguered millers, and meager revenues.[55] By 1869, the repeal of the grist tax became officially part of the political program of the parliamentary Left.[56]

In his speeches on this subject Ferrari showed a characteristic concern for the poorest classes of Italian society, but also a concern for the survival of the state. If he opposed the grist tax, it was not only because he sympathized with the poor and the powerless; it was also because he feared the effects of mass alienation upon a very young liberal state. Likewise, his concern for the survival of an imperfect but flexible political system made him wary of economic penetration by richer and more powerful countries. At times this fear made him take strongly nationalistic, even isolationist, positions on such issues as international trade agreements and the negotiation of loans with foreign banks. Such was the case, for example, with his speeches in 1863 against ratification of a commercial treaty with France.

Inspired by the principles of the free trade movement, it was patterned after the Cobden-Chevalier Treaty between England and France. It facilitated the export of agricultural products from Italy to France and of manufactured goods from France to

Italy. Contemporary economic historians generally agree that the treaty stimulated Italian agricultural production, albeit without leading to technical improvements, and that it retarded Italy's industrial development.[57] Critics of the treaty had predicted that this would happen. In the Chamber of Deputies, the strongest arguments against ratification came from the Lombard cotton manufacturer Ettore Lualdi and from Quintino Sella, whose family manufactured wool textiles in Piedmont. But despite their pleas for the protection of young domestic industries from foreign competition, the treaty was ratified by a large majority. The vote in the Chamber reflected the ideological commitment of Italy's political elites to the principles of free trade, but it also reflected the predominant economic interests of those elites, which were agricultural and commercial much more than industrial. Few members of Parliament spoke against the treaty on behalf of Italy's fledgling industrial sector; Ferrari alone spoke against it on behalf of the unrepresented lower classes. His criticism was aimed not at specific provisions of the treaty but at the principles of economic liberalism that had inspired it.[58]

Submitting this treaty for ratification, the Minghetti government had stressed its similarity to the highly publicized Cobden-Chevalier Treaty of 1860. Ferrari questioned the wisdom of such a comparison. The unrestricted international exchange of goods, he thought, made sense between countries which were approximately equal in economic strength and development. But what economic equality existed between Italy and a much older, larger, and richer nation whose politicians and publicists talked openly of "turning the Mediterranean into a French lake?" Under the aegis of free trade, he continued, the savages of North America had sold tracts of virgin forest in exchange for gunpowder and cheap liquor and the Africans had sold thousands of slaves in exchange for glass trinkets. These had been free exchanges—that is, not subject to government regulations. It could even be said that they had been equal exchanges, because both parties to the transaction had received something they wanted. In the long run, however, only one party had acquired the means for further economic development; the other had remained static and dependent. Ferrari feared that a similar situation might occur if Italy became dependent upon French manufactures while sticking to her traditional exports of nonessential agricultural products, like wine, and of semifinished products, like marble tiles.

But this was not his only reservation concerning the treaty. He also noted that the government's enthusiasm for international free trade seemed inconsistent with its domestic policies: "The theory of free trade is founded upon the theory of free production. But you do not accept free production. You interfere with strikes, you do not allow the workers to decide what is in their interest, you do not allow them to organize, and you regard their associations as subversive. You interfere with the freedom of the industrialists, and you oppose their mergers. . . . All these practices contradict your theories about free competition and free trade."[59] A majority of his colleagues, he charged, believed in laissez faire liberalism only when it suited their own particular interests; they did not hesitate to deny economic freedom to others. But lest his critique of free trade be mistaken for a defense of Italy's few industrial capitalists, he was careful to distinguish his position from that of Lualdi and Sella. To emphasize the point that economic liberalism was irrelevant to the lower classes, he reconstructed an imaginary dialogue between "a satisfied bourgeois and a dissatisfied worker":

"You are free as a bird," says the bourgeois.
"Yes, I am free to starve at the door of the cafés, restaurants, theaters, and other places where you go for entertainment. Some freedom!"
'Work, and you too shall prosper."
"But I cannot find work, and I have no machines, no tools, no raw materials."
"Buy them."
"I have no money."
"Go and see a banker."
"If his guards even let me in the door, the banker will ask for collateral. . . . "
"Then take a job in one of our factories."
"But you keep the wages so low, you dictate the working conditions; if I refuse to accept your terms, you send the police after me, you hand me over to the courts."

"We all have to start from scratch; look at how I made my fortune. . . . You must struggle; we are all equally free under law."

"Quite so, but you have money, assets, inheritances, you have an education; you can spend ten years learning a business; if I take so much as ten days off, I am dead. How can you talk about economic freedom, about free competition, when all the advantages are on your side and all the handicaps on ours?"[60]

This speech made little impact upon Ferrari's colleagues. And yet, the open rejection of economic liberalism by the Italian workers was closer at hand than they realized. While they moved quickly to approve the commercial treaty with France, European revolutionaries were gathering in London to prepare the groundwork for the First Workingmen's International. One of its most active, if unruly, branches would soon flourish on Italian soil.

Even a cursory reading of Ferrari's speeches and comments leaves no doubt that without him the Italian Parliament of the 1860s and 1870s would have been a much duller place. He had few rivals in the art of moving a habitually inattentive audience to anger or applause, to laughter or tears. But was he effective in his chosen role as Parliament's gadfly? That is, was he able to influence others? If we measure the influence of a politician by the number of bills that bear his name or by his power to swing large groups of votes, we must conclude that Ferrari was not effective. And this can be said, of course, of most members of the parliamentary Left up to 1876. But because the Italian Parliament of his day in no sense represented the entire population, we should perhaps measure his effectiveness by a different yardstick. On several occasions he claimed to be speaking on behalf of students, peasants or workers, people who enjoyed civil but not political rights. Many grateful letters from powerless citizens whose freedom of speech or economic interests he had defended suggest that he was quite effective in his role as a kind of "deputy-at-large." Moreover, he provided a political and intellectual role model for younger men, particularly Felice Cavallotti, who carried on the radical-socialist tradition after his death.[61]

[8]

The Twilight Years

FERRARI, WHO HAD always criticized the national obsession with "*Roma capitale*," felt vindicated by the Mentana crisis. But he was unable to rejoice over the humiliating defeat of his political adversaries. For several months after the crisis, he felt so despondent that he curtailed his political activities·to the minimum level compatible with his parliamentary mandate. As usual, he found relief from the frustrations of politics by turning to scholarly research and writing. Early in the summer of 1868 he returned to Paris, eager to resume his study of the laws of history. Although he spent much time alone in his apartment, he could not avoid occasional contacts with politically active old friends; nor could he ignore their growing excitement over the international implications of the recent dynastic crisis in Spain. His friends—especially Darimon, who remembered the Latin Democratic Committee of 1851—argued that the abdication of Queen Isabella II had precipitated a constitutional crisis from which the Spanish monarchy was unlikely to recover. They felt that a radical republican movement might have a chance to blossom south of the border, if it received moral and financial support from French and Italian opposition groups.[1] In fact, Ferrari became so fascinated by the implications of the Spanish crisis that he stayed on in France until the end of October 1868. While Parisian friends urged him to visit Madrid and to establish direct contacts with the Spanish republicans, Italian correspondents wrote him of a possible Garibaldian expedition.[2] He wrote: "If Spain is aroused, France will feel the impact, and then even Italy will change her ways. You know very well the current position of the French government, its corruption, its apathy, its unbelievable indifference to any scientific debate, the servile attitude of the press, the customary confusion within the democratic camp. These are things that could disappear overnight; if that happened, we might see a *joli tapage*, a marvelous uproar, as Voltaire said two or three years before the Revolution."[3] The *joli tapage* did begin shortly after his return to Italy. But in contrast to the crisis of 1848, it grew out of a seemingly old-fashioned dynastic quarrel, and not out of a revival of European radicalism. Ferrari paid little attention to the controversial Hohenzollern candidacy to the Spanish throne, and the diplomatic confrontation of 1869–70 between France and Prussia caught him by surprise. This happened in part because he was no longer as well informed about the inner workings of the Bonapartist regime as he had been in the 1850s. But there were other reasons for his failure to follow French foreign policy more closely.

During most of 1869 his attention was focused upon the forthcoming First Vatican Council, which Pope Pius IX inaugurated in December of that year. Political friends and admirers from various parts of Italy, especially Giuseppe Ricciardi, urged his participation in public lectures, rallies, mock religious ceremonies, and other activities designed to protest the Vatican Council.[4] But his Liberal Catholic friend, Jean Gustave Wallon, found the frantic activities of the Italian anticlericals ridiculous and unnecessary. He predicted that the most important item on the Council's agenda, the question of papal infallibility, would bring about a schism within the Church; and he speculated that the French bishops, mindful of their Gallican tradition, would reject any strengthening of papal authority. A schism and a revival of Gallicanism would inevitably result in the withdrawal of French troops from Rome.[5] Ferrari evidently found merit in Wallon's arguments; to Ricciardi's chagrin he urged the leaders of the anticlerical campaign to tone down their shrill rhetoric.[6]

While he was trying to keep abreast of his scholarly work, of his duties in Parliament, and of the anticlerical campaign, the issue of the Hohenzollern candidacy to the Spanish throne became more and more ominous.[7] By the early summer of 1870 the dangerous implications of that issue for the European international system had become so obvious that he hurried back to Paris in order to look after his financial affairs and to consult with his political friends. In July 1870, only hours before the French declaration of war on Prussia, he wrote to Cardani that he dreaded the thought of a Franco-Prussian conflict. Whatever its outcome, a war would certainly mean a setback for European democracy. In the political context of 1870, a French victory over Prussia was certain to make the Bonapartist regime more popular at home and to strengthen its influence in Madrid and in Rome. Ferrari did not want this to happen. But the prospect of a victory by conservative, militaristic Prussia seemed to him equally bleak.[8]

Upon the outbreak of hostilities, he departed reluctantly for Florence. As might have been expected, the international crisis had opened a new phase of the Roman question as an issue in Italian domestic politics. The Italian government was obviously hoping that a Prussian victory would force Napoleon III to withdraw his troops from Rome. As for the parliamentary opposition, its leaders were urging the Lanza government to occupy Rome without even awaiting the outcome of the war.[9] During the new round of debates on the Roman question, Ferrari took an independent stance. Wary of close ties with Prussia and convinced that a major Church schism was imminent, he urged the Lanza government to open immediate negotiations with France and to request again the evacuation of Rome in return for Italy's benevolent neutrality. He confessed that the current plight of France had made him "age ten years in ten days." With an emotional outburst that revealed his deep and persistent love for his adoptive homeland, he pleaded with the Italian government not to confuse the destiny of Bonaparte with the destiny of France, not to ignore the intimate relationship that existed between French and Italian civilization: "If the current disaster goes unchecked, if we lose a part of ourselves, if Paris fades away, our own sky will become drab and dull, the great star of the Latin world will set."[10]

The opposition deputies who were hounding Lanza to take Rome immediately had asked for his support; but they were disappointed. Their main objective, he argued, was and had always been to make Rome the capital of the Kingdom of Italy. His was to see the pope overthrown and, if at all possible, forced to flee abroad. As long as the Vatican Council was in progress, he felt that an Italian move into Rome might actually strengthen the pope's personal prestige and authority. It seemed preferable to wait for the definition of the dogma of papal infallibility and for the Church schism that was sure to follow. For a few days, his moderate counsel prevailed. But the Sedan debacle and the subsequent withdrawal of French troops from Rome eliminated the need for negotiations with France or other forms of Italian involvement in the conflict. The followers of Mazzini, Garibaldi, and Rattazzi both in and out of Parliament could no longer be restrained. On 20 September 1870 Italian troops entered the Eternal City at Porta Pia. Long thereafter, Ferrari remained convinced that this hasty move had aroused sympathy for the pope and had strengthened his moral authority among Catholics in Italy and abroad.[11]

Although he was chagrined by the actions of the Italian government, he watched with unabashed satisfaction the collapse of the Bonapartist regime in France under the blows of a superior Prussian army. He rejoiced over the proclamation of the Third French Republic and he was the first to announce in the Chamber of Deputies that the United States had extended diplomatic recognition to the new regime.[12] Hoping for a genuine revival of radical republicanism, at least in the Latin countries of Europe, he longed to return to France. In the meantime, through his friend Cernuschi he urged the French republicans to negotiate an armistice before the Prussians had reached Paris. A price would obviously have to be paid, but it was imperative to free the new regime from the burden of a war already lost.[13] Having acknowledged, however reluctantly, the military superiority of Prussia, he felt that a prolongation of hostilities could only jeopardize the fledgling republic. For that reason he refused to endorse Garibaldi's gallant intervention against the Prussians in the Dijon area. And he deplored publicly the decision of the Parisian radicals (among them his fellow *Quarante-huitards*) to defy the moderate republican leadership and to defend their besieged city to the bitter end. In the early months of 1871, having heard that most Frenchmen outside of Paris longed for peace, he feared that the independent stand of the radicals might precipitate a civil war between the French nation and its capital. The heroic and dreadful history of the Paris Commune was to prove him right.[14]

Between the outbreak of the Franco-Prussian war and the subjugation of the Communards by the Versailles government Ferrari wrote two articles that, together with his letters to Cernuschi, allow us to reconstruct his views on the events of 1870–71.[15] Upon reflection, he sensed that the Franco-Prussian war had been a turning point in European history, perhaps the beginning of a new era in which Paris would no longer be the heart of the Continent's political and intellectual life. The defeat of France was historically significant, he thought, because it offered important clues as to the changing direction of European civilization. It signalled the end of a historical phase that had begun with the French Revolution:

Accustomed as we are to thinking only of ourselves, of the Latin world, as if we were all alone in the universe, we are inclined to see the Revolution of 1789 as the prototype, the fountainhead of all contemporary revolutions; we are almost inclined to pity England, Germany, and other nations for having felt its impact only indirectly, thus remaining trapped within their feudal traditions. But this is a mere prejudice; in fact the Revolution of 1789 was an offshoot of the Anglo-American movement of 1775 . . . for which Locke, Collins, Taylor, Toland, not to mention Smith and Hume, prepared the ground. . . . Unfortunately for France, the recent events show that she has been slower than Prussia to understand the Anglo-American revolution.[16]

Both the Anglo-American movement of 1775–83 and the French Revolution of 1789–99, Ferrari wrote, had been inspired by the English radical thinkers of the seventeenth century. The concepts of natural rights and limited monarchy, the rejection of medieval Christianity, and the elimination of feudal restrictions upon the rights of property had been common to both revolutions. But during the early nineteenth century, the two currents of the European revolutionary tradition had diverged more and more. He stressed two major differences between the French (or Latin) and the English (or Anglo-Saxon) tradition.

As a result of the Revolution of 1789, he argued, France had forfeited a vast colonial empire. She had discovered, no doubt to her chagrin, that the Declaration of the Rights of Man and of the Citizen made the traditional forms of European imperialism wholly untenable. But England, having learned a lesson from the American rebellion, had devised a new, indirect, and very successful form of imperialism. She had advocated revolutionary ideas in order to subvert Spanish rule in the New World and the authority of native princes in India. The unprecedented expansion of her economic interests overseas had given her a political and military power that France could not match.[17] Prussia, he wrote, had never had the resources to engage in economic imperialism overseas. But at least she had learned from the Anglo-Americans (as France apparently had not) that military power depended upon a strong and prosperous economy.

Ferrari also found a significant difference between the Latin and the Anglo-Saxon traditions with regard to the rights of property. Anglo-Saxon civilization had defined those rights as nearly absolute; it had left inherited wealth alone; it had renounced any right to question the morality, the influence, and even the origin of private property. Such a definition seemed appropriate for a country like the United States, vast, sparsely populated, and blessed with enormous untapped wealth. But in France, where opportunities to accumulate great wealth were not as plentiful, "the rights of property, far from being defined as absolute, are subject to close scrutiny, they have to be justified; their source, use, or abuse, has to be explained; there are those who would legitimize property [only if] acquired by working, if limited to a specified amount, and if subject to expropriation in the name of the public interest."[18]

As the author of the *Filosofia della Rivoluzione*, Ferrari for twenty years had been firmly committed to that radical-socialist critique of bourgeois property of which Buonarroti and Babeuf had been the prophets. The Franco-Prussian war did not alter his conviction that such a critique was historically inevitable and much to be preferred to the "Protestant freedom of Adam Smith." But in these essays of 1870 he suggested, for the first time in his career, that the Anglo-Saxon definition of the rights of property could pay handsome political and military dividends. Wherever the rights of property were secure, he wrote, it became easier for the state to raise revenues for various purposes, including war. In addition, wherever the wealthy had no reason to fear the hostility and envy of the lower classes, as in England, Prussia, or the United States, they did not oppose the concept of "the nation-in-arms." It was obvious that a country like Prussia, which trained and armed every available man, was potentially much stronger than one that relied upon an army of professionals segregated from the rest of society.

He did not suggest that France should imitate Prussia. Indeed, he thought that the ongoing struggle "between Fourth and Third Estate" in France could end only with the introduction of a *legge agraria*, that is, with significant restrictions upon the rights of property. But he argued that European civilization was rapidly moving toward a historical phase in which the Anglo-Saxon concept of property would predominate over the Latin one. Consequently, those states that were most capable of expanding their economic interests and of fighting wars could be expected to control Europe, at least for a time, at the expense of those, like France, in which the class struggle was more intense.[19]

In the early part of 1871, the tragic confrontation between the Parisian Communards and the Versailles government confirmed Ferrari's view that a new phase of European civilization had indeed begun. The anguish he experienced during the Parisian insurrection was so great that he became physically ill. He worried about the well-being and the future of old friends like Darimon and Courbet. He felt a deep sympathy for the thousands of innocent citizens whose lives and property were in grave danger. And he worried about his own apartment and the rental properties which were his main source of income. In March 1871 he applied for a leave of absence from the Chamber of Deputies; but it was May before he was well enough to travel to Paris. In the meantime, he interpreted the meaning of the Commune for the readers of the *Nuova antologia*. In his essay once again he chided the Parisian radicals for their futile, if heroic, attempt to prolong the conflict. But he tried to understand their motives, even while condemning their actions. In the Communard mentality he saw a unique and distinctly French mixture of patriotism and class hatred. He observed that, like the Jacobins of 1792–93, the Communards had reacted to the Prussian victories and to the siege of Paris with a desperate determination to defend the national honor sullied by the Bonapartist generals. But, like the insurgents of June 1848, they had also waged war against the bourgeois republicans, whose claims to political power they refused to acknowledge.[20]

When this essay appeared, it had already been suggested in Italy as elsewhere that the Parisian insurrection had been masterminded by the First International. But Ferrari, who knew some prominent Communards personally, did not believe that the leaders or, for that matter, the ideas of the International had played a significant role in the insurrection. He wrote:

[Because] we live at a time when one hears all kinds of nonsense, while the truth remains hidden, it is important to refute those who argue that the Commune was the child of the International headquartered in London. . . . The Parisian insurrection has been a purely French affair, rooted in the ideas of French writers; it harks back to 1848 and to the republic of Robespierre in its way of raising and of evading issues, in its determination to avenge the defeat by Prussia. Besides, where would a cosmopolitan organization, limited by necessity to a small band of individuals and to the pursuit of philanthropic causes, ever find the strength to arouse a whole nation?[21]

He added that if the Communards had acted consistently with the ideals of European socialism they would not have taken sides in the Franco-Prussian war. Nor would they have opposed the peace negotiations undertaken by the bourgeois republicans. As he saw it, the real tragedy of the Paris Commune was precisely that its leaders had allowed a sense of wounded national pride to prevail upon the socialist principles of proletarian solidarity and of abstention from conflicts between bourgeois states.

But Ferrari's harsh critique of the Communards was in no sense an apology for the Versailles government. Indeed, he was among the first contemporary commentators to suspect the bourgeois republican leaders of having actually sought a confrontation with the revolutionaries in the capital. There was reason to suspect, he concluded, that the bourgeois republicans had taken advantage of the "heroic folly" of the Communards in order not only to thin out the ranks of radical and socialist groups, but more generally to reduce the population, the wealth, and the political influence of Paris, all of which had increased under the Second Empire.[22]

Like his writings of 1848 and 1851, Ferrari's essay on the Paris Commune deserves to be more widely read. It provides a fascinating contrast to Marx's famous pamphlet, *The Civil War in France*. While he never denied that class antagonism had indeed surfaced during the Parisian insurrection, Ferrari did not see the class struggle as the central theme. His interpretation of the Commune stressed the importance of frustrated nationalism and the traditional antagonism between capital and provinces, between city and countryside. On balance, his interpretation was more nuanced and convincing than Marx's. As a close friend of many *Quarante-huitards*, he knew that the romantic appeal of barricade fighting sometimes transcended the importance of specific issues or interests.[23]

In the summer of 1871 Ferrari found his beloved Paris dispirited and battle-scarred. The sight of smoldering ruins where once had stood the graceful Tuileries brought tears to his eyes and intensified his sense of outrage toward the Communards and toward their bourgeois enemies. His own properties had miraculously escaped looting, fires, and bombs. But during the months of siege and insurrection he had been unable to collect rents from his tenants; as a result, for the first time in his life he experienced serious financial difficulties.[24]

In September he returned to Florence for the opening of the

new legislative session. Despite an easy victory in the election of 1870, he was unhappy with the life of a deputy, and more than ever disenchanted with the economic policies of the Right. He could never actually bring himself to resign his seat. But from December 1871, when he reluctantly joined his colleagues who were already in Rome, until his death, he appeared infrequently in the Chamber, to the chagrin of Cardani and of many electors in Gavirate-Luino.[25] During this declining phase of his political career, there were three issues, however, about which he felt strongly enough to attend the parliamentary debates and to speak, as was his custom, "blunt and unadorned words." These were the changing international situation and Italy's place in it; the new developments in the cold war between the Italian government and the Holy See; and the national agitation in favor of universal suffrage.

The Franco-Prussian war had suggested to Ferrari that European civilization was entering a phase in which the Anglo-Saxon powers would be dominant. With the defeat of revolutionary forces first in Italy, then in Spain and France, the "Latin star" seemed to have set. Moreover, his visit to Paris had convinced him that a restoration of the monarchy "in the nest of Louis XIV" was probable and near at hand. If such a restoration occurred, the two victims of Prussian expansionism, Austria and France, might become allies and work together for the restoration of the temporal power. In any event, he argued, the steady growth of two old European Empires, the British and the Russian, and the birth of a new one in the heart of the continent were creating a potentially dangerous situation for weak countries like Italy. To make matters worse, the defeat of France and the occupation of Rome had left Italy without powerful friends in Europe.[26]

In Ferrari's view, Emilio Visconti-Venosta, although an able Foreign Minister, was not sufficiently attuned to the changing international situation. After a decade of patient and resourceful efforts to complete the territorial unification of Italy, he seemed to be drifting. In three parliamentary speeches of 1872, Ferrari pointed out that the occupation of Rome had ushered in a new

era in Italian foreign policy. From 1861 to 1871, he noted, the
parliamentary Left had loyally supported the great work of Italian unification. Its leaders had not always been happy with the
methods of moderate diplomacy. Nonetheless, except for a few
mavericks like himself, they had supported the efforts of the
moderates to attain those all-important national objectives, Venetia and Rome. But in the years ahead, he predicted, it would
become more difficult for at least two concurrent reasons to
conduct the nation's foreign policy. On the one hand, the European world was becoming more tense, competitive, even dangerous for countries with limited economic and military resources.
On the other hand, there was no longer one single objective of
overriding national importance that could be used to generate a
political consensus.

Ferrari expected Visconti-Venosta to remain at the helm of
the nation's foreign policy for a few more years. But he felt the
need for a change in the relationship between the foreign minister
and the Chamber of Deputies. Now that new foreign policy objectives had to be defined and pursued, the conduct of foreign
policy could no longer be left up to the King's government, with
little or no input from the nation's representatives. The time had
come, he insisted, for all Italian deputies to have easier access to
diplomatic documents and greater opportunity to debate the ideas
and the actions of the foreign minister. At the same time, he
urged his own colleagues of the Left to take a more active interest in international affairs. Unless they did so, they would either
remain deadlocked in a weak and sterile opposition or they would
be swept away by the ever-stronger tides of *trasformismo*.[27]

Visconti-Venosta's courteous yet evasive response to Ferrari's speeches of 19 April and 14 May 1872, and the editorial
comments of *La Perseveranza*, indicate that a very sensitive chord
had been struck.[28] The Foreign Minister was too intelligent a
man not to agree with Ferrari that domestic political considerations must henceforth have a far greater role in the formulation
of foreign policy. But Ferrari's insistence that such input must
come from open debates in the Chamber placed him in an embarrassing position. Indirectly, but, I think, intentionally, Ferrari

had raised the most important constitutional question left unresolved at the close of the Risorgimento—that is, the question of
ministerial responsibility. Visconti-Venosta could not accede to
Ferrari's requests, even if he sensed that they were justified and
popular, without acknowledging the principle of ministerial responsibility to the Chamber. This, as Ferrari knew very well,
would have meant de facto constitutional reform in the direction
of a parliamentary regime. The Kingdom of Italy did, in fact,
move steadily in that direction during the last quarter of the
nineteenth century, though with occasional attempts to defend
the prerogatives of the crown under the *Statuto* of 1848. Ferrari
did not live long enough to see that transformation. But he helped
to bring it about, because he believed that the domestic political
climate of the 1870s was not conducive to a constituent assembly
and that a de facto constitutional reform was better than no
reform at all.

In the 1870s the formulation of Italian foreign policy could
not be separated from new attempts to settle the dispute with the
Church that had been exacerbated by the occupation of Rome. In
search of a permanent settlement with the Vatican, the Lanza
government introduced the Law of Guarantees, which was passed
by the Chamber of Deputies on 21 March 1871. The law made
substantial territorial and financial concessions to the Church, in
return for recognition of the Kingdom of Italy. Not surprisingly,
Ferrari was among those 106 deputies who voted against it.

Before the Franco-Prussian war, he argued, the Italian government had had the option of completing the country's territorial unification while allowing Rome to remain the permanent
seat of the papacy. But by sending troops into Rome in September
1870, it had announced to the whole world its intention of
turning the pope's city into the capital of a modern nation-state.
Thus, Rome had entered a new phase in her very long history, and
it must be a secular phase. He found it politically unwise and
ideologicaly absurd to propose a "cohabitation" in Rome between the Italian state and the Roman Catholic Church, since
both were sovereign powers with exclusive jurisdiction over their
territory and other property.[29] Moreover, he rejected Visconti-

Venosta's argument that the Law of Guarantees was necessary in order to appease the Catholic powers of Europe. True, some governments had expressed concern over possible Italian inter-ference with the universal mission of the Church. But there was, he thought, no credible threat of intervention on behalf of Pius IX. On the contrary, the recent advent of Amedeo of Savoy to the Spanish throne indicated that Italy was still in good standing among the Catholic powers. His conviction that Italy had nothing to fear from the outside by allowing the cold war with the Church to continue was probably strengthened by the opinions of French correspondents well attuned to the Catholic world, especially Wallon.[30]

The domestic aspect of the Roman question, he conceded, was much more troublesome. But he refused to recognize Catholic intransigence as a major national problem. Ten years after its founding, the liberal state appeared viable, if not strong. Moderate Catholics, he thought, would eventually adjust to it as they had in France. As for the intransigents, if the Italian government abandoned its futile efforts to appease the Holy See and con-tinued instead to expropriate ecclesiastical properties and to emphasize secular education, they and the papal court might eventually leave Italy.[31]

In 1872–73, he continued to vote against Sella's attempts to balance the national budget through fiscal measures that weighed heavily upon the lower classes. But he made no major speeches on economic policy. Gradually he came to believe that no further progress toward social justice and toward a more equitable dis-tribution of wealth could be made within the existing political alignments. An infusion of new leaders and ideas was clearly needed; that could come only from social classes heretofore un-represented in the national Parliament. Some of those classes, especially factory workers and artisans in the major cities, were building a network of associations through which they proposed to press for political and economic reforms. Without becoming directly involved in these associations, in which followers of Mazzini and of Bakunin played a major role, Ferrari supported many of their demands, especially in the area of franchise reform. During his last years in Parliament, he followed with particular attention the campaign of a young southern firebrand, Salvatore Morelli, in favor of universal suffrage. A decade of political experience in Italy had changed his previous attitude on this important issue.[32]

The experience of 1849 in France had taught Ferrari that universal suffrage in the hands of a conservative majority could be a most effective weapon for the defense of existing political institutions, social divisions, and property relations. Shaken by that experience, in the early years of the Kingdom of Italy he had favored a very gradual extension of the franchise and the retention of literacy tests for prospective voters. But by the 1870s the introduction of a national system of public secular education and the growth of working-class associations led him to believe that even a radical franchise reform would not play into the hands of clerical elements.[33]

On this issue the Lanza-Sella government was considerably less sanguine. Although it was one of the longest lasting governments of the post-Risorgimento era (December 1869–July 1873), it felt threatened by parliamentary opposition to its fiscal and ecclesiastical policies and by a mounting wave of Catholic intransigence. In this context, it reacted sharply to the campaign in favor of universal suffrage, which it perceived as a dangerous challenge to the foundations of the liberal state. Thus, in November 1872 the minister of the interior instructed the prefect of Rome to ban a mass rally that Morelli and his supporters were planning to hold at the Roman Colosseo.[34]

Outraged by this action, Ferrari lost no time in questioning it on the floor of the Chamber, because he saw in the government's action a portent of things to come. He suspected that the moderate leadership had been frightened by recent editorials in Morelli's *Il Suffragio universale*, which had called upon the sponsors of the rally to debate not only the issue of franchise reform but also the broader and more controversial issue of constitutional reform. Until 1871 the spokesmen for Italian radicalism and republicanism had subordinated their interest in constitutional reform to the drive for unification. But now that Italy had achieved territorial unity they could be expected to resume the struggle for a constituent assembly. Would the moderate leadership, Ferrari asked, react to the inevitable revival of radicalism and republicanism by adopting repressive policies? The ban against the Colosseo rally suggested that this was happening.[35] Lanza's answer was quite as candid and blunt as Ferrari's query. He acknowledged that the decision to ban the Colosseo rally had been made in response to articles in *Il Suffragio universale* that had questioned the legitimacy of the *Statuto* and of the monarchy. The moderate government was taking the view that to advocate constitutional reform and republicanism in a public place such as the Colosseo was to endanger the public order.[36]

Both Ferrari and Lanza understood the far-reaching significance of this parliamentary confrontation. The leadership of the young Italian state was coming face to face with a problem that haunted the constitutional/liberal regimes of the nineteenth century and that continues to trouble the liberal/democratic regimes of our time. The problem was how to deal with the opposition groups and dissident minorities that obeyed the existing laws and operated within the existing institutions, but whose ultimate goal was the subversion of those laws and institutions. During the exchange with Ferrari, Lanza took the position that the liberal state, the monarchy, and the *Statuto* had to be protected from the attacks of dissident minorities even at the cost of occasional acts of repression. Ferrari believed, on the contrary, that preventive measures such as the ban against the Colosseo rally did more harm than good to the existing institutions. Repression, he argued, was certain to drive radicals and republicans underground and to produce a new generation of inflexible and alienated revolutionaries such as the Party of Action had spawned in the 1850s. In his view, the liberal state stood to suffer much more from violations of civil and political liberties by the government than by the activities of radical and republican minorities.

Until the end of his life Ferrari continued to argue that peaceful progress toward the reign of science and equality was possible, albeit slow, so long as a climate of civil and political liberty was maintained. Appropriately enough, his swan song in

the Chamber of Deputies (January 1875) was a protest against
the arrest of republican organizers at Villa Ruffi and the arbitrary
closing of their clubs.[37] His concern for the civil and political
rights of dissident minorities was certainly in keeping with his
radical past. But behind the facade of courage and ideological
consistency that he presented to the Chamber was a man troubled
by the awareness of a widening gap between his political values
and his philosophical reflections on the problem of historical
change. Those reflections, begun in the 1850s when he was writing the *Histoire des révolutions d'Italie*, were leading him away
from the concept of inevitable progress in history toward a generational theory of historical change, the subject of his last major
work. Ferrari's *Teoria dei periodi politici* was, in fact, the reason
why such twentieth-century proponents of generational theory
as François Mentré, Juliàn Marias Aguilera and José Ortega y
Gasset counted him among their intellectual ancestors along with
Wilhelm Dilthey, Justin Dromel and Gustav Ruemelin.[38]

The intellectual path by which Ferrari arrived at his *Teoria dei
periodi politici* was long and tortuous. This last among his major
works was the product of a lifelong search for an understanding
of the process of historical change. An interest in history in general and in the history of Italian thought in particular prompted
him to read and interpret Vico's *Scienza Nuova*. In a "new
science" based upon the study of the products of the human past
(religion, language, myths, and so forth) Ferrari saw an exciting
intellectual alternative to Cartesian philosophy. Later on, this
early interest in the products and patterns of history was refined
and strengthened through his association with Fauriel and Michelet.

But if Ferrari as a Romantically inclined young scholar was
attracted to Vico's philosophy of history, he rejected a cyclical
view of the human past. His essays for the *concours d'agrégation*
of 1840 and his lectures on the Italian Renaissance reflected
quite clearly the influence of the eighteenth century's faith in
historical "progress," to be attained through the application of
human reason to ever more complex societal problems. In turn,

this belief in historical progress and in reason nurtured his interest in politics and provided the intellectual foundation for his
radical-socialist convictions.

Like many radicals of 1848, however, Ferrari was deeply
shaken by the failure of the European revolutionary movement.
The experiences of exile, censorship, and political repression
obviously played a part in a gradual but irreversible rejection of
his youthful faith in historical progress. In fact, his major works
of the 1850s were suffused with a deep pessimism. The many
characters who acted out the drama of Italy's history in his
Révolutions d'Italie seemed to respond to inevitable and immutable historical laws. Their actions were determined by a dialectic
process in four stages (subversion, solution, combat, and victory),
which left little room for rational choices.

In the 1860s and early 1870s, Ferrari stuck to his radical
outlook in the realm of politics. But philosophically he moved
further and further away from the belief in historical progress
and from the optimistic view of human nature out of which that
outlook had grown. The result was, as I pointed out earlier, a
dichotomy between Ferrari the democratic politician and Ferrari
the philosopher of history. Gradually he became convinced that
the course of history was determined not by the rational choices
of individuals or classes but by laws that, if properly understood,
could be used to analyze the present and to predict the future.

In his last works—*La Chine et l'Europe* (1867), *Teoria dei
periodi politici* (1874) and *L'Aritmetica nella storia* (1875)—he
broke sharply with the humanistic approach to the study of the
past that he had learned within the Romagnosi circle and at the
Collège de France. Reflecting upon the tremendous advances of
science and technology that had occurred during his own lifetime, he was struck by the fact that modern man seemed willing
to measure, classify, and quantify every aspect of his experience
except his own past. Like his contemporaries Dromel and Ruemelin, he attempted to go one step beyond the study of patterns
in history. He hoped to arrive at a "science of history" based
upon the discovery of universally valid and immutable laws, in
much the same way as Newton and his contemporaries had

arrived at the foundation of modern physics. In the preface to the *Teoria dei periodi politici* he explained:

This is the background of my theory on the measurement of time and the mechanism of revolution. It was conceived when I was writing my *Histoire des révolutions d'Italie*; I developed it further in my *Histoire de la raison d'état*, and I generalized it in my *La Chine et l'Europe*. And now, freed from the shackles of narrative prose, it aspires to the accuracy of a mathematical theory, to the universality of science. I arrived at this theory while seeking something altogether different. While seeking a free man I discovered a man-machine, the laws that govern his constant changing, the forms that deceive and enlighten him. Nothing more can be asked of me. Herein lies my contribution.

Above all, Ferrari aspired to "a new way of writing history," one that would eliminate approximations, rhetorical statements, and didactic pretensions. In search of a "science of history" more attuned to the scientific and technological concerns of the 1870s than the Vichian new science of his youth, he tried to isolate the recurring and immutable aspects of the human past and to use them as reference points for the exploration and formulation of historical laws. The most important of these reference points was what he called the "political" or "thinking" generation. Unlike the natural generation (that is, the total number of people born at a given time), Ferrari's political generation comprised only those contemporaries whose various forms of interaction had left a mark upon the human past.

This was an important distinction but not, I think, an original one. It appears in almost identical form in Justin Dromel's *La loi des révolutions*, published in 1862 by Didier of Paris, the publisher of Ferrari's *Histoire des Révolutions d'Italie*. The chapters in which Dromel defined the difference between a natural and a political generation had appeared in the *Courrier de Paris* between 1856 and 1858, when Ferrari was revising the manuscript of the *Révolutions d'Italie* for publication. Because Ferrari was very well acquainted with Parisian press circles and because he read regularly the most important magazines of that day, we may assume that he had seen Dromel's essays. The lack of any reference to Dromel in Ferrari's correspondence and in the *Ré-*

volutions d'Italie precludes a direct assessment of the intellectual
relationship between the two men. But a textual analysis of their
works strongly suggests that Ferrari had read *La loi des révolutions* and accepted Dromel's basic premise that revolutions were
always preceded by a turnover of political generations. In turn,
Ferrari's *Teoria dei periodi politici* may have influenced the
thought of Dilthey and of the German emigré Gustav Ruemelin,
a participant in the Revolution of 1848, whose essay "Notion et
durée d'une génération" was written in the 1870s, although published much later.[39]

Demographic statistics, Ferrari wrote, showed that thirty
years was the average life span of western Europeans at mid-
nineteenth century. That is, a turnover of natural generations
occurred every thirty years or so. This also held true of political
generations, with one important difference: a man became a member of a natural generation upon his birth, but a member of a political generation only upon the beginning of his "public life," at
approximately thirty years of age. Like Dromel, Ferrari thought
that the study of natural generations was useful to economists
and demographers, but not to historians. In fact, the natural
generations that changed every thirty years included members
who died too early to participate in socially significant activities.
The historian, he wrote, must be concerned only with that span
of a man's life in which socially significant activities took place.
Until his early twenties a man was in most cases legally and
financially dependent upon his father. His public life—that is,
the span of time during which he enjoyed political rights and
exercised political responsibility—usually began after he was already married and financially independent, between the ages of
twenty-five and thirty. Those members of a natural generation
who survived long enough to have a public life were the historically significant ones, inasmuch as they led the political or
intellectual revolutions that marked the transition from one historical phase to another. These revolutions occurred when men
of a new generation, having entered public life, clashed with men
of previous political generations, who dominated all the important institutions of their society.

In order to single out and study the characteristics of a political generation, Ferrari reconstructed over six hundred biographical profiles of men who had made a contribution to the history of their native countries, particularly in the areas of politics and philosophy. His survey showed that, on the average, public life began in the third or fourth decade of a man's life and lasted until he was approximately sixty years old. Among the historical figures in his sample, he found a few, such as Wolfgang Goethe, whose public lives had spanned four, five, or even six decades. But these were exceptions; the mean for the entire sample was thirty-one years and three months. Although Ferrari's sample included men from many walks of life, he was most interested in those who had played a role in political revolutions. In particular, he wanted to know what had brought them into conflict with the political establishments of their day.

Whatever its origin and form, he wrote, government was by definition a conservative institution, resistant to change. Its very functions condemned it to death each time a new political generation reached maturity: "The [essential] function of government is to protect society, to defend it against foreign enemies; it therefore becomes a war machine, a living fortress; its raison d'être is summed up by the right to wage war and to make peace."[40] But government, he continued, could not exercise this function without resorting to secrecy, deceit, and violence. Ultimately, it became so corrupted by these practices that it lost sight of its initial goal. The weapons that it had forged for use against foreign enemies were then turned against real or suspected internal enemies and eventually against all citizens. Self-preservation rather than the welfare of society became the overriding concern of political elites, whether they had inherited their power from a previous government or had seized it by revolutionary means. But while the generation that dominated the political system or the culture became static and preoccupied only with self-preservation, other members of society were at work producing new ideas, values, and art forms. Every thirty years or so, as a new political generation emerged and asserted its own values, a confrontation with the dominant generation became inevitable. In this clash of political generations Ferrari found an explanation of historical change that seemed universally applicable, and as useful for the prediction of the future as it was for an understanding of the past. But more than one generation, he thought, was necessary for the transition from one historical phase to another. Returning to a theme of his *Révolutions d'Italie*, he argued that four "generational crises" (a period of approximately 125 years) had been necessary for the emergence and consolidation of such major innovations as Christianity in the world of imperial Rome or the concept of the social contract in the climate of Europe's traditional monarchies. Moreover, his comparative study of Chinese and Western history over a period of 2,000 years led him to believe that four periods of approximately 125 years—that is, sixteen generational crises—were necessary for the development of a totally new civilization.[41]

In fact, Ferrari wrote, the wheels of history moved so slowly that it was easy to overlook the emergence of a generational crisis in one's own lifetime. It was also easy to overestimate the historical significance of such "mutations" as wars, coups d'état, or assassinations. While such events often had a traumatic impact upon the history of a particular generation, they did not alter the basic character of a civilization. That could be altered only through a long chain of generational crises, which were more likely to go unnoticed by contemporary commentators and by future historians. In his *Révolutions d'Italie* Ferrari had argued that revolutions occurred in four stages. In the second part of the *Teoria* he used the same concept, though not the same terms, to explain the process of historical change. Using the history of France as an example and working backwards, he identified the following major changes (or "periods"): the emergence of the Encyclopedists around 1750, the growth of Cartesian philosophy around 1620, the Calvinist movement of the early 1500s, the peasant movement of 1378, the flourishing of poetry and of scholastic philosophy around 1270, and the flourishing of the troubadours around 1135.

Each of these milestones had required the efforts of four successive political generations. The generation of precursors worked quietly, spreading its ideas and values, while on the surface life went on as before. In his discussion of this generation Ferrari anticipated the most probable criticism. Because the present is always a product of the past, could it not be argued that *all* generations prepared the ground for future ones and were, therefore, generations of precursors? Not so, he answered. What set a generation of precursors apart from others was not the discovery of new principles per se, but rather the fact that, after an incubation period of some thirty years, those principles caused an intellectual revolution, undermining and replacing previously dominant ones.[42]

The precursors paved the way for the revolutionary or explosive generations. These, Ferrari wrote, were easiest to identify by their determination to break with tradition, to scoff at the wisdom of their elders.[43] A revolutionary generation had little time for intellectual discovery and reflection. Its mission was to translate the ideas of the precursors into action. Its leaders were as harried and brash as the previous generation had been serene and cautious. Thirty years of incessant activity on their part changed all institutions and all accepted norms of individual and social behavior. But in time the revolutionary generation became the victim of its own triumph. Eager to proclaim the superiority of its principles, it became suspicious, ruthless, and extremist, and therefore it jeopardized the very principles for which it had fought. These were ultimately safeguarded and carried on by the reactionary generation that followed.

Ferrari emphasized that reaction, at least in the context of his theory, did not mean a return to the principles of the preceding historical period: "Those who persecuted the revolutionary principles in the preparatory phase or fought them in the explosive phase were vanquished and have been dead for thirty to sixty years. ... The reactionaries do not reject the revolution, they simply want to tame it."[44] In every society, precursors and revolutionaries constituted small elites of dedicated intellectuals and men of action. They accomplished their mission with little regard for the great mass of their contemporaries. It was the task of the reactionary generation to popularize the ideas of the precursors even while curbing the excesses of the revolutionaries. If it succeeded, "the principles proclaimed by the innovators and by the revolutionaries . . . [became] the public and anonymous property of the masses." With a fourth and last generation (the resolutive generation), the new principles ceased to be the property of small elites and became instead the patrimony of a whole people. When this happened, a historical period came to a close. But the masses paid little attention to the origins of their shared heritage and took no interest in protecting its integrity. Thus, with the passing of time, a new historical period in four phases began.[45]

With an astonishing, if unconvincing, display of erudition, Ferrari then attempted to prove his theory of historical change with examples chosen from the history of many countries. Indeed, while he was writing this work he became obsessed with what he called "the arithmetic of history."[46] Like other historians then and now, he feared that the study of history would become obsolete and irrelevant to modern society unless it was established upon firm scientific foundations. But he hoped to go even beyond the critical tools for historical research developed by his contemporaries Ranke, Renan, and Strauss. He had never been particularly interested in history as a branch of literature, and toward the end of his career he was no longer satisfied with a philosophy of history either. His search for a science of history led him to pioneer, with imaginative flair if not with sound results, in those comparative and quantitative studies that are so much a part of contemporary historical scholarship.

The practitioner of history as science could not rely on older works of scholarship; he had to blaze new trails in the discovery, assembly, and interpretation of evidence. Ferrari realized that this new approach required an enormous amount of work, and he fretted that advancing age, ill health, and political responsibilities prevented him from doing more. On the night of 1 July 1876, when he suffered a fatal stroke, he was revising his last essay on "the arithmetic of history." His attempt to build a science of history along the same lines as the natural sciences may well have been appropriate to the spirit of the emerging industrial-technological society of the late nineteenth century, yet it was wholly incompatible with the radical ideology of his youth, to which he clung tenaciously as a politician. He was aware of the problem, a common one among European intellectuals of his generation. But the end came before he could really come to terms with it.

Conclusions

To Reach An overall assessment of Ferrari's significance three questions may be asked. What is the importance of his writings as a radical intellectual, a political theorist, and a philosopher of history? What do we learn about the nature of nineteenth-century European and Italian politics from his experiences in Paris in the 1840s and 1850s and from his parliamentary career in post-unification Italy? And finally, which aspects of his ideology and political career justify my initial assertion that he foreshadowed the attitudes and the concerns of the contemporary Italian Left to a greater extent than did either Cavour or Mazzini?

Ferrari was a very perceptive observer of the political and social trends of his time. His essays of the 1840s on the Italian question have stood the test of time remarkably well; they should be required reading for anyone interested in the Italian Risorgimento. But his writings on the French revolutionary tradition also deserve a wider audience than they have had thus far. They make especially stimulating reading for historians, because they anticipate important themes of recent historical scholarship. For example, Ferrari's argument in the *Filosofia della Rivoluzione* that the Revolution of 1789–99 had not reduced significantly the influence of the Church or changed the distribution of wealth in France reminded me more than a little of recent revisionist writings à la Cobban. Furthermore, the works that Ferrari wrote in France, like his personal correspondence, document very vividly the activities and the ideas in mid nineteenth-century Europe of an international brotherhood of radical intellectuals. He was a very typical member of that brotherhood, mostly based in Paris, which was consciously trying to carry on the secularization of European culture initiated by the libertine sects of the seventeenth and eighteenth centuries and the democratization of European politics initiated by the Jacobins of the 1790s. Like others of his generation, he hailed the outbreak of revolution in 1848 as a sign that the ancient alliance between throne and altar, already shaken by the French Revolution, was disintegrating at last. But in the 1850s he concluded that the industrial revolution was fostering the growth of another "unholy alliance," one between property and religion. While he continued to argue for a secular and democratic Europe, he became quite pessimistic about the ability of his contemporaries to move steadily in that direction. In the end, he departed from the intellectual tradition of the Lombard Enlightenment and also from the philosophical assumptions about human nature, rationality, and historical progress that were the foundation of nineteenth-century radicalism and socialism. If his *Filosofia della Rivoluzione* bears witness to the vitality of bourgeois radical ideology in the 1840s, his *Teoria dei periodi politici* points to a crisis of confidence among European intellectuals that coincided roughly with the triumph of Prussia over France in 1870.

Did Europe's radical intellectuals feel that their efforts to bring about a secular and democratic society had been in vain? Ferrari's career suggests that this was indeed the case. He sensed that the politicization of the lower classes, at least in the advanced countries of Europe, might eventually hasten the advent of the reign of science and equality. But in the 1860s and 1870s the political consciousness of the masses was still low, even in his adoptive homeland, and their reluctance to throw off the yoke of religion was evident everywhere. Toward the end of his life he felt the existential despair of the politically committed intellectual who realizes that he has few allies and few disciples. If he continued to believe that the attainment of a secular and democratic society was historically inevitable, he ceased to hope that this might happen during his lifetime. His obsession in the 1870s with the formulation of mathematically exact historical laws might be explained, in psychological terms, as a line of defense against despair concerning the political and intellectual condition of European civilization.

Ferrari's political disagreements with Proudhon after 1860 illustrate the most important reason why the intellectual brotherhood of earlier decades was breaking up. The emergence of new states like united Italy and of movements for national self-determination within the great dynastic empires of Europe forced Ferrari and his friends to choose between their concern for European civilization as a whole and their loyalty to a particular area or people. Men of that generation, particularly if they aspired to political office, found it difficult to reconcile their libertine and Jacobin intellectual heritage with the political realities of the age of nationalism.

Ferrari moved to Paris in 1838 in search of greater intellectual stimulation and political freedom than he enjoyed in his native Milan. In Paris he became interested in political issues, especially the Italian question, and there he began to develop his political ideology and style. While he was certainly influenced by French radical and socialist intellectuals, like Buchez and Leroux, he also spent much time in the company of other expatriates or exiles, among them Heine, Mickiewicz, and Herzen. Indeed, upon his arrival in Paris he was expected to play a role that others had already defined as the appropriate one for expatriates and political exiles. He was expected to write about his native country in a way that would arouse interest in its culture and sympathy for its political plight, and he was expected to establish a good rapport with all those fellow Italians who had suffered for the national cause. His reluctance to play this predetermined role and his merciless critique of the neo-guelph movement in the 1840s and of Mazzini later on led to his bitter quarrels with the Italian exiles in Paris and gave him a reputation as a gifted but volatile and divisive maverick. When he returned to Italy, he knew that such a reputation, whether deserved or not, was a political liability. He tried, with some success, to compensate for it by cultivating a solid political base in his electoral district and by working hard within the caucus of the parliamentary Left.

Ferrari's career after the unification of Italy is a very instructive case of politics in a liberal state of the nineteenth century. His correspondence with Longhi and Cardani allows us to see at very close range how an elected official of that era built his political base in the absence of structures that are familiar to us, such as the kinship and patronage networks of eighteenth-century England and Restoration France or the branches of contemporary mass parties. But his parliamentary career is also interesting for another reason: as a political "type" Ferrari stood at a midway point between the notable-in-politics characteristic of the early nineteenth century and the professional politician of later decades. He was himself a notable, in the sense that he was independently wealthy and that he was chosen by the electors of Gavirate-Luino on the basis of his intellectual reputation, not on the basis of proven political ability or of party affiliation. But he resembled the contemporary politician in the sense that he had neither property nor a kinship network in the district and also in the sense that he depended upon a political machine—albeit a rudimentary one—for reelection. Moreover, as a member of the first Italian Parliament he worked with several colleagues who were much further removed from the ideal of the notable-in-politics than he was himself. The difficulties experienced by able men who lacked independent wealth or important connections prompted him to ask that deputies be paid a salary.

Finally, Ferrari's political career is interesting for the effort he obviously made to steer his colleagues of the parliamentary Left away from revolutionary adventures and to make them face up to the overwhelming economic, social, and educational problems of united Italy. His awareness of those problems, especially the southern question, and his compassion justify, I believe, his self-image as the deputy-at-large of the disenfranchised, the inarticulate, and the oppressed. If the new state was to survive, it was imperative, he thought, to make the Italian masses feel part of it, even though they had played an insignificant role in the process of unification. His pleas for the distribution of Church lands to the peasantry, for fiscal policies less onerous to the lower classes, and for franchise reform were designed to strengthen the new political order by making it more acceptable to the masses. Ironically, the moderate liberals of the 1860s misunderstood his intentions and continued to regard him as an adversary of the existing institutions. Only two or three decades after his death, with the growth of Catholic and socialist organizations, did they begin to realize fully the danger of mass alienation from the liberal state.

Ferrari was among the first Italian politicians to sense and to object to the emerging practice that became known as *trasformismo*. He did not wish to see a merger between the moderate liberal and the radical currents of the Risorgimento. Such a merger, he thought, would stifle political debate and deprive the country of ideas and alternatives. Although he did not live long enough to see the triumph of *trasformismo* during the Depretis years, after the transfer of the capital to Rome he feared that the radical current was already running dry. He found personal satisfaction (but little political comfort) in the emergence of young disciples, especially Felice Cavallotti and his collaborators at the *Gazzettino Rosa*, who seemed willing to continue the radical tradition of the Risorgimento. But they were neither numerous nor experienced enough to press for the democratization of Italian institutions. At best, he thought, they might be able to fight a holding action against the increasingly illiberal attitudes of the governments of the 1870s in matters of civil and political rights.

This was, I believe, an accurate assessment of the withering of bourgeois radicalism at the close of the Risorgimento. But if the movement, of which Ferrari was one of the intellectual lights, was dying out, was there any hope for democratic progress in Italy? Ferrari believed that there was indeed hope for the future, provided that the middle-class heirs to the radical tradition could join hands with the emerging working-class organizations. It was probable, however, that if such a partnership ever came about, the bourgeois radicals would have to play second fiddle to the more numerous working-class cadres. By the end of his life Ferrari sensed that the younger generation of bourgeois radi-

cals would soon face a choice between two evils: either to remain isolated within the Italian Parliament in somewhat sterile
opposition to a large liberal majority or to cast their lot with
groups whose goals were as yet ill defined and whose strength
was untested in the area of national politics.

Ferrari's interest in the material and intellectual welfare of
the Italian masses is one obvious reason for regarding him as a
forerunner of the contemporary Italian Left. It certainly appears
to be the foremost reason why Italian scholars have generally
included him among the proto-socialist thinkers of the Risorgimento, alongside Pisacane, Montanelli, Luigi Pianciani, and
others. There are indeed socialist strains in his thought, particularly in his opposition to inherited wealth and to the accumulation of large amounts of capital in a few hands. Yet it must be
recognized that Ferrari's socialism was derivative and remained
very vague. Although his arguments against laissez faire liberalism were clear and trenchant, they were never developed into a
systematic and coherent critique of bourgeois society or into
alternate models of societal development. When he did offer an
alternate model, in the *Teoria dei periodi politici*, he departed
completely from radical and socialist principles.

There is, however, another aspect of Ferrari's thought that
is at once more original than his socialist beliefs and more significant for the history of the Italian Left since the unification.
That aspect is his lifelong commitment to the secularization of
Italian society. His ideological battle cry, *irreligione*, went far
beyond the emotional form of anticlericalism that was common
to the Parisian brotherhood of radical intellectuals before 1848
and to most Risorgimento radicals. Like them, he viewed the
temporal power of the papacy as a major obstacle to Italy's
unification. But he argued that the destruction of the temporal
power was not sufficient for achieving the political modernization of Italy. Nothing less than the radical secularization of Italian culture, strict controls over Catholic clergy and institutions,
and the expropriation of ecclesiastical property were required to
achieve that goal. Indeed, he was so very anxious to see the
Roman Catholic Church stripped of its influence and property

that he offended the sensibilities of men like Ricasoli, who wished to end the cold war between Church and state, and of many other moderate liberals who were committed to the principle of freedom of worship.

As a member of Parliament, Ferrari did his best to prevent any settlement between the Italian government and the Holy See. Moreover, he urged the moderate leadership to undermine the influence of the Church by training and appointing lay teachers at every level of the educational system, by encouraging the growth of cultural associations to rival those sponsored by religious orders, and by distributing expropriated Church lands to poor families. This last measure was especially important, he thought, if the Italian peasantry was ever to be weaned from its traditional dependence upon ecclesiastical authority, leadership, and charity.

Obviously, Ferrari never envisioned the growth of Catholic democracy in Italy. If he had, he would probably have denounced it as a sham, a contradiction in terms. Religion and property, he argued, were the pillars of nineteenth-century European society, just as throne and altar had been those of the Old Regime. Because political and social democracy, as he saw it, could not flourish in a climate of unrestrained economic freedom for the capitalists, democratic intellectuals and politicians could not avoid attacking property. But institutionalized religion (in Italy the Roman Catholic Church) was certain to rush to the aid of the propertied classes. Hence, the advocates of democracy would either have to stop their attack upon property or else they would have to fight against both property and religion. If they chose the former course of action, they remained democrats in name only. If they chose the latter, they forfeited their religious identity.

Contemporary Italy has moved very far away from the political model the great figures of Risorgimento liberalism had in mind when they worked for national unification. In the political sense, at least, she has become a democratic country, with important and active mass parties and with a high degree of popular participation in the political process. From an economic viewpoint, she is, for better or for worse, a far cry from the laissez faire ethos that Ferrari attacked in 1848–49 and then again in the 1860s. Cavour, I suspect, would find himself very ill at ease in this new Italy. Mazzini and most of his followers would approve of the republican and democratic constitution of 1948; yet because they believed that cooperation among all social classes was the key to political progress and economic prosperity, they might be ill at ease with the present political environment, highly charged as it is with social tensions. Indeed, among the major protagonists of the Italian Revolution, the maverick Giuseppe Ferrari is the only one who might still find a place within the present order of things.

Notes

CHAPTER I

1. For general background on Milanese politics and culture, see *Storia di Milano*, vol. 14.

2. Letters, personal documents, and business records concerning the Ferrari family are scattered throughout the thirty-four cartons of the Archivio Ferrari at the Museo del Risorgimento, Milan (hereafter cited as MRM).

3. See Archivio Giuseppe Ferrari, Cartella [Carton] VII, Plico [Folder] 7. Hereafter cited as GF/VII/7/MRM/(GF/roman number/ arabic number/MRM). See also GF/IX/12/MRM.

4. See Carlo Ferrari's comments on his mother in a letter to Giuseppe, Milan, 2 September 1846, GF/VIII/8/MRM.

5. See Giuseppe to Carlo Ferrari, Milan, 7 December 1833, GF/ XIII/17/MRM, and Carlo to Giuseppe Ferrari, Milan, 7 December 1833, GF/III/3/MRM.

6. See Silvia Rota Ghibaudi, *Giuseppe Ferrari*, pp. 7–8.

7. See Cesare Spellanzon and Ennio DiNolfo, *Storia del Risorgimento e dell'unità d'Italia*, 2:3–69; Renato Soriga, *Pavia nel Risorgimento italiano*; and Franco Della Peruta, *Mazzini e i rivoluzionari italiani*, ch. 1.

8. See Giuseppe to Carlo Ferrari, Milan, 8 November 1832, GF/ III/3/MRM, and 16 October 1834, GF/XIV/21/MRM.

9. MRM Archivio Generale, Carte di Giovanni Carozzi, 36524. The number denotes a folder; items within the folder are not numbered.

10. See Alessandro Levi, *Romagnosi*, and Giovanni Domenico Romagnosi, *Lettere edite ed inedite*.

11. On Milanese culture in the Age of Restoration, see especially Kent Roberts Greenfield, *Economics and Liberalism in the Risorgimento*.

12. For Ballanche, see Gaston Frainnet, *Essai sur la philosophie de Pierre-Simon Ballanche*.

13. For Ballanche, de Laprade, and Chenavard, see Joseph Buche, *L'école mystique de Lyon, 1776–1847*.

14. See Giuseppe Bucellati, *Introduzione alla vera vita sociale* and *Scogli della umanità e sua bussola di salvamento*. For a brief sketch of Bucellati's career, see Franco Della Peruta, "Note e documenti per la storia delle idee sociali in Italia, 1830–1849." *Annali dell'Istituto Giangiacomo Feltrinelli* (hereafter cited as *AIGF*), 5 (1962): 395–401.

15. For the ideas and activities of Milanese publicists in this period, see Alessandro Gianetti, *Trentaquattro anni di cronistoria milanese*; Antonio Monti, *Milano romantica*; and Raffaele Ciasca, *L'origine del programma per l'Opinione Nazionale Italiana del 1846–1847*.

16. See, for instance, Alessandro Luzio, "Giuseppe Acerbi e la *Biblioteca italiana*," *Nuova antologia* 148 (1896): 457–88.

17. For the thought of Terenzio Mamiani, see Marcella Pincherle, *Moderatismo politico e riforma religiosa in Terenzio Mamiani*. Ferrari's review appeared in the *Biblioteca italiana*, 2 (1835): 381–401. In the early 1830s Ferrari was already known in Florence as a contributor to this Milanese periodical. See Raffaele Ciampini, *Gian Pietro Vieusseux*. A check of the Vieusseux Papers at the Biblioteca Nazionale in Florence reveals, however, that the Parisian correspondent of Vieusseux's *Antologia* around 1838 mentioned by Ciampini was the Tuscan Jacopo Ferrari, and not Giuseppe Ferrari.

18. See Ferrari to Cattaneo, Milan, [1836], in "Contributo all'epistolario di Giuseppe Ferrari," *Rivista storica del socialismo* (article hereafter cited as *RSS*) 3 (1960): 181–211. For the revival of Catholic thought in Italy and for the role of Rosmini-Serbati, see Sandro Fontana, *La controrivoluzione cattolica in Italia, 1820–1830*, and Luigi Bulferetti, *Antonio Rosmini nella Restaurazione*.

19. *Opere di G.B. Vico* (1835–37). A second edition by the same publisher (1852–54) was used in the preparation of this work.

20. For details of Ferrari's controversy with his competitors, especially Francesco Predari, see Rota Ghibaudi, *Ferrari*, pp. 26–34.

21. See Ferrari to Cattaneo, Paris, 9 December 1838, in "Epistolario," *RSS*, 3 (1960): 181–211.

22. From "La sorte di Vico," reprinted in *Opere di G. B. Vico*, 6: v–xiv. All translations from Ferrari's works are mine.

23. See Rota Ghibaudi, *Ferrari*, pp. 34–40. For the intellectual and political implications of the Vico revival in the nineteenth century, see Emiliana P. Noether, "Giambattista Vico and the Risorgimento," *Harvard Library Bulletin*, 17 (1969): 309–19 and Francesco Brancato, *Vico nel Risorgimento*.

24. Ferrari to Cattaneo, Paris, 9 December 1838, in "Epistolario," *RSS*, 3 (1960): 181–211.

25. See Cattaneo to Gino Daelli, Castagnola, 23 July 1859, in Carlo Cattaneo, *Epistolario* 3:76.

26. See Clara M. Lovett, *Carlo Cattaneo and the Politics of the Risorgimento, 1820–1860*, pp. 12–36.

27. See the Ferrari Dossier in Archivio de Stato, Milan (ASM), Fondo Autografi, Serie Letterati.

28. See *Storia di Milano*, 14:149–238, and Della Peruta, *Mazzini*, pp. 113–22.

CHAPTER 2

1. See Jacques Hillairet, *Dictionnaire historique des rues de Paris*, and Albert Dauzat and Fernand Bournon, *Paris et ses environs*.

2. See Ferrari to Cattaneo, Paris, 4 August 1838, in "Epistolario," *RSS*, 3 (1960): 181–211.

3. See Giuseppe Ferrari, "Vico et son époque," *Revue des deux Mondes* (hereafter cited as *RDM*), 1 July 1838, pp. 103–16.

4. Though dated, David O. Evans, *Social Romanticism in France* remains the standard work on Leroux; but see also Frank Manuel, *Prophets of Paris*, and George Lichtheim, *The Origins of Socialism*.

5. See Ferrari's articles on Vico and on the humanist L. Vanini in *Encyclopédie nouvelle* 8 (1841): 588–92, 663–70.

6. See Leroux's review of Ferrari's *Idées sur la politique de Platon et d'Aristôte* in *Revue indépendante*, 2 (1842): 571–72.

7. On Reynaud's role in 1848, see David A. Griffiths, *Jean Reynaud*, ch. 4.

8. On Cerise, see Della Peruta, "Note e documenti," *AIGF*, 5 (1962): 395–401.

9. On Buchez and the Christian Socialist movement, see Sébastien Charlèty, *Histoire du Saint-Simonisme, 1825–1864*; Armand Cuvillier, *Hommes et idéologies de 1840* and his *Buchez et les origines du socialisme chrétien*; Jean-Baptiste Duroselle, *Les débuts du catholicisme social en France jusqu'à 1870*; and François-André Isambert, *De la Charbonnerie au Saint-Simonisme*.

10. On this issue, see, for instance, Hippolyte Auger, *Mémoires d'Auger, 1810–1859*, and Armand Cuvillier, *Un journal d'ouvriers: L'Atelier*.

11. Ferrari to Cattaneo, Paris, 4 August 1838 and early 1839, in "Epistolario," *RSS*, 3 (1960): 181–211.

12. Ferrari to Cattaneo, Paris, 25 February 1839, ibid.

13. Ferrari to Valerio, Paris, 9 February 1839, Turin, Biblioteca

della Provincia, Archivio Valerio, Cartella 8, Plico 14, Numero 1 (hereafter cited as Valerio/VIII/14/1/B. Prov. Turin).

14. See Aldobrandiro Malvezzi, *La principessa Belgiojoso*, and Maria Luisa Alessi, *Una giardiniera del Risorgimento italiano: Bianca Milesi*.

15. See Salvatore Carbone, *I rifugiati italiani in Francia*, and Salvo Mastellone, *Victor Cousin e il Risorgimento italiano*.

16. Ferrari to Cesare Cantù, Paris, 4 August 1838, Milan, Biblioteca Ambrosiana, Fondo Cantù.

17. Ferrari to Cattaneo, Paris, 9 December 1838, in "Epistolario," *RSS*, 3 (1960): 181–211.

18. See, for instance, Vincenzo Gioberti to Giuseppe Massari, Brussels, 13 March 1841, in Vincenzo Gioberti, *Epistolario*, 3:153–54.

19. *Vico et l'Italie*.

20. See, for instance, Marco Minghetti, *I miei ricordi*, 1:142, and Giuseppe Ricciardi's letter to Filippo Ugoni, in Della Peruta, "Per la storia dell'emigrazione meridionale," *Nuova rivista storica*, 50 (1966): 437.

21. See "Risposta del dottore Giuseppe Ferrario [*sic*] . . . all'articolo del Signor Libri," *Rivista europea* 3 (1840): 75–91.

22. *RDM*, 1 June 1839, pp. 690–720, and 15 February 1840, pp. 505–31. See, for instance, Biancamaria Frabotta, "Dialetto e popolo nella concezione critica di Giuseppe Ferrari," *La Rassegna della letteratura italiana*, 75 (1971): 460–79.

23. See, for instance, Massari to Gioberti, Paris, March 1841, in Gioberti, *Epistolario*, 3:156–59.

24. *De religiosis Campanellae opinionibus*.

25. *De l'erreur*.

26. See Rota Ghibaudi, *Ferrari*, pp. 69–72, and the important critique by Carmelo D'Amato, "Ideologia e politica in Ferrari." *Studi storici*, 11 (1970): 743–54.

27. *Journal général de l'instruction publique* 9 (1840): 541.

28. Paris, Archives Nationales, Dossier Ferrari, F. 17. 3151 (hereafter cited as Ferrari/F. 17. 3151/AN/Paris).

29. F. 17. 20732/AN/Paris.

30. Strasbourg, November 1841, Rome, Museo Centrale del Risorgimento, Busta [Carton] 322, Plico [Folder] 83 (hereafter cited as 322/83/MCR).

31. For the background of Ferrari's experience in Strasbourg, see Félix Ponteil, "La renaissance catholique à Strasbourg," *Revue historique*, 55 (1930): 225–87, and his *L'opposition politique à Strasbourg sous la Monarchie de Juillet*, pp. 658–70.

32. See Charles Pfister, "Un épisode de l'histoire de la Faculté des Lettres de Strasbourg," *Revue internationale de l'enseignement*, 66

(1926): 334–55 and Charles Staehling, *Histoire contemporaine de Strasbourg et de l'Alsace*, pp. 206–7.

33. Ferrari/F. 17. 20732/AN/Paris.

34. Other articles against Ferrari appeared in the issues of 6 February, 15 March, and 20 April 1842.

35. Rota Ghibaudi, *Ferrari*, p. 116.

36. See Paul Bonnefon, "Saint-René Taillandier et Edgar Quinet," *Revue des études historiques*, 88 (1918): 1–40.

37. See *L'Univers*, 29 January 1842.

38. Ferrari to Villemain, Paris, 26 January 1842, Ferrari/F. 17. 20732/AN/Paris.

39. See Cottard to Villemain, 5 and 7 February 1842, ibid.

40. See, in addition to the articles in *L'Univers*, the interventions of *L'Union catholique*, *Le Courrier français*, and *Le Courrier du Bas-Rhin* during the period February–April 1842.

41. See Cottard to Villemain, Strasbourg, 7 February and 10 March 1842, Ferrari/F. 17. 20732/AN/Paris. See also Ponteil, *L'opposition politique*, pp. 658–70.

42. See Villemain to Laurent Delcasso, Paris, 18 March 1842, Ferrari/F. 17. 20732/AN/Paris.

43. Years later Ferrari still bore the scars of this traumatic moment in his life. See, for instance, his letter to Carlo Ferrari, Lugano, 20 January 1847, GF/VIII/8/MRM.

44. Gioberti, *Epistolario*, 3:340–42.

45. See Ferrari to Valerio, Valerio/VIII/14/3/B. Prov. Turin.

46. Gioberti to Massari, Brussels, 28 April 1842, in Gioberti, *Epistolario*, 4:44–50.

47. Interesting details concerning Ferrari's social life in this period emerge from Massari's letters to Costanza Arconati. See, for instance, Massari to Arconati, Paris, 31 May 1843, 56/27/12/MCR, and Paris, 1 October 1843, 56/27/8/MCR.

48. See Marie-Louise Pailleron, *François Buloz et ses amis*, and her *La Revue des deux Mondes et la Comédie française*; and Samuel Edwards, *Georges Sand*.

49. *Idées sur la politique de Platon et d'Aristote*.

50. "La philosophie catholique in Italie." *RDM*, 15 March 1844, pp. 956–994, and 15 May 1844, pp. 643–88.

51. Ferrari's position can be inferred by Valerio's reply from Turin on 9 April 1844, GF/XVIII/29/T–Z/MRM.

52. "La philosophie catholique en Italie," Part II, *RDM*, 15 May 1844, pp. 686–87. It is obvious from Ferrari's comments that he was familiar with Gioberti's *Del primato morale e civile degli Italiani* (Brussels: Meline et Cans, 1843).

53. For the struggle of anticlerical professors within the Université

in the 1840s, see Jules Barthèlemy-Saint-Hilaire, M. *Victor Cousin, sa vie et sa correspondance*, 1:441–502. See also Joseph N. Moody, "The French Catholic Press in the Education Conflict of the 1840s." *French Historical Studies*, 7 (1972): 393–415.

54. See the account of Ferrari's visit in Pietro Borsieri, *Avventure letterarie di un giorno ed altri scritti editi ed inediti*, pp. 355–59.

55. "La révolution et les réformes en Italie," *RDM*, 16 November 1844, pp. 571–614 and 1 January 1845, pp. 150–94.

56. Ibid., part II, p. 172.

57. Ibid., p. 190.

58. Ibid., p. 189.

59. See Massari to Arconati, Paris, 12 October 1843, 56/27/9/ MCR.

60. Giuseppe to Carlo Ferrari, Paris, 26 October 1845, GF/II/2/ MRM.

61. See Giuseppe to Rosalinda Ferrari, Paris, 3 July 1846, ibid., and Giulio Caimi to Ferrari, Milan, 19 August 1846, GF/XVIII/27/C/ MRM.

62. "De l'aristocratie italienne." *RDM*, 15 August 1846, pp. 580–616.

63. GF/XIV/19/MRM.

64. See especially Alessandro Porro to Ferrari, Milan, 10 July 1846, GF/XIX/31/MRM.

65. Giuseppe to Carlo Ferrari, Paris, 26 July 1846, GF/II/2/MRM.

66. Giuseppe to Rosalinda Ferrari, Paris, 28 July 1846, ibid.

67. In early 1848 Porro revealed what his thoughts had been during this difficult period in a letter to Ferrari hand-delivered by their common friend Giulio Caimi. See GF/XIX/31/MRM.

68. GF/XIV/19/MRM.

69. Carlo to Giuseppe Ferrari, Milan, 24 November 1846, GF/ VIII/8/MRM.

70. Giuseppe to Carlo Ferrari, Paris, 1 April 1847, ibid.

71. See Onofrio Moja to Ferrari, Milan, 29 September 1847, GF/ XVIII/28/M/MRM.

72. GF/XIX/31/MRM.

CHAPTER 3

1. See *Revue indépendante*, 10 November 1847, pp. 104–45, and 10 January 1848, pp. 85–119.

2. For background on the Leroux-Sand circle, see Louis-Eugène Hatin, *Bibliographie historique et critique de la presse périodique française*; Georges Weill, *Histoire du parti républicain en France*; Griffiths,

Jean Reynaud, Ch. 3; André Maurois, *Lèlia, ou la vie de Georges Sand*; Leonard Sainville, *Victor Schoelcher, 1804–1893*; and Edith Thomas, *Pauline Roland*.

3. See fragments of two Ferrari letters of January 1848 in Angelo Mazzoleni, ed., *Giuseppe Ferrari. I suoi tempi e le sue opere*, p. 22.

4. See *Le Peuple constituant*, issues of 29 February, 1 March, and 6 March 1848. At this stage Ferrari's position was close to that of Louis Blanc. For a comparison see Louis Blanc, *1848: Historical Revelations*, and Leo Loubère, *Louis Blanc*.

5. "La Renaissance italienne," *Revue indépendante*, 10 November 1847, p. 110.

6. Ibid., p. 143.

7. Ibid., p. 144.

8. "Question italienne," ibid., 10 January 1848, pp. 85–119.

9. Ibid., p. 90.

10. Ibid., p. 91.

11. Ibid., p. 92.

12. Ibid., p. 94.

13. For background, see Giorgio Candeloro, *Storia dell'Italia moderna*, 3: 23–148.

14. AJ 18.9/AN/Paris and AJ 18.119/AN/Paris.

15. Caimi to Ferrari, Milan, 24 March 1848, GF/XVIII/27/C/MRM.

16. Carlo to Giuseppe Ferrari, Milan, 24 April 1848, GF/VIII/8/MRM.

17. See *Storia di Milano*, vol. 14, chs. 3 and 4; Lovett, *Cattaneo*, pp. 37–63; and Ferdinand Boyer, *La Seconde République, Charles Albert et l'Italie du Nord en 1848*.

18. See, for instance, Caimi to Ferrari, Milan, 3 May 1848, GF/XVIII/27/C/MRM.

19. For an account of this meeting, see Antonio Monti, *Un dramma fra gli esuli*, part I.

20. For background on the situation in other Italian states, see Candeloro, *Storia dell'Italia moderna*, 3:177–224.

21. For Ferrari's recollections, see his letter of March 1852 to Cattaneo, in Monti, *Un dramma*, pp. 77–86. This published version, however, contains numerous errors.

22. See *Storia di Milano*, vol. 14, ch. 4, and Lovett, *Cattaneo*, pp. 44–47.

23. Ferrari's views can be inferred from the reply of his friend Emile Egger, Paris, 16 June 1848, GF/XVIII/27/D–E/MRM.

24. See, for instance, Charpenne to Ferrari, Paris, 21 June 1848, GF/XVIII/27/C/MRM.

25. Charpenne to Ferrari, Paris, 4 July 1848, ibid.
26. Carozzi to Ferrari, Milan, 30 July 1848, GF/XVIII/27/C/ MRM.
27. Ferrari to Carozzi et al., [Strasbourg, August 1848], ibid.
28. ASM, Fondo Autografi, Serie Letterati [1848].
29. See Lovett, *Cattaneo*, pp. 47–51.
30. See *Le Peuple constituant*, editorial of 11 July 1848.
31. On the work of Reynaud and Carnot, see Roger Price, *The French Second Republic*, pp. 225–45, and Frederick A. de Luna, *The French Republic under Cavaignac*, pp. 238–47.
32. See Joseph C. Sloane, *Paul-Marc-Joseph Chenavard, Artist of 1848*.
33. See Lovett, *Cattaneo*, p. 52–58.
34. See Price, *The French Second Republic*, pp. 225–45.
35. See Rota Ghibaudi, *Ferrari*, pp. 177–82.
36. Charles de Rémusat, *Mémoires de ma vie*, 4:424–25.
37. See Rota Ghibaudi, *Ferrari*, pp. 180–81.
38. See Price, *The French Second Republic*, pp. 225–45.
39. See Aristide Douarche, *Michel de Bourges et le parti républicain*, and Judah Tchernoff, *Associations et societés secrètes sous la Deuxième République*.
40. See Rota Ghibaudi, *Ferrari*, pp. 189–93.
41. Ibid., pp. 194–99.
42. See Giovanni Arrivabene, *Memorie della mia vita*, 1:278. For Ferrari's sojourn in Belgium see Mario Battistini, *Esuli italiani nel Belgio, 1815–1861*. Battistini has shown, however, that the information on Ferrari available in the Belgian State Archives is not reliable, because his dossier was combined with that of a military leader from Modena by the same name.
43. Mazzini to Ferrari, Lausanne, 2 October 1849, in Monti, *Un dramma*, pp. 86–88.
44. See Ferrari to Cattaneo, [Paris, December 1849] in Cattaneo, *Epistolario*, 1:515–16.
45. See Rota Ghibaudi, *Ferrari*, p. 209.
46. See, for instance, Ferrari to Cattaneo, Paris, [September or October 1850], in Monti, *Un dramma*, pp. 90–92.
47. See, for instance, Cattaneo to Ferrari, Lugano, 27 June 1850, in Cattaneo, *Epistolario*, 2:23–26.
48. Mazzini to Ferrari, London, 25 October 1850, in Monti, *Un dramma*, p. 88.
49. Ferrari to Mazzini, Paris, [October 1850], ibid., pp. 88–90. For the debate among the political leaders of 1848, see Della Peruta, *I democratici e la rivoluzione italiana*, and his *Democrazia e socialismo nel Risorgimento*.

50. See Ferrari to Giuseppe Montanelli, Capolago, 26 July 1851, Livorno, Biblioteca Labronica, Autografoteca Bastogi, Cartella FER, Plico 418, Numero 9 (hereafter cited as Bastogi/FER/418/9/B. Labr.).

51. See especially Cattaneo to Ferrari, Lugano, 12 September 1851, in Cattaneo, *Epistolario*, 2:95–97; Ferrari to Cattaneo, Paris, [September 1851], ibid., pp. 473–77; and Gino Daelli to Ferrari, Turin, 30 September 1851, GF/XIV/20/MRM.

52. See Della Peruta, *I democratici*, pp. 220–31.

53. Ferrari to Cattaneo, Paris, [September 1851], in Cattaneo, *Epistolario*, 2:473–77.

54. Ferrari's Manifesto was attached to a letter of September 1851 to Cattaneo. See Monti, *Un dramma*, pp. 99–112.

55. Ibid., p. 105.

56. See Ferrari to Cattaneo, Paris, 20 October 1851, in Cattaneo, *Epistolario*, 2:485–87.

57. See Daelli to Ferrari, Turin, 21 November 1851, GF/XIV/20/MRM.

58. See, for instance, Georges Doutrepont, *Les proscrits du coup d'état du deux décembre 1851 en Belgique*, and Judah Tchernoff, *Le parti républicain au coup d'état et sous le Second Empire*.

59. Ferrari's critique began to emerge in the last pages of his *Machiavel, juge des révolutions de nos temps* [1849]. In the preparation of this work, however, I have used a recent Italian translation, available in *Scritti politici di Giuseppe Ferrari*, pp. 159–268. But see also Ferrari's *Les philosophes salariés*.

60. In an article of 1875, Ferrari acknowledged the influence of Proudhon's economic writings on his interpretation of the Revolution of 1848 in France. Because the personal and intellectual relationship between the two men flourished only in the 1850s, however, it will be discussed in the following chapter.

61. For background, see, in addition to the previously cited works, Paul Bastid, *Doctrines et institutions politiques de la Seconde République*.

62. See Ferrari to Carozzi, [Strasbourg, August 1848], GF/XVIII/27/C/MRM. At this time Ferrari was assisting Cattaneo in the preparation of *L'insurrection de Milan en 1848*, which contained a devastating critique of the Lombard referendum. See Lovett, *Cattaneo*, pp. 52–56.

63. See Ferrari, *Machiavelli*, in *Scritti politici*, pp. 246–47.

64. *Filosofia della Rivoluzione* [1851], ibid., p. 888.

65. Ibid., "Proemio."

66. Ibid.

67. Ibid., p. 864.

68. Ibid., pp. 854–57.

69. Ibid.

70. Ibid., p. 860. Ferrari seems to be referring here to the Free-thinkers or Libertines of the 1720s.

71. Ibid., p. 863.

72. Ibid., pp. 774–82. The psychological predisposition of women to be "more interested in the individual than in mankind" and their submissive nature (p. 773) make it advisable, according to Ferrari, to have male heads of household. But in a modern society men and women should enjoy equal rights, including the right to own property and to seek a divorce.

73. Ibid., p. 867.

74. Ibid., p. 871.

75. Ibid., pp. 872–80.

76. Ibid., pp. 774–82, 877–78, and 901–8.

77. Ibid., pp. 877–78.

78. Ibid., pp. 880–82.

79. See Della Peruta, "Il socialismo risorgimentale di Ferrari, Pisacane, Montanelli" *Movimento operaio*, 8 (1956): 3–41 and "Un capitolo di storia del socialismo risorgimentale: Proudhon e Ferrari," *Studi storici*, 3 (1962): 307–42; S. Rota Ghibaudi, "Ferrari e Proudhon," *Il Pensiero politico*, 1 (1968): 190–207; and D'Amato, "Ideologia e politica," *Studi storici*, 11 (1970): 743–54.

80. *La Federazione repubblicana* [1851], in *Scritti politici*, p. 380.

81. See *Storia di Milano*, vol. 14, chs. 1 and 3.

82. *La Federazione repubblicana*, in *Scritti politici*, pp. 297–335.

83. Ibid., p. 336.

84. Ibid., p. 356.

85. Ibid., pp. 344–58.

86. See Ferrari to Cernuschi, Turin, [May or June 1851], in Della Peruta, *I democratici*, p. 440. For Ferrari's political plans at this point, see ibid., pp. 207–18.

87. *La Federazione repubblicana*, in *Scritti politici*, pp. 390–91.

88. Ibid., pp. 395–96.

89. See Carlo Pisacane, *La rivoluzione in Italia* [1849]. The 1970 Einaudi edition was used in the preparation of this work.

90. See Antonio Gramsci, *Il Risorgimento*. For the controversy surrounding the Gramscian thesis on the Italian Risorgimento, see Walter Maturi, *Interpretazioni del Risorgimento*; Rosario Romeo, *Il giudizio storico sul Risorgimento*; Salvatore Russo, "Interpretazioni sul Risorgimento," *Rassegna storica del Risorgimento* (hereafter cited as *RSR*) 55 (1968): 397–401; and A. William Salomone, "The Risorgimento between Ideology and History," *American Historical Review* (hereafter cited as *AHR*) 68 (1962): 38–56.

91. *La Federazione repubblicana*, in *Scritti politici*, p. 169.

CHAPTER 4

1. See Pascal Duprat, *Les tables de proscription de Louis Bonaparte et de ses complices*, pp. 111–53.
2. Cattaneo to Repetti, Lugano, 6 December 1851, in Cattaneo, *Epistolario*, 2:135.
3. Daelli to Ferrari, Turin, 25 December 1851, GF/XIV/20/MRM.
4. Ibid.
5. Cattaneo to Ferrari, Castagnola, 21 March 1852, in Cattaneo, *Epistolario*, 2:145–47.
6. Ferrari to Cattaneo, Paris, [March 1852], ibid., pp. 494–95.
7. See Cattaneo to Repetti, Lugano, 14 March 1852, in Rinaldo Caddeo, *Le edizioni di Capolago, 1830–1853*, p. 435.
8. Cattaneo to Repetti, Castagnola, 10 May 1852, in Cattaneo, *Epistolario*, 2:163–64.
9. Ferrari to Gorresio, [Paris, November 1852], cited in Rota Ghibaudi, *Ferrari*, p. 246.
10. Ferrari to an unknown correspondent, Paris, 5 May 1852, GF/XIV/20/MRM.
11. Ferrari to Cernuschi, [Canton Ticino, summer 1852], in Della Peruta, *I democratici*, pp. 443–44.
12. Pisacane to Cattaneo, Genoa, 10 August 1852, in Carlo Pisacane, *Epistolario*, pp. 148–49.
13. For the most important interpretations of the Bonapartist coup d'état, see *December 2, 1851. Contemporary Writings on the Coup d'Etat of Louis Napoleon*.
14. See Mazzini to Ferrari, Lausanne, 2 October 1849, in Monti, *Un dramma*, pp. 86–88.
15. See Duprat, *Les tables de proscription*, pp. 111–53, and Victor Schoelcher, *Histoire des crimes du deux décembre*.
16. See Tocqueville's letter of 11 December 1851 to the London *Times*, in *December 2, 1851*, pp. 35–46.
17. *L'Italia dopo il colpo di stato*, pp. 28–30.
18. Ibid., pp. 40–41.
19. Karl Marx, *The Eighteenth Brumaire of Louis Bonaparte* (abridged version), in *December 2, 1851*, pp. 141–205.
20. *L'Italia dopo il colpo di stato*, pp. 22–25.
21. See Ferrari's preamble to *L'Italia dopo il colpo di stato* and Proudhon's *La révolution sociale*, in *December 2, 1851*, pp. 299–304.
22. See Loubère, *Louis Blanc*, chs. 3 and 4.
23. Proudhon to Mazzini, Paris, March 1852, in Pierre-Joseph Proudhon, *Correspondance*, 4:262–65.
24. *L'Italia dopo il colpo di stato*, Conclusions.
25. Proudhon to Louis Napoleon Bonaparte, Paris, 29 July 1852, in *December 2, 1851*, pp. 225–27.

26. Ferrari to Cernuschi, [Canton Ticino, June or July 1852], in Della Peruta, *I democratici*, pp. 443–44, and Mazzini to an unknown correspondent, London, 12 April 1853, ibid., pp. 512–15.

27. Paris, 15 August 1852, in Monti, *Un dramma*, p. 124.

28. See Carozzi to Cattaneo, Paris, 24 December 1853, Cattaneo/VI/19/72/MRM.

29. Proudhon to Bergmann, Besançon, 8 February 1842, in Proudhon, *Correspondance*, 2:14.

30. On Proudhon's life and writings see Georges Gurvitch, *Proudhon*; George Woodcock, *Pierre-Joseph Proudhon*; Robert Hoffman, *Revolutionary Justice*; and Alan Ritter, *The Political Thought of Proudhon*.

31. Woodcock, *Proudhon*, pp. 150–80.

32. Daniel Halèvy, *Le mariage de Proudhon*, pp. 250–87.

33. See Alfred Darimon, *A travers une révolution, 1847–1855*, pp. 250–90.

34. See Proudhon to Ferrari, Passy, 10 May 1864, in Proudhon, *Correspondance*, 13:290–92. Several references to Ferrari are found in Proudhon's *Lettres à sa femme*.

35. For Proudhon's views on the family and on the role of women in society, see *De la Justice dans la Révolution et dans l'Eglise*, 3:335–413.

36. See, for instance, Ferrari to Proudhon, Milan, 25 July 1859, in "Lettere di Giuseppe Ferrari a Pierre-Joseph Proudhon." *AIGF*, 4 (1961): 260–90.

37. See Ferrari, "Pierre-Joseph Proudhon," in *Scritti politici*, pp. 1048–96.

38. The interpretive passages that follow are based upon a comparison between Ferrari's *Les philosophes salariés* [1849] and *Filosofia della Rivoluzione* [1851] and Proudhon's *Qu'est-ce que la propriété* [1840]; *Système des contradictions économiques* [1846]; and *De la création de l'ordre dans l'humanité* [1843].

39. Ferrari to Proudhon, Paris, [May 1855], in "Lettere di Ferrari a Proudhon," *AIGF*, 4 (1961): 269–70.

40. *De la Justice dans la Révolution et dans l'Eglise*, 1:285–305, 347–422.

41. "Lettere di Ferrari a Proudhon," *AIGF*, 4 (1961): 273.

42. Paris, 12 January 1854, ibid., pp. 261–62.

43. Ferrari to Proudhon, Paris, 16 January 1854, ibid., pp. 262–63.

44. Ferrari to Proudhon, Paris, [end of April 1854], ibid., pp. 267–68.

45. For background, see Lynn M. Case, *French Opinion on War and Diplomacy during the Second Empire*; Werner Mosse, *The Rise and Fall of the Crimean System 1855–1871*; Paul W. Schroeder, *Austria,*

Great Britain, and the Crimean War; and Ann Pottinger Saab, *The Origins of the Crimean Alliance*.

46. Paris, 25 February 1854, in Proudhon, *Correspondance*, 5: 355–59.

47. Paris, [end of April 1854], in "Lettere di Ferrari a Proudhon," *AIGF*, 4 (1961): 267–68.

48. Proudhon to Ferrari, Brussels, 6 February 1859, in Proudhon, *Correspondance*, 9:15–19.

49. *La fédération et l'unité en Italie*, p. 5.

50. Proudhon, *Du principe fédératif* [1863].

51. Ferrari to Proudhon, Paris, 14 September 1859, in "Lettere di Ferrari a Proudhon," *AIGF*, 4 (1961): 276–77.

52. For background, see Stuart J. Woolf et al., *Storia d'Italia dal primo Settecento all'unità*, pp. 436–66, and Alfonso Scirocco, *I democratici italiani da Sapri a Porta Pia*, ch. 1.

53. See Della Peruta, *I democratici*, ch. 9, and Lovett, *Cattaneo*, ch. 3.

54. See, for instance, Mazzini to Giovanni Grilenzoni, London, 30 August 1853, in Mazzini, *Scritti editi ed inediti* (hereafter cited as *SEI*), 49:330.

55. See, for instance, Ferrari to Osvaldo Perini, Paris, 1 June 1853, in "Epistolario," *RSS*, 3(1960): 181–211.

56. Paris, [March 1852], in Monti, *Un dramma*, pp. 77–86.

57. See Scirocco, *I democratici*, ch. 1. For Ferrari's reaction, see his letter of 14 July 1857 to Mauro Macchi, in "Epistolario," *RSS*, 3 (1960): 181–211.

58. Ibid.

59. For the diplomacy leading to the Italian War of 1859, see *Plombières. Secret Diplomacy and the Rebirth of Italy*; *La guerra del 1859 nei rapporti fra la Francia e l'Europa*; Franco Valsecchi, *Italia ed Europa nel 1859*; and Denis Mack Smith, *Victor Emmanuel, Cavour and the Risorgimento*, ch. 5.

60. For Mazzini's protest against the Franco-Sardinian alliance, see *The Making of Italy*, pp. 263–265.

61. Lovett, *Cattaneo*, ch. 4.

62. Ferrari to Montanelli, Paris, [1858], in "Epistolario," *RSS*, 3 (1960): 181–211.

63. See Nino Bixio to Girolamo Ramorino, Paris, 28 August 1851, in Nino Bixio, *Epistolario*, 1:48.

64. See Fiorella Bartoccini, *Il Murattismo*, pp. 123–96.

65. In a parliamentary speech of 1861, Ferrari made a flattering reference to the reign of King Joachim Murat in Naples. The letter of thanks which Lucien Murat sent him on that occasion demonstrates that they were not personally acquainted. See Murat to Ferrari, Paris, 14 April 1861, published in "Giuseppe Ferrari e la Questione Meri-

dionale—con lettere inedite," *RSR*, 61 (1974): 74–88.

66. Paris, [end of 1858], in "Epistolario," *RSS*, 3 (1960): 181–211.

67. Cattaneo, *Epistolario*, 3:82.

68. For contemporary critiques, see Ernest Renan, *Essais de morale et de critique*, pp. 243–68; P. Brisset, "Critique historique," *RDM*, 15 November 1858, pp. 230–40; Luigi Ferri, *Essais sur l'histoire de la philosophie en Italie au XIXe siècle*, 2: chapter 5; and Carlo Cattaneo "La città considerata come principio ideale delle istorie italiane," in *Scritti storici e geografici*, 2:383–437.

69. Benedetto Croce, *Storia della storiografia italiana nel secolo XIX*, 2:114–20.

70. See George P. Gooch, *History and Historians in the Nineteenth Century*, p. 403.

71. See Alfredo Oriani, *La lotta politica in Italia* [1892].

72. See, for instance, the *Proceedings* of the International Colloquium on Failed Transitions to Modern Industrial Society (Montreal: Interuniversity Center for European Studies, 1976).

73. *Histoire des révolutions d'Italie*, 1:i–xi.

74. See chs. 2 and 3 of this work.

75. See Ferrari's "Machiavelli," in *Scritti politici*, pp. 221–23.

76. *Révolutions d'Italie*, 1:3.

77. Ibid., 1:26–40, 95–112; and 3:159–70.

78. Ibid., 1:xvi.

79. Ibid., 3:453–55.

80. Ibid., 1:xvi

81. Ibid., 1:465.

82. Ibid., 4:157–73.

83. Ibid., 1:461.

84. See Carozzi to Cattaneo, Paris, 24 December 1853, Cattaneo/VI/19/72/MRM, and Ferrari to Felice LeMonnier, Paris, 15 June, 15 August, and 30 August 1858, Biblioteca Nazionale (Florence), Fondo LeMonnier, Buste 26, 29 (hereafter cited as LeMonnier/B 26, 29/BNF).

85. Ferrari to Cattaneo, Paris, 9 December 1838, in "Epistolario," *RSS*, 3 (1960): 181–211.

86. *Révolutions d'Italie* 4:272–324.

87. Ibid., 1:264–77.

88. See Ferrari's preface to his *La Chine et l'Europe*. This aspect of Ferrari's thought is discussed in the last chapter of this work.

89. See *Histoire de la raison d'état*, ch. 9.

90. Ibid., p. vi.

91. See, for instance, Della Peruta, "Il socialismo risorgimentale," *Movimento operaio*, 8 (1956): 3–41. Rota Ghibaudi's important study devotes more space to contemporary criticism of Ferrari's works than to the works themselves (*Ferrari*, pp. 253–61).

CHAPTER 5

1. Ferrari to Proudhon, Paris, [early 1859], in "Lettere di Ferrari a Proudhon," *AIGF*, 4 (1961): 274.
2. See Piero Pieri, *Storia militare del Risorgimento*, ch. 16, and Candeloro, *Storia dell'Italia moderna*, 4:333–41.
3. Ferrari to Proudhon, Milan, 25 July 1859, in "Lettere di Ferrari a Proudhon," *AIGF*, 4 (1961): 275.
4. The relationship between Ferrari and Cristina Arpagans is discussed in the following chapter.
5. Ferrari to Proudhon, Milan, 25 July 1859, in "Lettere di Ferrari a Proudhon," *AIGF*, 4 (1961): 275.
6. Ibid.
7. See for instance, Macchi to Cattaneo, Turin, 1 January 1859, in Cattaneo, *Epistolario*, 4:663–65.
8. Ferrari to Proudhon, Paris, 14 September [1859], in "Lettere di Ferrari a Proudhon," *AIGF*, 4 (1961): 276–77.
9. Proudhon to Ferrari, Brussels, 24 September 1859, in Proudhon, *Correspondance*, 9:167–70.
10. Ferrari to Proudhon, Paris, 14 September [1859], in "Lettere di Ferrari a Proudhon," *AIGF*, 4 (1961): 276–77.
11. Proudhon to Ferrari, Brussels, 7 November 1859, in Proudhon, *Correspondance*, 9:222–30.
12. Ferrari to Proudhon, Paris, 12 November 1859, in "Lettere di Ferrari a Proudhon," *AIGF*, 4 (1961): 279–81.
13. Ferrari to Carozzi, Milan, [late August or early September 1859], AG/Carozzi/36524/MRM.
14. Ferrari to Michele Sartorio, Milan, 15 July 1859, GF/XIV/20/MRM.
15. Ferrari to Proudhon, Paris, 12 November 1859, in "Lettere di Ferrari a Proudhon," *AIGF*, 4 (1961): 279–81.
16. See Daelli to Cattaneo, Milan, 18 December 1859, in Cattaneo, *Epistolario*, 3:246.
17. For background on the electoral campaign of March 1860, see *Storia di Milano*, 15:47–54; Scirocco, *I democratici*, chs. 1 and 2; and Raymond Grew, *A Sterner Plan for Italian Unity*, ch. 9.
18. Ferrari to Proudhon, Paris, 5 February 1860, in "Lettere di Ferrari a Proudhon," *AIGF*, 4 (1961): 281.
19. Proudhon to Ferrari, Ixelles, 6 February 1860, in Proudhon, *Correspondance*, 9:327–30.
20. See Giuseppe Leti, *Henri Cernuschi*, ch. 17.
21. See, for instance, Ferrari to Carozzi, Milan, [March 1860], AG/Carozzi/36524/MRM.
22. Lovett, *Cattaneo*, pp. 98–110.

23. See, for instance, Daelli to Cattaneo, Milan, 12 February 1860, in Cattaneo, *Epistolario*, 3:265.

24. See Ferrari to Carozzi, Milan, 21 April 1860, AG/Carozzi/ 36524/MRM.

25. See Ferrari to Circolo Elettorale di Luino, Milan, 20 March 1860, Archivio Agostino Bertani/XI/12–2/11/MRM, and Ferrari to Proudhon, [Milan, March 1860], in "Lettere di Ferrari a Proudhon," *AIGF*, 4 (1961): 283–84.

26. Ibid.

27. Ibid.

28. Ferrari to Montanelli, Turin, 27 May 1860, in "Epistolario," *RSS*, 3 (1960): 181–211.

29. Ferrari to Carozzi, Milan, 21 April 1860, AG/Carozzi/36524/ MRM.

30. Ferrari to Cattaneo, Milan, 14 April 1860, in *Scritti editi ed inediti di Ferrari* (hereafter cited as *SEIGF*). Only one volume of this projected multivolume edition was ever published, under the title *Giuseppe Ferrari e la politica interna della Destra*. Due to an unusually high number of editorial errors, all letters cited from this volume have been checked against the original items in the Archivio Ferrari.

31. See Macchi to Cattaneo, Turin, 14 May 1860, in Cattaneo, *Epistolario*, 3:341.

32. Ferrari to Proudhon, [Paris, June 1860], in "Lettere di Ferrari a Proudhon," *AIGF*, 4 (1961): 284–86.

33. For Cavour's policy early in 1860, see especially Ettore Passerin d'Entrèves, *L'ultima battaglia politica di Cavour*. For the attitudes of the Left toward his policy see Scirocco, *I democratici*, ch. 2.

34. "Savoja e Nizza," in Carlo Cattaneo, *Scritti politici*, 4:46–61.

35. See Ferrari to Carozzi, Turin, [early June 1860], AG/Carozzi/ 36524/MRM.

36. Cattaneo to Ferrari, Castagnola, 12 April 1860, in Cattaneo, *Epistolario*, 3:329–31.

37. See Atti Parlamentari. Camera dei Deputati. Discussioni (hereafter cited as APCD), 27 May 1860.

38. See Ferrari to Carozzi, Paris, 11 May 1860, AG/Carozzi/ 36524/MRM.

39. See Ferrari to Michele Cavaleri, Paris, 5 July 1860, in *SEIGF*, pp. 131–32.

40. Ferrari to Proudhon, [Paris, June 1860], in "Lettere di Ferrari a Proudhon," *AIGF*, 4 (1961): 284–86.

41. Ferrari to Cavaleri, Paris, 17 July 1860, in *SEIGF*, pp. 132–33. See also Ferrari's pamphlet *L'annexion des deux Siciles*.

42. For background on the political struggle in the South in 1860 see especially, Denis Mack Smith, *Cavour and Garibaldi*; Giuseppe

Berti, *I democratici e l'iniziativa meridionale nel Risorgimento*; A. Scirocco, *Governo e paese nel Mezzogiorno nella crisi dell'unificazione*; Aurelio Lepre, *Storia del Mezzogiorno nel Risorgimento*; and Rosario Romeo, *Il Risorgimento in Sicilia*.

43. See Lovett, *Cattaneo*, pp. 112–17.

44. Cattaneo to Daelli, Castagnola, 7 January 1861, in Cattaneo, *Epistolario*, 3:444.

45. For Cavour's policy, see especially *La liberazione del Mezzogiorno e la formazione del Regno d'Italia. Carteggi di Cavour*, vols. 3 and 4.

46. APCD, 8 October 1860.

47. Francesco Cardani to Ferrari, Milan, 3 January 1861, GF/ VIII/54/1/MRM.

48. Achille Longhi to Ferrari, Lavello, 14 October 1860, GF/ XXXIV/54/1/MRM.

49. Milan, 8 November 1860, in "Epistolario," *RSS*, 3 (1960): 181–211.

50. Ferrari to Cattaneo, Milan, 14 April 1860, in *SEIGF*, pp. 127–28, and Ferrari to Longhi, Milan, 18 January 1861, ibid., p. 37.

51. APCD, 16 April 1861. See also Ferrari's marginal notes to Marco Minghetti's proposal for regional administrative decentralization (March 1861), GF/XXXII/52/MRM.

52. Ferrari to Cavaleri, Turin, 15 March 1861, in *SEIGF*, pp. 137–39.

CHAPTER 6

1. Ferrari to Proudhon, [Milan, March 1860], in "Lettere di Ferrari a Proudhon," *AIGF*, 4 (1961): 283–84.

2. See, for instance, Ferrari to Montanelli, Milan, 8 November 1860, in "Epistolario," *RSS*, 3 (1960): 181–211, and Ferrari to Massarani, Rome, 17 August 1874, in Tullo Massarani, *Carteggio inedito*, 1:205–6.

3. See Ferrari to Carozzi, Paris, 7 July 1871, AG/Carozzi/36524/ MRM.

4. See, for instance, Agostino Depretis to Ferrari, [Turin], 19 August 1864, in *SEIGF*, pp. 199–201.

5. Ferrari to Carozzi, Florence, 11 February 1868, AG/Carozzi/ 36524/MRM.

6. Ferrari to Cavaleri, [Turin, early February 1861], in *SEIGF*, pp. 130–31. The date of May 1860 attributed to this letter by Monti is obviously incorrect, because Ferrari refers here to the parliamentary debate concerning the king's title.

7. For an account of Ferrari's death see Angelo Mazzoleni, *Giuseppe Ferrari*, pp. 160–65.

8. See Ferrari to Cardani, Florence, 27 December 1867, GF/ XXXIV/55/MRM.

9. Ferrari to Cardani, Rome, 26 February 1872, ibid.

10. Ferrari to Cardani, Florence, 27 December 1867, ibid.

11. See Cristoforo to Giuseppe Ferrari, Canzo, 31 March and 22 July 1862, GF/IX/11/MRM.

12. For the dispute concerning Carlo Ferrari's will, see GF/VIII/8/ MRM and Ferrari to Cavaleri, Paris, 28 June 1869, GF/XXXIV/55/ MRM.

13. Ibid.

14. See numerous items (1869–75) in GF/VIII/8/MRM.

15. See Giorgio Asproni, *Diario politico, 1855–1876*, vol. 1.

16. The letters of Giuseppe Zanardelli to A. Bargoni (late 1860s) offer an excellent example of a deputy hard-pressed to keep up with his political obligations in the capital, while practicing law in Bergamo in order to support his family (Bargoni/234/20–21/MCR).

17. See *Risorgimento italiano. Memorie di A. Bargoni*.

18. See, for instance, Depretis to Ferrari, [Stradella], 29 September [1864], GF/XIX/30/MRM.

19. On the Ferrari-Dassi relationship, see numerous items (1861– 62) in GF/XIX/31/MRM.

20. See Euryale Cazeaux to Ferrari, Paris, 15 and 17 October 1867, GF/XVIII/27/C/MRM.

21. See Ferrari to Proudhon, [Milan, March 1860], in "Lettere di Ferrari a Proudhon," *AIGF*, 4 (1961): 283–84.

22. See, for instance, Ernesta Margarita to Ferrari, Connobbio, 4 September 1871, GF/XVIII/28/M/MRM.

23. For background on Lombardy in the first decades after the unification, see Nicola Raponi, *Politica ed amministrazione in Lombardia agli esordi dell'unità*; Giovanni Grilli, *Como e Varese nella storia della Lombardia*; and *Guida alla Lombardia misteriosa*.

24. For background on the economy and social structure of Lombardy in the nineteenth century, see Armando Sapori, *Attività manifatturiera in Lombardia dal 1600 al 1914*; Mario Romani, *L'agricoltura in Lombardia dal periodo delle riforme al 1859*; and Alberto Caracciolo, *L'inchiesta agraria Jacini*.

25. See Giuseppe Talamo, *La scuola dalla legge Casati all'inchiesta del 1864*, and Dina Bertoni Jovine, *Storia della scuola popolare in Italia*.

26. See *Indice generale degli atti parlamentari e storia dei collegi elettorali* and *Compendio di statistiche elettorali dal 1848 al 1914*.

27. See Achille Longhi to Ferrari, numerous items (1862–74), in GF/XIX/31/MRM. See especially Longhi to Ferrari, Lavello, 21 April 1862, ibid.

28. Longhi to Ferrari, Lavello, 4 March 1867, ibid.
29. See E. Margarita's reference to the move of a Mrs. Balestrini from the village of Besozzo to another district (GF/XVIII/28/M/MRM) and Longhi's numerous references to the political interests of his wife, Gina (GF/XIX/31/MRM).
30. Ferrari to Carozzi, Turin, 11 May 1864, AG/Carozzi/36524/MRM.
31. Giuseppe Parietti to Ferrari, Bosco Val Travaglia, numerous items (fall 1874), GF/XVIII/N–Q/MRM.
32. Cardani, for instance, complained that Ferrari, having changed residence in Rome, had failed to notify his correspondents of that fact. See GF/VIII/10/MRM, undated letter, written between 1872 and 1875.
33. See Giovanni Secondi to Ferrari, Melegnano, 15 February 1863, GF/XVIII/29/R–S/MRM.
34. See Ferrari's open letters to his electors, Florence, 7 February 1866 and 8 December 1870, in *SEIGF*, pp. 209–12, 253–55.
35. Ferrari to Cavaleri, Rome, 16 May 1876, ibid., p. 294.
36. See A. Mazzoleni to Ferrari, Dorno Lomellina, 24 August 1874, GF/XVIII/28/M/MRM.
37. See Longhi to Ferrari, Lavello, 8 July 1874 and Turin, 18 August 1874, GF/XIX/31/MRM.
38. See Parietti to Ferrari, Bosco Val Travaglia, 15 October 1874, GF/XVIII/29/R–S/MRM.
39. See numerous petitions, drafts, and reports sent to Ferrari by his constituents during the decade 1862–72, GF/XIV/22/MRM.
40. See ibid., for example, the letters of Giovanni Bricchi, mayor of Germignaga for over thirty years and a very influential landowner and elector in Ferrari's district.
41. See *Storia di Milano*, 15:1034–35.
42. For the Ferrari-Cardani relationship, see the hundreds of letters (1861–76) in GF/VIII/10/MRM and GF/XXXIV/55/MRM.
43. See Cardani to Ferrari, Milan, 19 January 1873 and 4 December 1874, GF/VIII/10/MRM.
44. [Turin, 16 April 1861], in "Lettere di Ferrari a Proudhon," *AIGF*, 4 (1961): 287–89.
45. For background on the problems of the Italian Left in the 1860s, see Scirocco, *I democratici*; Franco Catalano, *Storia dei partiti politici italiani*; Giovanni Spadolini, *I repubblicani dopo l'unità*; and the collection of essays "La Sinistra italiana dal 1861 al 1870 nel quadro delle opposizioni democratiche europee," in *Rassegna storica toscana*, 11 (1965).
46. Ferrari to F. D. Guerrazzi, [Turin, January 1862], in *SEIGF*, pp. 166–67.
47. See Scirocco, *I democratici*, ch. 9.

48. Ferrari to Crispi, Turin, 13 October and 2 November 1860, Archivio di Stato, Palermo, Carte di Francesco Crispi, Cartella 54, Plico 84.

49. See APCD, 2 December 1861. For Ferrari's views on the southern question see the following chapter of this work.

50. For background on the Aspromonte crisis, see Scirocco, *I democratici*, and Renato Composto, *I democratici dall'unità ad Aspromonte*.

51. See APCD, 3 August 1862, and Ferrari to Carozzi, Turin, 2 August 1862, AG/Carozzi/36524/MRM.

52. See the press clippings on Ferrari's speech in a letter from Cardani, Milan, 20 March 1863, GF/VIII/10/MRM.

53. Ibid.

54. See Ferrari to Bargoni, Paris, 27 August 1863, Bargoni/233/59/MCR.

55. See Cardani to Ferrari, Milan, 21 March 1863, GF/VIII/10/MRM.

56. See Ferrari to Cavaleri, [Turin, early 1862], GF/XXXIV/55/MRM.

57. See Ferrari to Cavaleri, [Turin, late March 1863], in *SEIGF*, pp. 164–65. The date of December 1861 attributed to this letter by Monti is obviously wrong.

58. See Valerio Castranovo, *La stampa italiana dall'unità al fascismo*, ch. 1.

59. For background on the repression of banditry, see Franco Molfese, *Storia del brigantaggio dopo l'unità*.

60. See Scirocco, *I democratici*, pp. 241–43.

61. For background on this political crisis, see Jessie White Mario, *Agostino Bertani e i suoi tempi*, 2: ch. 20, and *Risorgimento italiano. Memorie di A. Bargoni*, ch. 7.

62. See Cardani to Ferrari, Milan, 22 June 1864, GF/VIII/8/MRM.

63. See several letters of 1868 by Ferrari to Cardani, GF/XXXIV/55/MRM.

64. See Talamo, *La scuola*, but also Augusto Romizi, *Storia del ministero della pubblica istruzione*.

65. Ferrari to Cavaleri, Turin, 29 May 1861, in *SEIGF*, pp. 139–40.

66. Ibid.

67. Ferrari's twenty-nine lectures were published in *Il Diritto* and later brought together in the volume *Corso sugli scrittori politici italiani*.

68. General Cibrario to Ferrari, Turin, 1 June 1862, GF/XIV/19/MRM, and Ferrari to Cavaleri, Turin, 6 June 1862, in *SEIGF*, p. 185.

69. See Carlo Matteucci, *Raccolta di scritti vari intorno all'istruzione pubblica*, and Domenico Zanichelli, *La questione universitaria in Italia*.

70. See Matteucci to Ferrari, Turin, [April and June 1862], in *SEIGF*, pp. 178–80.

71. See GF/XIV/19/MRM, documents dated 16 February 1864, 30 August 1864, 7 November 1864, and 21 December 1865.

72. For background on the Council on Public Education see Romizi, *Storia del ministero della pubblica istruzione*; D. Zanichelli, *La questione universitaria*; and Mario Di Domizio, *L'università italiana*.

73. For Ferrari's correspondence with the ministry on this matter, see several items in GF/XIV/19/MRM (summer 1865).

74. See Ferrari to his electors, Florence, 7 February 1866, in *SEIGF*, pp. 213–14.

75. Ferrari to Cavaleri, Florence, [early 1866], ibid., pp. 194–95. The date of February 1863 attributed to this letter by Monti is obviously incorrect.

76. For the Ferrari-Berti correspondence concerning the Florentine Istituto and other academic matters see GF/XIV/19/MRM (October 1866 to February 1867).

77. Ferrari to Bertani, Florence, 9 December 1866, Bertani/LXVI/24-4/15/MRM.

78. Berti did present an ex post facto proposal to Parliament, but no action was taken during his tenure or that of his successors. In 1870, during a debate on the budget for public education, Ferrari again raised this issue. See APCD, 12 April 1870.

CHAPTER 7

1. For background on the southern question in the 1860s, see, in addition to the works cited in ch. 5 n. 42, Alfonso Scirocco, *Democrazia e socialismo a Napoli dopo l'unità*; *Il Sud nella storia d'Italia*; Umberto Zanotti-Bianco, *Meridione e meridionalisti*; Gaetano Salvemini, *Scritti sulla Questione Meridionale*; and Massimo Salvadori, *Il mito del buon governo*. See also *Giustino Fortunato. Antologia dei suoi scritti*.

2. Ferrari to Cattaneo, Paris, 25 February 1839, in "Epistolario," *RSS*, 3 (1960): 181–211.

3. Ferrari to Cavaleri, Paris, 20 July 1860, GF/XXXIV/55/ MRM.

4. See, for instance, Depretis to Ferrari, [Stradella], 24 September 1864, in *SEIGF*, pp. 204–6.

5. For the Ferrari-Dassi relationship in 1861–62 see numerous items in GF/XIX/31/MRM and five items at the Biblioteca Marucelliana (Florence), Carteggio Generale, Sezione Autografi.

6. On the problem of banditry see especially Pasquale Soccio, *Unità e brigantaggio*; Molfese, *Storia del brigantaggio dopo l'unità*; and Aldo De Jaco (ed.), *Il brigantaggio meridionale*.

7. APCD, 2–6 April 1861.

8. Ibid., 4 April 1861.

9. Ibid.

10. References to Murat's activities in Paris are found in the letters of Jean Gustave Wallon, a neo-Gallican intellectual who opposed Napoleon III's policy in Italy. See Wallon to Ferrari, Paris, 8 October 1861, GF/XVIII/29/T–Z/MRM.

11. For the Ferrari-Savarese correspondence see numerous items (1861–62) in GF/XIV/21/MRM.

12. Ferrari to Cavaleri, Turin, 15 December 1861, in *SEIGF*, pp. 162–63.

13. Ferrari to Cavaleri, Turin, 3 February 1862, GF/XXIV/55/MRM.

14. See, for instance, the emotionally charged exchange between Crispi and Ferrari during the making of the Aspromonte crisis. APCD, 3 August 1862.

15. For Ferrari's intervention on this issue see pp. 183–86 of this chapter.

16. See several letters and reports in GF/XXXII/52/MRM (early 1860s) and GF/XIV/22/MRM (late 1860s).

17. Ferrari to Cavaleri, Palermo, 1 October 1861, in *SEIGF*, pp. 159–160.

18. Ferrari to Cavaleri, on board the S.S. *Venezia*, 6 November 1861, in *SEIGF*, pp. 161–62.

19. APCD, 2 December 1861.

20. For background on the complicated question of the *beni demaniali* in the Kingdom of the Two Sicilies, see Pasquale Villari, *La vendita dei beni dello stato nel Regno di Napoli*; Rosario Villari, *Mezzogiorno e contadini nell'età moderna*; and Aurelio Lepre, *Contadini, borghesi e operai nel tramonto del feudalesimo napoletano*.

21. See Antonino De Stefano's introduction to Giuliana D'Amelio, *Stato e Chiesa*, pp. xiii–xvi.

22. For background on state-church relations in the 1860s, see, in addition to the work cited above, Arturo Carlo Jemolo, *Chiesa e stato in Italia negli ultimi cento anni*, ch. 3; Gabriele De Rosa, *Storia del movimento cattolico in Italia*, vol. 1; Renato Mori, *La questione romana, 1861–1865*, and his *Il tramonto del potere temporale, 1866–1870*; Pietro Pirri, *La questione romana, 1856–1864*, and his *La questione romana dalla Convenzione di Settembre alla caduta del potere temporale*. For the Roman policy of Napoleon III see Ivan Scott, *The Roman Question and the Powers*, and Jean Maurain, *La politique ecclésiastique du Second Empire de 1852 à 1869*.

23. See especially "La religione del Regno," [1865], *Scritti politici*, pp. 932–35.

24. APCD, 2 December 1861.

25. Ibid.

26. Ibid., 29 November 1862.

27. For Ferrari's views on this subject see, in addition to the previously cited works of the 1840s and 1850s, his parliamentary speeches in APCD, 10 November 1864, 13 July 1867, and 25 November 1868.

28. APCD, 24 April 1867.

29. See "La religione del Regno," *Scritti politici*, pp. 932–35.

30. APCD, 10 November 1864.

31. For the crisis among the leaders of the parliamentary Left after the Aspromonte affair, see Scirocco, *I democratici*, ch. 7.

32. For the background of the September Convention, see Mori, *La questione romana*, ch. 3, and Jemolo, *Chiesa e stato*, ch. 3. The standard work in English is Lynn M. Case, *Franco-Italian Relations*.

33. On the transfer of the capital to Florence see Giovanni Spadolini, *Firenze capitale*. For the Lombard reaction see the Ferrari-Cardani correspondence in "Milano e la Convenzione di Settembre—dalla corrispondenza inedita di Giuseppe Ferrari," *Nuova rivista storica*, 59 (1975): 186–90.

34. For the opposition to the Convention, especially in Turin, see Candeloro, *Storia dell'Italia moderna*, 5:207–12.

35. Cardani to Ferrari, Milan, 27 October 1864, in "Milano e la Convenzione di Settembre," *Nuova rivista storica*, 59 (1975): 186–90.

36. APCD, 10 November 1864.

37. For the background of the liberation of Venetia in 1866, see Letterio Briguglio, *Correnti politiche nel Veneto dopo Villafranca*.

38. On the financial crisis of 1866–68 and its relationship to Ricasoli's ecclesiastical policy, see Jemolo, *Chiesa e stato*, ch. 11, and Candeloro, *Storia dell'Italia moderna*, 5: 296–323.

39. See Luigi Izzo, *La finanza pubblica nel primo decennio dell'unità italiana*, pp. 59–68.

40. APCD, 13 July 1867.

41. Ibid.

42. Ibid.

43. Ibid.

44. See Mori, *Il tramonto del potere temporale*, ch. 5, and Paolo Dalla Torre, *L'anno di Mentana*.

45. APCD, 11 December 1867.

46. APCD, 25 November 1868.

47. For background, see especially Achille Plebano, *Storia della finanza italiana nei primi quarant'anni dell'unificazione*, vol. 1, and Francesco Repaci, *La finanza pubblica italiana nel secolo 1861–1960*, vol. 1.

48. APCD, 26 June 1861.

49. APCD, 4 July 1864.

50. APCD, 10 November 1864.

51. See Domenico Novacco, "I tumulti del macinato," *Nuovi quaderni meridionali*, 6 (1968): 427–35; Emilio Sereni, *Il capitalismo nelle campagne, 1860–1900*, ch. 2; and Antonio Fappani, *Il movimento contadino in Italia*.

52. APCD, 7 March 1868.

53. APCD, 14 March 1868.

54. APCD, 16 March 1868.

55. See several items (1869–70) in GF/XIV/22/MRM.

56. APCD, 21–22 January 1869.

57. See especially Izzo, *Storia delle relazioni commerciali tra l'Italia e la Francia dal 1860 al 1875*, chs. 1–3.

58. APCD, 25–27 November 1863.

59. Ibid.

60. Ibid.

61. See, for instance, Cavallotti to Ferrari, Milan, early 1870s, GF/XIX/30/MRM.

CHAPTER 8

1. Ferrari to Cardani, Paris, 11 October 1868, in *SEIGF*, pp. 232–33.

2. Giovanni Pantaleo to Ferrari, Naples, 22 November 1868, GF/XVIII/29/N–Q/MRM.

3. Ferrari to Cardani, Paris, 11 October 1868, in *SEIGF*, pp. 232–33.

4. See, for instance, Luigi Guardabassi et al. to Ferrari, Loreto, 3 December 1869, GF/XIV/22/MRM.

5. Wallon to Ferrari, Paris, 20 June 1869?, GF/XVIII/29/T–Z/MRM.

6. Ricciardi to Luigi Pianciani, Naples, 27 November 1869, Archivio di Stato (Rome), Carte Pianciani, Busta 41.

7. For a summary of recent scholarship on the Hohenzollern candidacy to the Spanish throne see S. William Halperin, "The Origins of the Franco-Prussian War Revisited," *Journal of Modern History*, 45 (1973): 183–191.

8. Ferrari to Cardani, Paris, 18 July 1870, in *SEIGF*, pp. 245–46.

9. Ferrari to Carozzi, Florence, 6 August 1870, AG/Carozzi/36524/MRM.

10. APCD, 19 August 1870.

11. Ferrari to Cernuschi, Florence, 5 September 1870, in "Epistolario," *RSS*, 3 (1960): 181–211.

12. Ferrari to Cernuschi, Florence, 9 September 1870, ibid.

13. Ferrari to Cernuschi, Florence, 9, 11 and 18 September 1870, ibid.

14. Ferrari to Cernuschi, Florence, 22 February 1871, ibid.
15. See *Scritti politici*, pp. 961–1018.
16. Ibid., pp. 968–69.
17. Ibid., pp. 975–78.
18. Ibid., p. 972.
19. Ibid., pp. 974–75.
20. Ibid., pp. 1019–1047.
21. Ibid., p. 1034. See also Ferrari to Mazzoleni, Paris, 25 June 1871, in *SEIGF*, pp. 256–58.
22. Ibid., p. 1033.
23. Two recent works on the controversial history of the Paris Commune summarize decades of, respectively, liberal-democratic and Marxist scholarship: Georges Bourgin, *La guerre de 1870–1871 et la Commune*, and Jean Bruhat, *La Commune de 1871*.
24. Ferrari to Mazzoleni, Paris, 25 June 1871, in *SEIGF*, pp. 256–58.
25. Cardani to Ferrari, Milan, 16 March 1872, GF/VIII/10/MRM.
26. For his views on foreign policy see APCD, 19 April 1872.
27. See ibid. as well as the speech of 14 May 1872.
28. Cardani to Ferrari, Milan, 21 April, 7 May, 18 May 1872, GF/VIII/10/MRM.
29. Ferrari to his electors, Florence, 8 December 1870, in *SEIGF*, pp. 253–55.
30. See especially Wallon's letters of 20 May 1872, 25 October 1872, and 26 February 1873, GF/XVIII/29/T–Z/MRM.
31. See his intervention on a bill to close some religious orders, APCD, 12 May 1873.
32. Morelli to Ferrari, Rome, 11 November 1872, GF/XVIII/28/M/MRM.
33. APCD, 21 November 1872 and 25 January 1875.
34. For background see especially Aldo Berselli, *La Destra storica dopo l'unità*, vol. 1.
35. APCD, 21 November 1872.
36. Ibid.
37. Ibid., 25 January 1875.
38. For an introduction to generational theory and some of its contemporary applications in the social sciences see Paul R. Abramson, *Generational Change in American Politics*; Hans Brocher, *Aufstand gegen die Tradition*; Herbert Butterfield, *The Discontinuities between the Generations in History*; Donald E. Stokes, *The Study of Political Generations*; and Alan Spitzer, "The Historical Problem of Generations," *AHR* 78 (1973): 1364–96.
39. Gustav Ruemelin, *Problèmes d'économie politique et de statistique*, pp. 153–71.

40. *Teoria*, p. 17.
41. Ibid., pp. 113–15 and 189–96.
42. Ibid., p. 115.
43. Ibid., p. 134.
44. Ibid., p. 151.
45. Ibid., p. 167.
46. See his last essay, *L'aritmetica nella storia*, which he read exactly one year before his death at the Istituto lombardo di Scienze e Lettere.

Bibliography

I. MANUSCRIPT SOURCES

Museo del Risorgimento, Milan
(MRM)
    Archivio Giuseppe Ferrari
    Archivio Carlo Cattaneo
    Archivio Agostino Bertani
    Carteggio Crispi-Bertani
Biblioteca Ambrosiana, Milan
    Fondo Cesare Cantù
Archivio di Stato, Milan (ASM)
    Sezione Autografi, Serie Letterati
Biblioteca Nazionale, Florence
(BNF)
    Carteggio G. P. Vieusseux
    Carteggio Niccolò Tommaseo
Biblioteca Marucelliana, Florence
    Carteggi Vari (Carte Dassi)
Museo del Risorgimento,
Florence (MRF)
    Carteggi Vari

Biblioteca della Provincia, Turin
    Archivio Lorenzo Valerio
Biblioteca Labronica, Livorno
    Autografoteca Bastogi
Museo Centrale del Risorgimento,
Rome (MCR)
    Archivio Angelo Bargoni
    Carteggio Massari-Arconati
    Archivio Adriano Lemmi
    Manoscritti Ferrari
Archivio Centrale dello Stato,
Rome (ACS)
    Ministero della Pubblica
    Istruzione, Carteggi del
    Consiglio Superiore di
    Pubblica Istruzione
Archivio di Stato, Rome
    Carte Luigi Pianciani
Archivio di Stato, Palermo
    Carte Francesco Crispi
Archives Nationales, Paris (AN)
    Dossier Giuseppe Ferrari

II. PUBLISHED SOURCES

A) *Works by Giuseppe Ferrari*

L'annexion des deux Siciles. Paris: Dentu, 1860.
L'aritmetica nella storia. Milan: Bodoni, 1875.

La Chine et l'Europe; leur histoire et leurs traditions comparées. Paris: Didier, 1867.

Corso sugli scrittori politici italiani. Milan: Manini, 1862.

"De l'aristocratie italienne." *Revue des deux Mondes,* 15 August 1846, pp. 580–615.

"De la littérature populaire en Italie." *Revue des deux Mondes,* 1 June 1839, pp. 690–720, and 15 February 1840, pp. 505–31.

De l'erreur. Paris: Moquet, 1840.

De religiosis Campanellae opinionibus. Paris: Moquet, 1840.

"Des idées et de l'école de Fourier depuis 1830." *Revue des deux Mondes,* 1 August 1845, pp. 389–434.

Essai sur le principe et les limites de la philosophie de l'histoire. Paris: Joubert, 1843.

La Federazione repubblicana [1851]. See *Scritti politici.*

Filosofia della Rivoluzione [1851]. See *Scritti politici.*

Histoire de la raison d'état. Paris: Michel Lèvy Frères, 1860.

Histoire des Révolutions d'Italie. 4 vols. Paris: Didier, 1858.

Idées sur la politique de Platon et d'Aristôte. Paris: Capelle, 1842.

L'Italia dopo il colpo di stato del 2 dicembre 1851. Capolago: Tipografia Elvetica, 1852.

Lettere chinesi sull'Italia. Milan: Tipografia della Gazzetta di Milano, 1869.

Lettere politiche. Milan: Tipografia della Gazzetta di Milano, 1869.

Machiavelli giudice delle rivoluzioni dei nostri tempi [1849]. See *Scritti politici.*

"La mente di G. B. Vico." Introduction to *Opere di G. B. Vico.* 2nd edition.

La mente di G. D. Romagnosi. Florence: La Voce, 1924.

La mente di Pietro Giannone. Milan: Tipografia del Libero Pensiero, 1868.

Opuscoli politici e letterari. Capolago: Tipografia Elvetica, 1852.

Les philosophes salariés. Paris: Sandré, 1849.

"La philosophie catholique en Italie." *Revue des deux Mondes,* 15 March 1844, pp. 956–95, and 15 May 1844, pp. 643–88.

"Question italienne." *Revue indépendante,* 10 January 1848, pp. 85–119.

"La Renaissance italienne." *Revue indépendante,* 10 and 15 November 1847, pp. 104–45.

"La révolution et les réformes en Italie." *Revue des deux Mondes,* 16 November 1844, pp. 573–614, and 1 January 1845, pp. 150–94.

Scritti editi ed inediti di Giuseppe Ferrari. Edited by Antonio Monti. Milan: Vallardi, 1925.

Scritti politici di Giuseppe Ferrari. Edited by Silvia Rota Ghibaudi. Turin: UTET, 1973.

Teoria dei periodi politici. Milan: Hoepli, 1874.

"Vanini." *Encyclopédie nouvelle,* 8 (1841): 663–70.

"Vico." *Encyclopédie nouvelle,* 8 (1841): 588–92.

Vico et l'Italie. Paris: Eveillard, 1839.

"Vico et son époque." *Revue des deux Mondes,* 1 July 1838, pp. 103–16.

B) *Published Correspondence of Giuseppe Ferrari*

"Contributo all'epistolario di G. F." In Franco Della Peruta, *I democratici e la rivoluzione italiana.* Milan: Feltrinelli, 1958.

"Contributo all'epistolario di G.F." Edited by F. Della Peruta. *Rivista storica del socialismo* 3 (1960): 181–211.

"G.F. e la Questione Meridionale—con lettere inedite." Edited by Clara M. Lovett. *Rassegna storica del Risorgimento* 61 (1974): 74–88.

"Lettere di G.F. a Pierre-Joseph Proudhon." Edited by F. Della Peruta. *Annali dell'Istituto Giangiacomo Feltrinelli* 4 (1961): 260–90.

"Milano e la Convenzione di Settembre—dalla corrispondenza inedita di G.F." Edited by C. M. Lovett. *Nuova rivista storica* 59 (1975): 186–90.

"Il 1848 in Lombardia dalla corrispondenza inedita di G.F." Edited by C. M. Lovett. *Nuova rivista storica* 59 (1975): 470–80.

"Il Secondo Impero, il Papato e la Questione Romana. Lettere inedite di Jean Gustave Wallon a G.F." Edited by C. M. Lovett. *Rassegna storica del Risorgimento* 63 (1976): 441–48.

C) *Other Published Sources*

Amari, Michele. *Carteggio.* 3 vols. Edited by Alessandro D'Ancona. Turin: Roux, Frassati & Co., 1896.

Anelli, Luigi. *Storia d'Italia dal 1814 al 1867.* 6 vols. Milan: Vallardi, 1868.

Arnaud [de l'Ariège], Frédéric, *L'indépendance du Pape et les droits des peuples.* Paris: Dentu, 1860.

————. *L'Italie.* 2 vols. Paris: Paguerre, 1864.

————. *La Papauté temporelle et la nationalité italienne.* Paris: Dentu, 1860.

Arrivabene, Giovanni. *Memorie della mia vita.* 2 vols. Florence: Barbera, 1880.

Asproni, Giorgio. *Diario politico, 1855–1876.* 2 vols. Edited by Bruno Josto Anedda. Milan: Giuffrè, 1974–77.

Auger, Hippolyte. *Mémoires d'Auger, 1810–1859*. Edited by Paul Cottin. Paris: Au Bureau de la Revue rétrospective, 1891.

Augustin Thierry d'après sa correspondance et ses papiers de famille. Edited by Amédée-Augustin Thierry. Paris: Plon-Nourrit, 1922.

Beslay, Charles. *Mes souvenirs*. 3d ed. Paris: Sandoz & Fischbacher, 1874.

Bixio, Nino. *Epistolario*. 4 vols. Edited by Emilia Morelli. Rome: Istituto per la storia del Risorgimento italiano, 1939–54.

Blanc, Louis, *1848: Historical Revelations* [1858]. New York: Fertig, 1971.

Borsieri, Pietro. *Avventure letterarie di un giorno ed altri scritti editi ed inediti*. Edited by Giorgio Alessandrini. Rome: Edizioni dell'Ateneo, 1967.

Brambilla, Giuseppe. *Ricordi, 1848–1870*. Como: Vanossi, 1884.

Brisset, P. "Critique historique." *Revue des deux Mondes*, 15 November 1858, pp. 230–41 [review of Ferrari's *Révolutions d'Italie*].

Bucellati, Giuseppe. *Introduzione alla vera vita sociale*. Milan: Pirola, 1834.

———. *Scogli dell'umanità e sua bussola di salvamento*. Milan: Manini, 1834.

Carnazza, Gabriele. *La rivoluzione e l'unità d'Italia. Lettera a Ferrari*. Paris: [n.p.], 1851.

Cattaneo, Carlo. *Epistolario*. 4 vols. Edited by Rinaldo Caddeo. Florence: Barbera, 1949–56.

———. *Scritti politici*. 4 vols. Edited by Mario Boneschi. Florence: LeMonnier, 1964–65.

———. *Scritti storici e geografici*. 4 vols. Edited by Gaetano Salvemini and Ernesto Sestan. Florence: LeMonnier, 1957–67.

Comin, Jacopo. *Il Parlamento e il Regno nel 1860. Scritti e profili politici*. Milan: Sanvito, 1860.

D'Ancona, Alessandro. *Ricordi storici del Risorgimento italiano*. Florence: Sansoni, 1913.

Daniele Manin e Giorgio Pallavicino. Epistolario politico. Edited by B. E. Maineri. Milan: Bortolotti, 1878.

Darimon, Alfred. *A travers une révolution, 1874–1855*. Paris: Dentu, 1884.

———. *Les Cinq sur l'Empire*. Paris: Dentu, 1885.

December 2, 1851. Contemporary Writings on the Coup d'Etat of Louis Napoleon. Edited by John B. Halsted. Garden City: Doubleday, 1972.

Dromel, Justin. *La loi des révolutions*. Paris: Didier, 1862.

Duprat, Pascal. *Les tables de proscription de Louis Bonaparte et de ses complices*. Liège: Redouté, 1852.

Fauvety, Charles. *Du principe de la nationalité*. Paris: Dentu, 1859.

Feugueray, Henri. *L'Association ouvrière, industrielle et agricole*. Paris: Havard, 1851.

Fortunato, Giustino. *Antologia dei suoi scritti*. Edited by Manlio Rossi-Doria. Bari: Laterza, 1948.

Galati, Domenico. *Gli uomini del mio tempo*. 2nd ed. Bologna: Zanichelli, 1882.

Gioberti, Vincenzo. *Epistolario*. 11 vols. Edited by Giovanni Gentile and Gustavo Balsamo-Crivelli. Florence: Vallecchi, 1927–37.

————. *Réponse à un article de la Revue des deux Mondes*. Brussels: Méline et Cans, 1844.

Greppo, Jean Louis. *Cathéchisme social où exposé succinct de la doctrine de la solidarité*. Paris: Sandré, 1849.

Hodde, Lucien de la. *Histoire des sociétés secrètes et du parti républicain de 1830 à 1848*. Brussels: Méline et Cans, 1850.

La Farina, Giuseppe. *Scritti politici*. 2 vols. Edited by Ausonio Franchi. Milan: Salvi, 1870.

Lamartine, Alphonse de. *Histoire de la révolution de 1848*. Paris: Vent du large, 1948.

La liberazione del Mezzogiorno e la formazione del Regno d'Italia. Carteggi di Camillo Cavour. 5 vols. Bologna: Zanichelli, 1949–54.

Mamiani, Terenzio. *Del rinnovamento della filosofia antica italiana*. Florence: [n.p.], 1836.

Marias Aguilera, Juliàn. *Generations: A Historical Method*. University of Alabama Press, 1970.

Massarani, Tullo. *Carteggio inedito*. 3 vols. Edited by Raffaello Barbiera. Florence: LeMonnier, 1909.

Matteucci, Carlo. *Raccolta di scritti vari intorno alla istruzione pubblica*. Prato: [n.p.], 1867.

Mazzini, Giuseppe, *Scritti editi ed inediti*. 99 vols. Imola: Galeati, 1906–43.

Memorie di Giorgio Pallavicino-Trivulzio. 3 vols. Edited by Anna and Nini Pallavicino-Trivulzio. Turin: Roux, Frassati & Co., 1882–95.

Mentré, François. *Les générations sociales*. Paris: Bossard, 1920.

1840–1851. Luigi Dottesio di Como e la Tipografia Elvetica di Capolago. Ricordi di Alessandro Repetti. Rome: Tipografia Nazionale, 1887.

Minghetti, Marco. *I miei ricordi*. 4th ed. 3 vols. Turin: Roux, 1889.

Montanelli, Giuseppe. *Introduzione ad alcuni appunti sulla rivoluzione d'Italia*. Edited by Alberto Alberti. Turin: Chiantore, 1945.

————. *Mémoires sur l'Italie*. 2 vols. Paris: Chamerot, 1851.

Petruccelli della Gattina, Ferdinando. *I moribondi del Palazzo Carignano e memorie di un ex-deputato* [1861–62]. Rome: Edizioni moderne, 1960.

Pisacane, Carlo. *Epistolario*. Edited by Aldo Romano. Rome: Albrighi & Segati, 1937.

————. *La guerra combattuta in Italia negli anni 1848–1849* [1851]. Turin: Loescher, 1968.

————. *La rivoluzione in Italia*. Edited by Franco Della Peruta. Turin: Einaudi, 1970.

Proudhon, Pierre-Joseph. *Correspondance*. 14 vols. Edited by J.-A. Langlois. Paris: Lacroix, 1875.

————. *De la création de l'ordre dans l'humanité*. Paris: Rivière, 1927.

————. *De la Justice dans la Révolution et dans l'Eglise* [1858]. 3 vols. Paris: Rivière, 1930–35.

————. *Du principe fédératif*. Paris: Dentu, 1863.

————. *La fédération et l'unité d'Italie*. Paris: Dentu, 1862.

———— *Lettres à sa femme*. Edited by Suzanne Henneguy. Paris: Grasset, 1950.

Quinet, Edgar. *Correspondance. Lettres à sa mère*. 2 vols. Paris: Hachette, 1877.

————. *Lettres d'exil à Michelet et à divers amis*. 4 vols. Paris: Calmann Lèvy, 1886.

————. *Qu'est-ce que la propriété?* Paris: Rivière, 1938.

————. *Système des contradictions économiques*. Paris: Flammarion, 1954.

Quinet, Hermione Asaki. *Cinquante ans d'amitié: Michelet-Quinet, 1825–1875*. Paris: Colin, 1903.

Rémusat, Charles de. *Mémoires de ma vie*. 5 vols. Edited by Charles Pouthas. Paris: Plon, 1958–62.

Renan, Ernest. *Correspondance*. 2 vols. Paris: Calmann Lèvy, 1926.

————. *Essais de morale et de critique*. Paris: Michel Lèvy Frères, 1860.

Ricciardi, Giuseppe. *Opere*. Naples: Rondinella, 1861.

Risorgimento italiano. Memorie di Angelo Bargoni. Edited by Attilio Bargoni. Milan: Hoepli, 1911.

Romagnosi, Giovanni Domenico. *Lettere edite ed inedite*. Edited by Stefano Fermi. Milan: Vallardi, 1935.

Rosa, Gabriele. *Autobiografie*. Edited by Giuseppe Tramarollo. Pisa: Domus Mazziniana, 1963.

Ruemelin, Gustav. *Problèmes d'économie politique et de statistique*. Paris: Guillaumin, 1896.

Schoelcher, Victor. *Histoire des crimes du deux décembre*. London: Chapman, 1852.

Wallon, Jean Gustave. *La Cour de Rome et la France*. Paris: Lachaud, 1871.

III. Secondary Works

A) *Works about Giuseppe Ferrari*

Auletta, Gennaro. "Anticlericali dell'Ottocento: G.F. impegno falso e storto." *L'Osservatore della Domenica*, 10 March 1968, p. 11.
Barillari, Bruno. "G.F. critico di Mazzini." *Pensiero mazziniano* 18 (1963): 4.
Brancato, Francesco. *G.F. e i Siciliani*. Trapani: Vento, 1959.
Brunello, Bruno. "Ferrari e Proudhon." *Rivista internazionale di filosofia del diritto* 27 (1951): 58–75.
————. *Il pensiero di G.F*. Rome: Albrighi & Segati, 1933.
Cantoni, Carlo. *G.F.* [Eulogy]. Milan: Brigola, 1878.
Cavaleri, Michele. *G.F.* Milan: Manini, 1861.
D'Amato, Carmelo. "La formazione di G.F. e la cultura italiana della prima metà dell'Ottocento." *Studi storici* 12 (1971): 693–717.
————. "Ideologia e politica in G.F." *Studi storici* 11 (1970): 743–54.
Della Peruta, Franco. "Il socialismo risorgimentale di Ferrari, Pisacane e Montanelli." *Movimento operaio* 8 (1956): 3–41.
————. "Un capitolo di storia del socialismo risorgimentale: Proudhon e Ferrari." *Studi storici* 3 (1962): 307–42.
Druart, Marise. "Le carte di G.F. nel Museo del Risorgimento di Milano." *Movimento operaio* 7 (1955): 799–801.
Ferrari, Aldo. *G.F. Saggio critico*. Genoa: Formiggini, 1914.
Ferri, Luigi. "Cenno su G.F. e le sue dottrine." In *La mente di G. D. Romagnosi*. Milan: Libreria editrice milanese, 1913.
————. *Essai sur l'histoire de la philosophie en Italie au XIXᵉ siècle*. 2 vols. Paris: Durand, 1869.
Frabotta, Biancamaria. "Dialetto e popolo nella concezione critica di G.F." *La Rassegna della letteratura italiana* 75 (1971): 460–79.
Levi, Alessandro. "Il pensiero politico di G.F." *Nuova rivista storica* 15 (1931): 217–58, 365–97.
Limentani, Ludovico. "G.F. e la scienza degli ingegni." *Rivista di filosofia e scienze affini* 9 (1907): 525–58.
Lioy, Diodato. "G.F." In *I contemporanei italiani*, vol. 68. Turin: UTET, 1864.
Lovett, Clara M. "Europa e Cina nell'opera di G.F." *Rassegna storica del Risorgimento* 59 (1972): 398–401.
Mazzoleni Angelo. *G.F. Il pensatore, lo storico, lo scrittore politico*. Rome: Libreria politica moderna, 1925.
————. *G.F. I suoi tempi e le sue opere*. Milan: [n.p.], 1877.

Mola, Aldo Alessandro. "Non parliamo degli eretici." *Gazzetta del Popolo* (Turin), 2 January 1977.
Monti, Antonio. "La posizione di G.F. nel primo Parlamento italiano." *Critica politica* 3 (1923): 180–86.
_____. "Il ritorno di G.F." *Nuova antologia* 442 (1948): 107–13.
Oriani, Alfredo. *La lotta politica in Italia. Origini della lotta attuale.* Bologna: Cappelli, 1956.
Ottaviani, Dario. "Il Mefistofele del Risorgimento." *Pensiero mazziniano* 31 (1976): 61–62.
Perticone, Giacomo. "La concezione etico-politica di G.F." *Rivista internazionale di filosofia del diritto* 2 (1922): 259–74.
Pfister, Charles. "Un épisode de l'histoire de la Faculté des Lettres de Strasbourg: l'affaire Ferrari." *Revue internationale de l'enseignement* 56 (1926): 334–55.
Rosselli, Nello. "Italia e Francia nel pensiero di G.F." [Published posthumously.] *Il Ponte* 33 (1967): 750–56.
Rota Ghibaudi, Silvia. "Ferrari e Proudhon." *Il Pensiero politico* 1 (1968): 190–207.
_____. *G.F. L'evoluzione del suo pensiero, 1838–1860.* Florence: Olschki, 1969.
Solimani, Antonio. "La filosofia della storia di G.F." *La Rassegna nazionale* 60 (1891): 509–24.
Tabarrini, Marco. "G.F." [Eulogy.] *Archivio storico italiano* 24 (1876): 358–63.
Taviani, Paolo Emilio. *Problemi economici nei riformatori sociali del Risorgimento italiano.* Florence: LeMonnier, 1968.
Tranfaglia, Nicola. "G.F. e la storia d'Italia." *Belfagor* 25 (1970): 1–32.
Troccoli, Antonio. "G.F. e l'unificazione italiana." *Amministrazione civile* 3 (1959): 39–41.
Vertua, Giovanni Battista. *Sulle opere di Ausonio Franchi, di G.F., di un anonimo, del Pernet, del De Sanctis e del Valle.* Milan: Pirola, 1854.

B) *Other Secondary Works*

Abramson, Paul R. *Generational Change in American Politics.* Lexington: Lexington Books, 1975.
Alessi, Maria Luisa. *Una giardiniera del Risorgimento italiano: Bianca Milesi.* Genoa: Streglio, 1906.
Arbib, Edoardo. *Pensieri, sentenze e ricordi di uomini parlamentari.* Florence: Barbera, 1901.
Avenel, Henri. *Histoire de la presse française depuis 1789 jusqu'à nos jours.* Paris: Flammarion, 1900.

Barbey d'Aurevilly, Jules-Amedée. *Le XIXe siècle. Des oeuvres et des hommes.* 2 vols. Paris: Mercure de France, 1954.

Barbiera, Raffaello. *Passioni del Risorgimento. Nuove pagine sulla Principessa Belgiojoso.* Milan: Treves, 1903.

_____. *Il salotto della contessa Maffei e la società milanese, 1834–1886.* Milan: Treves, 1895.

Barthèlemy-Saint-Hilaire, Jules. *M. Victor Cousin, sa vie et sa correspondance.* 3 vols. Paris: Hachette, 1895.

Bartoccini, Fiorella. *Il Murattismo.* Milan: Giuffrè, 1959.

_____. *La Roma dei Romani.* Rome: Istituto per la storia del Risorgimento italiano, 1971.

Bastid, Paul. *Doctrines et institutions politiques de la Seconde République.* Paris: Hachette, 1945.

_____. *Institutions politiques de la monarchie parlementaire française, 1814–1848.* Paris: Sirey, 1954.

Battistini, Mario. *Esuli italiani in Belgio, 1815–1861.* Florence: Brunetti, 1968.

Belardinelli, Mario. *Il conflitto per gli exequatur, 1871–1878.* Rome: Edizioni dell'Ateneo, 1971.

Berselli, Aldo. *La Destra storica dopo l'unità.* 2 vols. Bologna: Il Mulino, 1963–65.

Berti, Giuseppe. *I democratici e l'iniziativa meridionale nel Risorgimento.* Milan: Feltrinelli, 1962.

Bertoni Jovine, Dina. "La legge Casati." In *Problemi dell'unità d'Italia. Atti del II Convegno di studi gramsciani.* Rome: Editori Riuniti, 1962, pp. 441–47.

_____. *Storia della scuola popolare in Italia.* Bari: Laterza, 1965.

Bertrand, Louis. *Histoire de la démocratie et du socialisme en Belgique depuis 1830.* 2 vols. Paris: Cornèly, 1906.

Bianchi, Nicomede. *Carlo Matteucci e l'Italia del suo tempo.* Turin: Bocca, 1874.

Bonnefon, Paul. "Saint-René Taillandier èt Edgar Quinet." *Revue des études historiques* 84 (1918): 1–40.

Bourgin, Georges. *La guerre de 1870–1871 et la Commune.* Paris: Flammarion, 1971.

Boyer, Ferdinand, *La Seconde République, Charles Albert et l'Italie du Nord en 1848.* Paris: Pedone, 1967.

Brancato, Francesco. *Vico nel Risorgimento.* Palermo: Flaccovio, 1969.

Il brigantaggio meridionale. Cronaca inedita dell'unità d'Italia. Edited by Aldo De Jaco. Rome: Editori Riuniti, 1969.

Briguglio, Letterio. *Correnti politiche nel Veneto dopo Villafranca, 1859–1866.* Rome: Edizioni di storia e letteratura, 1965.

Brocher, Hans. *Aufstand gegen die Tradition: ueber den Konflikt zwischen den Generationen.* Stuttgart: Kreuz Verlag, 1972.

Bruhat, Jean. *La Commune de 1871*. Paris: Editions Sociales, 1970.
Buche, Joseph. *L'école mystique de Lyon, 1776–1847*. Paris: Alcan, 1935.
Bulferetti, Luigi. *Antonio Rosmini nella Restaurazione*. Florence: LeMonnier, 1942.
Bury, J. P. T. *Napoleon III and the Second Empire*. London: English University Presses, 1964.
Butterfield, Herbert. *The Discontinuities between the Generations in History: Their Effect on the Transmission of Political Experience*. London: Cambridge University Press, 1972.
Caddeo, Rinaldo, *Le edizioni di Capolago, 1830–1853*. Milan: Bompiani, 1934.
————. *La Tipografia Elvetica di Capolago*. Milan: Casa editrice Alpes & Archetipografia di Milano, 1931.
Calani, Aristide. *Il Parlamento del Regno d'Italia*. 3 vols. Milan: Civelli, 1860–66.
Candeloro, Giorgio. *Storia dell'Italia moderna*. 8 vols. Milan: Feltrinelli, 1956–78.
Capone, Alfredo. *L'opposizione meridionale nell'età della Destra*. Rome: Edizioni di storia e letteratura, 1970.
Caracciolo, Alberto. "Autonomia o centralizzazione degli studi nell'età della Destra." *Rassegna storica del Risorgimento* 45 (1958): 573–603.
————. *L'inchiesta agraria Jacini*. Turin: Einaudi, 1958.
————. *Il Parlamento nella formazione del Regno d'Italia*. Milan: Giuffrè, 1960.
Carbone, Salvatore. *I rifugiati italiani in Francia*. Rome: Istituto per la storia del Risorgimento italiano, 1962.
Case, Lynn M. *Franco-Italian Relations. The Roman Question and the Convention of September*. Philadelphia: University of Pennsylvania Press, 1932.
————. *French Opinion on War and Diplomacy during the Second Empire*. Philadelphia: University of Pennsylvania Press, 1954.
Cassese, Leopoldo. *La spedizione di Sapri*. Bari: Laterza, 1969.
Castronovo, Valerio. *La stampa italiana dall'unità al fascismo*. Bari: Laterza, 1970.
Catalano, Franco. *Storia dei partiti politici italiani*. Turin: ERI, 1965.
Ceccuti, Cosimo. *Il Concilio Vaticano I nella stampa italiana, 1860–1870*. Rome: Edizioni Cinque Lune, 1970.
Charlèty, Sébastien. *Histoire du Saint-Simonisme, 1825–1864*. Paris: Hartmann, 1931.
————. *La Monarchie de Juillet*. Paris: Hachette, 1921.
Choury, Maurice. *Paris Communard*. Paris: Perrin, 1970.
Ciampini, Raffaele. *Gian Pietro Vieusseux*. Turin: Einaudi, 1953.

Ciasca, Raffaele. *L'origine del programma per l'Opinione Nazionale Italiana del 1846–1847.* 2nd ed. Milan: Giuffrè, 1965.

Cipolla, Carlo. *Storia dell'economia italiana.* Turin: Einaudi, 1959.

Clough, Shepard B. *The Economic History of Modern Italy.* New York: Columbia University Press, 1964.

Collins, Irene, *The Government and the Newspaper Press in France, 1814–1881.* London: Oxford University Press, 1959.

Compendio di statistiche elettorali dal 1848 al 1914. 2 vols. Rome: ISTAT, 1946.

Composto, Renato. *I democratici dall'unità ad Aspromonte.* Florence: LeMonnier, 1967.

Crippin, Gary R., and Lovett, Clara M. "Federalism in Modern Italian Politics: The Historical Background." *Italian Quarterly* 19 (1975):5–32.

Croce, Benedetto. *Storia della storiografia italiana nel secolo XIX.* 2 vols. Bari: Laterza, 1921.

Cuvillier, Armand. *Hommes et idéologies de 1840.* Paris: Rivière, 1956.

————. *Buchez et les origines du socialisme chrétien.* Paris: Presses Universitaires de France, 1948.

————. *Un journal d'ouvriers: L'Atelier.* Paris: Alcan, 1914.

Dalla Torre, Paolo. *L'anno di Mentana.* 2nd ed. Milan: Il Martello, 1968.

D'Amelio, Giuliana. *Stato e Chiesa. La legislazione ecclesiastica fino al 1867.* Milan: Giuffrè, 1961.

Dansette, Adrien. *Histoire religieuse de la France contemporaine.* 2 vols. Paris: Flammarion, 1948–51.

Dauzat, Albert, and Bournon, Fernand. *Paris et ses environs.* Paris: Larousse, 1925.

Della Peruta, Franco. *I democratici e la rivoluzione italiana. Dibattiti ideali e contrasti politici all'indomani del 1848.* Milan: Feltrinelli, 1958.

————. *Democrazia e socialismo nel Risorgimento.* Rome: Editori Riuniti, 1965.

————. *Mazzini e i rivoluzionari italiani.* Milan: Feltrinelli, 1974.

————. "Note e documenti per la storia delle idee sociali in Italia, 1830–1849." *Annali dell'Istituto Giangiacomo Feltrinelli* 5 (1962): 395–401.

De Rosa, Gabriele. *Storia del movimento cattolico in Italia.* 2 vols. Bari: Laterza, 1966.

Di Domizio, Mario. *L'università italiana. Lineamenti storici.* Milan: Nicola, 1952.

Dollèans, Edouard, and Puech, Jules. *Proudhon et la Révolution de 1848.* Paris: Presses Universitaires de France, 1948.

Douarche, Aristide. *Michel de Bourges et le parti républicain*. Paris: Pedone-Lauriel, 1882.

Doutrepont, Georges. *Les proscrits du coup d'état du deux décembre 1851 en Belgique*. Brussels: [n.p.], 1938.

Duclos, Jacques. *La Commune de Paris à l'assaut du ciel*. Paris: Editions Sociales, 1970.

Duroselle, Jean-Baptiste. *Les débuts du catholicisme social en France jusqu'à 1870*. Paris: Presses Universitaires de France, 1951.

Edwards, Samuel. *Georges Sand: A Biography of the First Modern Liberated Woman*. New York: McKay, 1972.

Evans, David O. *Social Romanticism in France*. Oxford: The Clarendon Press, 1951.

Fappani, Antonio. *Il movimento contadino in Italia*. 2nd ed. Rome: ACLI, 1960.

Fontana, Enea. *Indice alfabetico per autori delle relazioni sui disegni di legge*. Rome: Tipografia della Camera dei Deputati, 1883.

_____. *Prontuario generale per materia e per ordine alfabetico e di data degli atti parlamentari dall'unificazione del Regno d'Italia al 17 giugno 1875*. Rome: Botta, 1875.

Fontana, Sandro. *La controrivoluzione cattolica in Italia, 1820–1830*. Brescia: Morcelliana, 1968.

Frainnet, Gaston. *Essai sur la philosophie de Pierre-Simon Ballanche*. Paris: Picard, 1903.

Galante Garrone, Alessandro. *I radicali in Italia*. Milan: Garzanti, 1973.

Gay, Jules. *Un siècle d'histoire italienne*. Paris: Alcan, 1931.

Ghisalberti, Carlo. *Stato e costituzione nel Risorgimento italiano*. Milan: Giuffrè, 1972.

_____. *Storia costituzionale d'Italia, 1849–1948*. Bari: Laterza, 1974.

Gianetti, Alessandro. *Trentaquattro anni di cronistoria milanese*. Milan: Cogliati, 1903.

Gooch, George P. *History and Historians in the Nineteenth Century*. Boston: The Beacon Press, 1959.

Gramsci, Antonio. *Il Risorgimento*. Turin: Einaudi, 1949.

Greenfield, Kent R. *Economics and Liberalism in the Risorgimento*. 2nd ed. Baltimore: Johns Hopkins University Press, 1965.

Grew, Raymond. *A Sterner Plan for Italian Unity. The Italian National Society in the Risorgimento*. Princeton: Princeton University Press, 1963.

Griffiths, David A. *Jean Reynaud*. Paris: Rivière, 1965.

Grifone, Pietro. *Il capitale finanziario in Italia*. Turin: Einaudi, 1971.

Grilli, Giovanni. *Como e Varese nella storia della Lombardia*. Azzate: La Varesina grafica, 1968.

La guerra del 1859 nei rapporti tra la Francia e l'Europa. 5 vols. Edited by Armando Saitta. Rome: Istituto storico italiano per l'età moderna e contemporanea, 1960–62.

Guerrini Angrisani, Isa. "La questione della libertà d'insegnamento in Francia nei primi decenni del secolo XIX e il corso di Michelet e Quinet al Collège de France nel 1843." In *Annali dell'Istituto italiano per gli studi storici* (Naples), 1970, pp. 275–360.

Guida alla Lombardia misteriosa. Milan: Sugar, 1968.

Guillemin, Henri. *Le coup d'état du deux décembre.* Paris: Gallimard, 1951.

Gurvitch, Georges. *Proudhon. Sa vie et son oeuvre.* Paris: Presses Universitaires de France, 1965.

Halèvy, Daniel. *Le mariage de Proudhon.* Paris: Stock, Delamain & Boutelleau, 1955.

Halperin, S. William. "The Origins of the Franco-Prussian War Revisited." *Journal of Modern History.* 55 (1973): 83–91.

Hatin, Louis-Eugène. *Bibliographie historique et critique de la presse periodique française.* Paris: Firman Didot Frères, 1866.

————. *Histoire politique et littéraire de la presse en France.* 8 vols. Paris: Poulet-Malassis, 1859–61.

Hemmings, F. W. J. *Culture and Society in France, 1848–1898.* New York: Scribner, 1972.

Hillairet, Jacques. *Dictionnaire historique des rues de Paris.* 2 vols. Paris: Editions du minuit, 1963.

Hoffbauer, Théodore. *Paris à travers les ages.* 2 vols. Paris: Didot, 1875–85.

Hoffman Robert. *Revolutionary Justice: The Social and Political Theory of Proudhon.* Urbana: University of Illinois Press, 1972.

Indice generale degli atti parlamentari e storia dei collegi elettorali. 2 vols. Rome: Tipografia della Camera dei Deputati, 1898.

Isambert, François-André. *De la Charbonnerie au Saint-Simonisme. Etudes sur la jeunesse de Buchez.* Paris: Editions du minuit, 1966.

————. *Politique, religion et science chez Philippe Buchez, 1796–1865.* Paris: Editions Cujas, 1967.

Izzo, Luigi, *La finanza pubblica nel primo decennio dell'unità d'Italia.* Milan: Giuffrè, 1962.

————. *Storia delle relazioni commerciali tra l'Italia e la Francia dal 1860 al 1875.* Naples: ESI, 1965.

Jacini, Stefano. *La proprietà fondiaria e le popolazioni agricole in Lombardia.* Milan: Crivelli, 1856.

Jackson, John Hampden, *Marx, Proudhon, and European Socialism.* London: English University Presses, 1964.

Jemolo, Arturo Carlo. *Chiesa e stato negli ultimi cento anni.* Turin: Einaudi, 1963.

Kluback, William. *Wilhelm Dilthey's Philosophy of History*. New York: Columbia University Press, 1955.
Lèger, Charles. *Courbet et son temps*. Paris: Editions universelles, 1948.
Lepre, Aurelio. *Contadini, borghesi e operai nel tramonto del feudalesimo napoletano*. Milan: Feltrinelli, 1963.
————. *Storia del Mezzogiorno nel Risorgimento*. Rome: Editori Riuniti, 1969.
Leroy, Maxime. *Histoire des idées sociales en France*. 3 vols. Paris: Gallimard, 1946.
Leti, Giuseppe. *Henri Cernuschi*. Paris: Presses Universitaires de France, 1936.
Levi, Alessandro. *Romagnosi*. Rome: Formiggini, 1935.
Lichtheim, George. *The Origins of Socialism*. New York: Praeger, 1968.
Loubère, Leo. *Louis Blanc: His Life and his Contribution to the Rise of French Jacobin-Socialism*. Evanston: Northwestern University Press, 1961.
Lovett, Clara M. *Carlo Cattaneo and the Politics of the Risorgimento, 1820–1860*. The Hague: Nijhoff, 1972.
————. "Nineteenth Century Italian Radicals and the American Republic: A Study in Ambivalence." In *Proceedings of the Seventh Annual Meeting of the American-Italian Historical Association*. New York, 1977, pp. 29–38.
Luna, Frederick A. de. *The French Republic under Cavaignac*. Princeton: Princeton University Press, 1969.
Luzio, Alessandro. "Giuseppe Acerbi e la *Biblioteca Italiana*." *Nuova Antologia* 148 (1896): 457–88.
Mack Smith, Denis. *Cavour and Garibaldi. A Study in Political Conflict*. New York: Kraus Reprint, 1968.
————. *Italy. A Modern History*. Ann Arbor: University of Michigan Press, 1959.
————. *Victor Emmanuel, Cavour and the Risorgimento*. New York: Oxford University Press, 1971.
The Making of Italy, 1796–1870. Edited by Denis Mack Smith. New York: Harper and Row, 1968.
Malvezzi, Aldobrandino. *La Principessa Belgiojoso*. 3rd edition. Milan: Treves, 1937.
Manuel, Frank. *Prophets of Paris*. Cambridge: Harvard University Press, 1962.
Maranini, Giuseppe. *Storia del potere in Italia, 1848–1967*. Florence: Vallecchi, 1967.
Mario, Jessie White. *Agostino Bertani e i suoi tempi*. 2 vols. Florence: Barbera, 1888.
Mastellone, Salvo. "La composition sociale de l'émigration italienne en France." *Rassegna storica toscana*, 8 (1962): 223–38.

————. *Victor Cousin ed il Risorgimento italiano*. Florence: LeMonnier, 1955.

Maturi, Walter. *Interpretazioni del Risorgimento*. Turin: Einaudi, 1962.

Maurain, Jean. *La politique ecclésiastique du Second Empire de 1852 à 1869*. Paris: Alcan, 1930.

Maurois, André. *Lèlia, ou la vie de Georges Sand*. Paris: Hachette, 1952.

Mazzarella, Bonaventura. *Critique de la science*. Genoa: Lavagnino, 1860.

Ministri, deputati e senatori dal 1848 al 1922. 3 vols. Edited by Alberto Malatesta. Rome: Istituto editoriale italiano, 1941.

Molfese, Franco. *Storia del brigantaggio dopo l'unità*. Milan: Feltrinelli, 1964.

Monti, Antonio. *L'idea federalistica nel Risorgimento italiano*. Bari: Laterza, 1922.

————. *Milano romantica*. Milan: Edizioni Domus, 1946.

————. *Un dramma fra gli esuli*. Milan: Caddeo, 1921.

Moody, Joseph N. "The French Catholic Press in the Education Conflict of the 1840's." *French Historical Studies* 7 (1972): 393–415.

Mori, Renato. *La questione romana, 1861–1865*. Florence: Le Monnier, 1963.

————. *Il tramonto del potere temporale, 1866–1870*. Rome: Edizioni di storia e letteratura, 1967.

Moscati, Ruggero. *La diplomazia ed il ministero degli affari esteri, 1861–1870*. Milan: Giuffrè, 1961.

Mosse, Werner. *The Rise and Fall of the Crimean System, 1855–1871*. London: Macmillan, 1963.

Noether, Emiliana P. "Giambattista Vico and the Risorgimento." *Harvard Library Bulletin* 17 (1969); 309–19.

————. *Seeds of Italian Nationalism, 1700–1815*. 2nd ed. New York: AMS Press, 1969.

————. "Vatican Council I: Its Political and Religious Setting." *Journal of Modern History* 40 (1968): 218–23.

Novacco, Domenico. "I tumulti del macinato." *Nuovi quaderni meridionali* 6 (1968): 427–35.

Pailleron, Marie-Louise. *François Buloz et ses amis*. Paris: Perrin, 1923.

————. *La Revue des deux Mondes et la Comédie française*. Paris: Didot, 1930.

Passerin d'Entrèves, Ettore. *L'ultima battaglia politica di Cavour*. Turin: ILTE, 1956.

Pieri, Piero. *Storia militare del Risorgimento*. Turin: Einaudi, 1962.

Pincherle, Marcella. *Moderatismo politico e riforma religiosa in Terenzio Mamiani*. Milan: Giuffrè, 1973.

Pirri, Pietro. *La questione romana, 1856–1864.* Rome: Pontificale Università Gregoriana, 1951.

———. *La questione romana dalla Convenzione di Settembre alla caduta del potere temporale.* Rome: Pontificale Università Gregoriana, 1963.

Pitocco, Francesco. *Utopia e riforma religiosa nel Risorgimento.* Bari: Laterza, 1972.

Plebano, Achille. *Storia della finanza italiana nei primi quarant'anni dell'unificazione.* Padova: Cedam, 1960.

Plombières. Secret Diplomacy and the Rebirth of Italy. Edited by Mack Walker. New York: Oxford University Press, 1968.

Ponteil, Felix. *La monarchie parlementaire, 1815–1848.* Paris: Colin, 1949.

———. "La renaissance catholique à Strasbourg. L'affaire Bautain." *Revue historique* 55 (1930): 225–87.

———. *L'opposition politique à Strasbourg sous la Monarchie de Juillet.* Paris: Hartmann, 1932.

Price, Roger. *The French Second Republic. A Social History.* Ithaca: Cornell University Press, 1972.

Procacci, Giuliano. *Le elezioni del 1874 e l'opposizione meridionale.* Milan: Feltrinelli, 1956.

———. *La lotta di classe in Italia agli inizi del XX secolo.* Rome: Editori Riuniti, 1970.

Quazza, Guido. *La lotta sociale nel Risorgimento.* Turin: [n.p.], 1951.

Raponi, Nicola. *Politica ed amministrazione in Lombardia agli esordi dell'unità. Il programma dei moderati.* Milan: Giuffrè, 1967.

Repaci, Francesco. *La finanza pubblica italiana nel secolo 1861–1960.* 2 vols. Bologna: Zanichelli, 1962.

Righetti, Carlo. *I 450 deputati del presente ed i deputati dell'avvenire.* 7 vols. Milan: Tipografia degli Autori-Editori, 1864–65.

Ritter, Alan. *The Political Thought of Proudhon.* Princeton: Princeton University Press, 1969.

Romani, Mario. *L'agricoltura in Lombardia dal periodo delle riforme al 1859.* Milan: Vita e Pensiero, 1957.

Romeo, Rosario. *Il giudizio storico sul Risorgimento.* Catania: Bonanno, 1966.

———. *Il Risorgimento in Sicilia.* Bari: Laterza, 1950.

Romizi, Augusto. *Storia del ministero della pubblica istruzione.* 2 vols. Milan: Albrighi & Segati, 1902.

Rosselli, Nello. *Saggi sul Risorgimento.* Edited by Gaetano Salvemini. Turin: Einaudi, 1946.

Rubel, Maximilien. *Karl Marx devant le Bonapartisme.* Paris: Mouton, 1960.

Ruffili, Roberto. *La questione regionale dall'unificazione alla dittatura.* Milan: Giuffrè, 1971.

Ruini, Meuccio. *Pensatori politici del Prerisorgimento e del Risorgimento d'Italia.* Milan: Giuffrè, 1962.

Russo, Salvatore. "Interpretazioni sul·Risorgimento," *Rassegna storica del Risorgimento* 55 (1968): 397–401.

Saab, Ann Pottinger. *The Origins of the Crimean Alliance.* Charlottesville: University of Virginia Press, 1977.

Sainville, Leonard. *Victor Schoelcher, 1804–1893.* 2 vols. Paris: Fasquelle, 1950.

Salomone, A. William. "The Risorgimento between Ideology and History: The Political Myth of *rivoluzione mancata.*" *American Historical Review* 68 (1962): 38–56.

Salvadori, Massimo. *Il mito del buon governo. La questione meridionale da Cavour a Gramsci.* 2nd ed. Turin: Einaudi, 1962.

Salvatorelli, Luigi. *Il pensiero politico italiano.* Turin: Einaudi, 1949.

Salvemini, Gaetano. *Scritti sulla questione meridionale.* Turin: Einaudi, 1955.

Sapori, Armando. *Attività manifatturiera in Lombardia dal 1600 al 1914.* Milan: Associazione industriale lombarda, 1959.

Schroeder, Paul W. *Austria, Great Britain, and the Crimean War.* Ithaca: Cornell University Press, 1972.

Scirocco, Alfonso. *I democratici italiani da Sapri a Porta Pia.* Naples: ESI, 1969.

──────. *Democrazia e socialismo a Napoli dopo l'unità.* Naples: Libreria scientifica editrice, 1973.

──────. *Governo e paese nel Mezzogiorno nella crisi dell'unificazione.* Milan: Giuffrè, 1963.

Scott, Ivan. *The Roman Question and the Powers.* The Hague: Nijhoff, 1968.

Sereni, Emilio. *Il capitalismo nelle campagne, 1860–1900.* Turin: Einaudi, 1947.

Silvestre, Théophile. *Histoire des artistes vivantes.* Paris: Blanchard, 1856.

Simon, Jules. *Victor Cousin.* Paris: Hachette, 1891.

"La Sinistra italiana dal 1861 al 1870 nel quadro delle opposizioni democratiche europee." *Rassegna storica toscana* 11 (1965): entire issue.

Sloane, Joseph C. *Paul-Marc-Joseph Chenavard, Artist of 1848.* Chapel Hill: University of North Carolina Press, 1962.

Soccio, Pasquale. *Unità e brigantaggio.* Naples: ESI, 1969.

Soltau, Roger. *French Political Thought in the Nineteenth Century.* New York: Russell & Russell, 1959.

Soriga, Renato. *Pavia nel Risorgimento italiano*. Pavia: Ateneo pavese, 1925.

Spadolini, Giovanni. *Firenze capitale*. Florence: LeMonnier, 1967.

————. *I radicali dell'Ottocento*. Florence: LeMonnier, 1972.

————. *I repubblicani dopo l'unità*. 2nd ed. Florence: LeMonnier, 1963.

Spano, Nicola. *La legislazione universitaria italiana dal 1859 al 1947*. Rome: Edizioni dell'Ateneo, 1967.

Spellanzon, Cesare, and DiNolfo, Ennio. *Storia del Risorgimento e della unità d'Italia*. 7 vols. Milan: Rizzoli, 1951–60.

Spitzer, Alan. "The Historical Problem of Generations." *American Historical Review* 78 (1973): 1364–96.

Staehling, Charles. *Histoire contemporaine de Strasbourg et de l'Alsace*. Paris: Fischbacher, 1884.

Stokes, Donald E. *The Study of Political Generations*. London: Longmans, 1969.

Storia di Milano. 15 vols. Milan: Fondazione Treccani degli Alfieri, 1953–60.

Il Sud nella storia d'Italia. Edited by Rosario Villari. Bari: Laterza, 1961.

Tabarrini, Marco. *Vite e ricordi di Italiani illustri del secolo XIX*. Florence: Barbera, 1884.

Talamo, Giuseppe. *La scuola dalla legge Casati all'inchiesta del 1864*. Milan: Giuffrè, 1960.

Talmon, Jacob L. *Political Messianism: The Romantic Phase*. London: Secker & Warburg, 1960.

Tchernoff, Judah. *Associations et sociétés secrètes sous la Deuxième République*. Paris: Alcan, 1905.

————. *Le parti républicain au coup d'état et sous le Second Empire*. Paris: Pedone, 1906.

Thomas, Edith, *Pauline Roland: socialisme et féminisme au XIXe siècle*. Paris: Rivière, 1956.

Thompson, J. M. *Louis Napoleon and the Second Empire*. Oxford: Blackwell, 1954.

Tocci, Giovanni. *Terra e riforme nel Mezzogiorno moderno*. Bologna: Patron, 1971.

Torre, Augusto. *La politica estera dell'Italia dal 1870 al 1896*. Bologna: Patron, 1959.

Totomiantz, Victor. "Un coopérateur française inconnu: Henri Feugueray." *Revues des études coopératives* 6 (1926–27): 114–17.

Treves, Paolo. *Profeti del passato. Maestri e discepoli della controrivoluzione francese*. Florence: Barbera, 1952.

Treves, Renato. *La dottrina sansimoniana nel pensiero italiano*. Turin: Istituto giuridico dell'Università di Torino, 1931.

Tuttle, Howard N. *Wilhelm Dilthey's Philosophy of Historical Understanding*. Leiden: Brill, 1969.
Un Italiano vivente. *Il libro dei profeti dell'idea repubblicana in Italia*. Milan: Battistelli, 1898.
Valsecchi, Franco. *L'Europa e il Risorgimento. L'alleanza di Crimea*. Florence: Vallecchi, 1968.
_____. *Italia ed Europa nel 1859*. Florence: LeMonnier, 1965.
Villari, Pasquale. *La vendita dei beni dello stato nel Regno di Napoli, 1806–1815*. Milan: Banca Commerciale Italiana, 1964.
Villari, Rosario. *Mezzogiorno e contadini nell'età moderna*. Bari: Laterza, 1962.
Weill, Georges. *Histoire du mouvement social en France*. Paris: Alcan, 1911.
_____. *Histoire du parti républicain en France, 1815–1870*. Paris: Alcan, 1928.
White, Hayden V. *Metahistory. The Historical Imagination in Nineteenth Century Europe*. Baltimore: The Johns Hopkins University Press, 1973.
Wohl, Robert. *The Generation of 1914*. Cambridge: Harvard University Press, 1979.
Woodcock, George. *Pierre-Joseph Proudhon: A Biography*. London: Routledge & Kegan Paul, 1969.
Woolf, Stuart J. *Storia d'Italia dal primo Settecento all'unità*. Turin: Einaudi, 1973.
Zanichelli, Domenico. *La questione universitaria in Italia*. Bologna: [n.p.], 1890.
Zanotti-Bianco, Umberto. *Meridione e meridionalisti*. Rome: Collezione meridionale, 1964.
Zeldin, Theodore. *The Political System of Napoleon III*. New York: Norton, 1971.

Index

A

Adamoli, Giulio, 141
Allart de Méritens, Hortense, 23
Amari, Michele, 39, 153, 155, 160
Amedeo of Savoy, King of Spain.
  See Savoy, House of
Annali universali di statistica, 9, 10, 19
Antonelli, Giacomo, 172
Archivio storico italiano, 99
Archivio triennale delle cose d'Italia, 65, 78, 96
Arconati, Costanza (Visconti), 227 (n. 47), 228 (n. 59)
Arnaud (de l'Ariége), Frédéric, 25
Arrivabene, Giovanni, 64
Aspromonte crisis (1862), 147, 148, 149, 165, 166
Asproni, Giorgio, 133
L'Atelier, 25
L'Ateneo, 19
Auger, Hippolyte, 25

B

Babeuf, Gracchus, 24
Bagehot, Walter, 83
Bakunin, Mikhail, 202
Balbo, Cesare, 45
Ballanche, Pierre-Simon, 10, 11, 22, 224 (n. 12)
Banditry, 150–51, 162–63, 165, 167, 168, 169, 170
Bargoni, Angelo, 134, 149, 150, 240 (n. 16), 242 (n. 54)
Bastogi, Pietro, 181, 182
Battaglia, Giacinto, 6
Bautain, Louis-Eugène-Marie, 33, 34
Beccaria, Cesare, 12, 16
Belgiojoso, Cristina Trivulzio di, 27, 38, 47
Bentham, Jeremy, 16
Bergmann, Frédéric-Guillaume, 35, 87, 234 (n. 29)
Bertani, Agostino, 125, 144, 146, 147–51, 243 (n. 77)
Berti, Domenico, 158, 243 (n. 76)
Beslay, Charles, 88
Biblioteca italiana, 12, 224 (n. 16)
Bixio, Nino, 150, 235 (n. 63)
Blanc, Louis, 86, 229 (n. 4)
Bonaparte, Napoleon (Emperor Napoleon I), 3, 43, 44, 74, 86

Bonaparte, Louis Napoleon (Emperor Napoleon III), 63, 65, 68, 81, 83–87, 89, 91, 93, 96, 97, 98, 112, 116, 121, 123, 127, 174, 180, 233 (n. 25)
Borgatti, Francesco, 176
Bourbons, House of: France, 85, 96; Kingdom of the Two Sicilies, 162, 165, 168, 169
Bourges, 51, 62, 63, 88
Brénier, Alexandre-Anatole, 65, 97
Brénier, Isabelle (Woodcock), 61
Bricchi, Giovanni, 241 (n. 40)
Brigandage. See Banditry
Brisset, Pierre, 99
Brofferio, Angelo, 67
Bruno, Giordano, 173
Brussels, 42, 64, 124
Bucellati, Giuseppe, 11
Buchez, Philippe, 24, 25, 31, 47, 50, 75, 216, 225 (n. 9)
Buloz, François, 23, 32, 39, 40

C

Cabet, Etienne, 73, 94
Cadolini, Giovanni, 149
Caimi, Giulio, 56, 133, 228 (n. 61), 229 (nn. 15, 18)
Cairoli, Benedetto, 148
Cambray-Digny, Guglielmo di, 181, 183, 184
Campanella, Tommaso, 31, 173
Cantù, Cesare, xii, 6, 226 (n. 16)
Cantù, Ignazio, 6
Carbonarism, 55
Cardani, Francesco, 118, 132, 142, 143, 192, 199, 217, 239 (n. 47), 240 (n. 8), 241 (nn. 42, 43), 242 (nn. 52, 62, 63), 245 (n. 35), 246 (nn. 1, 2, 8), 247 (nn. 25, 28)
Carnazza, Gabriele, 162

Carnot, Hippolyte, 24, 56, 61, 62, 63
Carozzi, Giovanni, 8, 60, 67, 87, 115, 116, 117, 230 (n. 26), 231 (n. 62), 234 (n. 28), 236 (n. 84), 237 (n. 13), 238 (nn. 24, 29, 35, 38), 239 (n. 3), 241 (n. 30), 242 (n. 51), 246 (n. 9)
Casati, Gabrio, 152
Casati Law (1859), 152, 153, 155
Cassinis, Giovanni Battista, 163
Castelli, Angiolino, 9
Cattaneo, Anna (Woodcock), 8, 18, 22, 23, 27, 60, 65
Cattaneo, Carlo, xii; in the Romagnosi circle, 7, 8, 9, 10, 13; literary cooperation with Ferrari, 15, 18, 19, 20, 21; correspondence with Ferrari after 1838, 26, 27, 28, 29; role in Milanese Revolution of 1838, 58, 59, 60, 61; editor of *Archivio triennale*, 65, 66, 67, 68, 69; critique of Ferrari's *Federazione repubblicana*, 78, 79, 80; political attitude in 1859–60, 97; attitude in 1860–61, 117, 118, 119, 120, 122, 125
Cattaneo, Giovanni, 82
Cavaignac, Louis-Eugène, 59, 61, 63, 70
Cavaleri, Michele, xii, 118, 124, 238 (nn. 39, 41), 239 (nn. 52, 6), 240 (n. 12), 241 (n. 35), 242 (nn. 56, 65), 243 (nn. 75, 3), 244 (nn. 12, 13, 17, 18)
Cavallotti, Felice, 189, 218, 246 (n. 61)
Cavour, Camillo Benso di, xi, xii, 82, 96, 97, 111, 113, 116, 117, 119, 121–29, 144, 146, 161, 163, 171, 172, 174, 175, 177, 178, 214, 221, 239 (n. 45)

Cazeaux, Euryale, 135, 240
(n. 20)
Cerise, Lorenzo (Laurent), 24, 25,
27, 28, 225 (n. 8)
Cernuschi, Enrico (Henri), 58, 59,
67, 87, 117, 120, 181, 193, 232
(n. 86), 233 (n. 11), 234 (n. 26),
246 (nn. 11, 12, 13), 247
(n. 14)
Charles Albert, King of Sardinia.
See Savoy, House of
Charpenne, Pierre, 59, 229
(n. 24), 230 (n. 25)
Chenavard, Joseph, 11, 61, 224
(n. 13)
Cibrario, Luigi, 242 (n. 68)
Clarke, Mary, 23, 38
Cobden-Chevalier Treaty, 186,
187
Cola di Rienzo, 103, 114
Collège de France, 10, 22, 23, 25,
49, 51, 63, 100
Commedia dell'arte, 29, 30
Comte, Auguste, 107
Condillac, Etienne Bonnot de, 16
Congress of Paris (1856), 96
Congress of Vienna (1815), 43, 44
Consiglio Superiore della Pubblica
Istruzione. *See* Ministry of
Public Education, Italy
Il Convegno, 141, 143
Correnti, Cesare, 6, 158
Costantini, Giuseppe, 162
Cottard, Louis Magloire, 34–38,
59, 227 (nn. 39, 41)
Courbet, Gustave, 88, 196
Cousin, Victor, 23, 37, 40, 62, 64
Il Crepuscolo, 99
Crimean War, 91, 93, 95
Crispi, Francesco, 125, 134, 144,
146, 147, 166, 184, 242 (n. 48),
244 (n. 14)
Croce, Benedetto, 99, 100
Cuoco, Vincenzo, 12, 15

Czoernig, Karl von, 20

D

Daelli, Gino, 67, 68, 81, 115, 225
(n. 25), 231 (n. 51), 233 (n. 3),
237 (n. 16), 238 (n. 23), 239
(n. 44)
Darimon, Alfred, 88, 89, 190, 196
Dassi, Giuseppe, 134, 161, 166,
167, 240 (n. 19), 243 (n. 5)
De Boni, Filippo, 125, 145, 146
Delcasso, Laurent, 227 (n. 42)
De Luca, Francesco, 149
Del Zio, Floriano, 149
Depretis, Agostino, 134, 181,
184, 218, 239 (n. 4), 240
(n. 18), 243 (n. 4)
De Sanctis, Francesco, 153
Descartes, René, 17, 71, 205
Destra storica, xii
Dilthey, Wilhelm, 205, 207
Il Diritto, 134, 149, 156
Dottesio, Luigi, 68
Il Dovere, 149
Dromel, Justin, 205, 207
Duchies (of central Italy). *See*
Parma; Modena
Duprat, Pascal, 51, 52, 61, 84

E

Egger, Emile, 229 (n. 23)
Elgin, Thomas Bruce, 39
Encyclopédie nouvelle, 23, 24
Enlightenment, 5, 9, 18, 40, 70,
104, 215
European Democratic Central
Committee, 67
L'Européen, 25

F

Farini, Luigi Carlo, 117, 149, 174

Fauriel, Claude, 26, 27, 30, 32, 43, 104, 152, 205
Federalism, 29, 30, 65, 68, 93, 95. *See also* Ferrari, Giuseppe; Proudhon, Pierre-Joseph
Ferdinand I, Emperor. *See* Habsburg, House of
Ferrari, Carlo, xii, 4, 5, 7, 8, 20, 47, 48, 49, 57, 112, 133, 223 (nn. 4, 5, 8), 227 (n. 43), 228 (nn. 60, 69), 229 (n. 16), 240 (n. 12)
Ferrari, Cristoforo, 57, 112, 133, 240 (n. 11)
Ferrari, Francesco, 4, 5, 48
Ferrari, Giovanni (d. 1820), 4, 5, 48
Ferrari, Giovanni (d. 1854), 57, 60
Ferrari, Giuditta, 57
Ferrari, Giuseppe: youth in Milan, 3–8; in the Romagnosi-Cattaneo circle, 9–13; interest in Vichian philosophy, 15–18; intellectual experiences in Paris, 22–26; influence of Fauriel, Michelet, Quinet, 27–31; federalist ideology, 29–30, 65–68, 77–78, 100–103; *l'affaire Ferrari* in Strasbourg, 32–38; polemic with Gioberti, 38–42; financial settlement with family, 47–50; involvement in February Revolution (Paris), 52–53; analysis of Italian revolutionary movement, 52–56; return to Milan during revolution, 57–58; appointment to faculty of Bourges lycée, 62–64; exile in Belgium, 64–65; political activities in France and Switzerland (1849–51), 67–69; interpretations of the Revolutions of 1848, 69–79; secularist

ideology, 71–73; socialist ideology, 73–79; interpretation of Bonapartist coup (December 1851), 82–85; view of Second Empire, 85–87; friendship with Proudhon, 87–95; view of Crimean War, 92, 93, 95; differences with Mazzini and Italian National Society, 95–98; interpretation of Italian revolutionary tradition, 99–104; emergence of generational theory of historical change, 104–7; return to Italy after War of 1859, 111–16; political campaigns of 1860–61, 116–21; speech against cession of Nice and Savoy, 121–24; speech against annexation of South, 126–27; development of parliamentary career, 130–35; characteristics of electoral district, 135–43; relationship with Italian Left, 144–52; educational activities, 152–57; views on southern question, 160–70; on church-state relations, 170–80; on economic and fiscal issues, 180–89; on War of 1870, 192–97; on Paris Commune, 197–98; on Italian foreign policy, 199–202; on universal suffrage, 202–4; development of generational theory, 205–12
Ferrari, Maria Cristina (Arpagans), 112, 132, 133, 237 (n. 4)
Ferrari, Marietta (Caimi), 133
Ferrari, Rosalinda, 5, 20, 48, 49, 228 (n. 61)
Feugueray, Henri, 25
First Workingmen's International, 189, 197
Flaubert, Gustave, 22

Fortunato, Giustino, 170
Fourierist movement, 10, 11, 94
Franchetti, Leopoldo, 170
Francis Joseph I, Emperor. *See*
　Habsburg, House of
Franco-Prussian War, 192, 194,
　197, 199, 201
Franco-Sardinian alliance (1859),
　96, 97, 111, 235 (n. 60)
Franco-Spanish Democratic Com-
　mittee. *See* Latin Democratic
　Committee.
Free Trade movement, 186, 187,
　188
French Empire: First, 3, 28, 44;
　Second, xiii, 87, 92, 111, 180,
　191, 192, 193, 197, 198, 233
　(n. 13)
French Republic: First (*see* French
　Revolution); Second, 59, 70,
　84, 85, 147; Third, 193
French Revolution (1789–99), xii,
　18, 27, 40, 43, 44, 47, 59, 71,
　72, 74, 76, 91, 194, 214, 215

G

Gargantini, Antonio, 20, 26, 48,
　50, 60, 89
Gargantini, Luisa (Carozzi), 60
Garibaldi, Giuseppe, 122, 124,
　125, 126, 145, 147, 148, 151,
　161, 164, 168, 170, 172, 175,
　179, 191, 193, 194
Il Gazzettino rosa, 218
Generational theory, 205, 207,
　208, 209, 210, 212
Giannone, Pietro, 12, 173
Gioberti, Vincenzo, 37, 38, 42,
　45, 98, 104, 127, 226 (nn. 18,
　23), 227 (n. 56)
Gorresio, Gaspare, 233 (n. 9)
Gramsci, Antonio, 80, 232 (n. 90)
Grilenzoni, Giovanni, 235 (n. 54)

Grist tax, 167, 183, 184
Guardabassi, Luigi, 246 (n. 4)
Guerrazzi, Francesco Domenico,
　241 (n. 46)
Guerzoni, Giuseppe, 147
Guizot, François, 49, 90, 100

H

Habsburg Empire, 12, 13, 19, 43,
　45, 48, 49, 55, 56, 76, 80, 94,
　95, 111, 116, 127, 148
Habsburg, House of: Ferdinand I,
　54; Francis Joseph I, 112;
　Joseph II, 3; Leopold II, 3;
　Maria Theresa, 3
Hartig, Franz von, 20
Hegelian idealism, 14, 104
Heine, Heinrich, 31, 216
Herzen, Alexander, 88, 216
Hobbes, Thomas, 10
Hohenzollern candidacy, 191, 192
Holy Roman Empire, 53
Hugo, Victor, 83
Hume, David, 10, 16

I

Imperialism, xiii, 186, 187, 195
Irreligione. *See* Ferrari, Giuseppe,
　secularist ideology
Isabella II, Queen of Spain, 190
Italian National Society, 97, 98,
　116
Italian Question, 45, 46, 51, 68,
　81, 82, 83, 101

J

Jacobin, 52, 69, 74, 197, 215, 216
Janet, Paul, 62, 63
Joseph II, Emperor. *See* Habs-
　burg, House of
Jouffroy, Théodore, 32

Jourdain, C. M., 62
Journal des savants, 29
*Journal général de l'instruction
publique*, 32, 99
July Monarchy, xiii, 24, 37, 51,
70
July Revolution (1830), 6, 33

K

Kingdom of Italy (Napoleonic), 3,
12
Kingdom of Italy (1861–1946), 6,
144, 153, 160, 164, 173, 174,
193, 201, 203
Kingdom of Lombardy-Venetia,
xiii, 3, 11, 12, 22, 25, 32, 37,
43, 48, 50, 57, 58, 60, 69
Kingdom of Sardinia, 22, 24, 45,
57, 58, 68, 69, 76, 81, 82, 93,
112, 114, 116, 123, 125, 183
Kingdom of the Two Sicilies, 97,
124, 125

L

La Marmora, Alfonso, Ferrero de,
151, 152, 175
Lamartine, Alphonse de, 23
Lamennais, Félicité de, 52, 67, 68
Lampato, Francesco, 11, 19
Lanza, Giovanni, 151, 192, 193,
201, 203, 204
La Pappe de Trévern, J.-F., 33, 34
Laprade, Victor de, 11, 224
(n. 13)
Latin Democratic Committee, 67,
68, 190
Law of Guarantees (1871), 201,
202
Legge agraria. See Ferrari,
Giuseppe, socialist ideology
Legion d'Antibes, 178, 180
Legitimist, 33, 63, 84, 87, 162,
180

Le Monnier, Felice, 236 (n. 84)
Leopold II, Emperor. *See* Habs-
burg, House of
Lerminier, Jean-Louis-Eugène, 10,
26, 27
Leroux, Pierre, xii, 23, 24, 25, 31,
32, 39, 47, 50, 51, 54, 75, 86,
104, 216, 225 (n. 4), 228 (n. 2)
La Liberté, 65
Libertine movement, 75
Libri, Guglielmo, 29
Locke, John, 75
Longhi, Achille, 140, 141, 142,
143, 217, 239 (n. 50), 240
(n. 27), 241 (n. 29)
Longhi, Gina, 241 (n. 29)
Louis-Philippe, King of the
French. *See* Orleans, Louis-
Philippe
Lualdi, Ettore, 187, 188

M

Macchi, Mauro, 115, 235 (n. 57),
237 (n. 7), 238 (n. 31)
Machiavelli, Niccolò, 29, 59, 100,
114, 173
Macinato. See Grist tax
Malebranche, Nicolas de, 31
Mamiani della Rovere, Terenzio,
13, 14, 22, 27, 40, 153, 224
(n. 17)
Mancini, Pasquale Stanislao, 153,
154
Manin, Daniele, 68, 95
Margarita, Ernesta, 240 (n. 22),
241 (n. 29)
Maria Theresa, Empress. *See*
Habsburg, House of
Marìas Aguilera, Juliàn, 205
Mario, Alberto, 125, 147, 149,
150
Marx, Karl, xiii, 75, 76, 83, 85,
106, 107, 181, 198

Massarani, Tullo, 239 (n. 2)
Massari, Giuseppe, xii, 226
(nn. 18, 23), 227 (n. 56), 228
(n. 59)
Matteucci, Carlo, 153, 154, 243
(n. 70)
Mazzini, Giuseppe, xi, xii, 19, 46;
Ferrari's critique of his *pro-gramma unitario*, 55, 58, 77,
78, 79; rapprochement with
Ferrari after 1848, 64, 65, 66;
feud with French socialists, 82,
83; political attitude in 1858–
59, 95, 96, 97, 111; opposition
to federalist candidates in 1860,
118, 119; political views of his
followers in early 1860s, 147,
149; differences with Ferrari,
214, 216, 221
Mazzoleni, Angelo, 229 (n. 3),
241 (n. 36), 247 (n. 21)
Menabrea, Federico, 151, 179,
180, 183
Mentana crisis (1867), 178, 179,
180, 183, 190
Mentré, François, 205
Metternich, Klemens von, 49, 54
Miceli, Luigi, 150
Michel (de Bourges), Louis, 51,
63, 67
Michelet, Jules, 10, 26, 27, 43,
100, 104, 152, 205
Mickiewicz, Adam, 31, 216
Milesi Mojon, Bianca, 27
Mill, John Stuart, 107
Minghetti, Marco, 148, 149, 151,
163, 174, 175, 187, 239 (n. 51)
Ministry of Public Education:
France, 23, 24, 56, 61, 152,
153, 155, 156, 158; Italy, 153,
156, 158
Mirecourt, Eugène de, 90
Modena, Duchy of, 114, 121
Moja, Onofrio, 228 (n. 71)

Montalembert, Charles de, 178
Montanelli, Giuseppe, 67, 68, 95,
122, 127, 219, 231 (n. 50), 235
(n. 62), 238 (n. 28), 239 (n. 2)
Mordini, Antonio, 129, 144, 148,
150, 151
Morelli, Salvatore, 203, 247
(n. 32)
Morny, Charles-Auguste de, 87
Murat, Joachim (King), 97, 98,
165, 235 (n. 65)
Murat, Lucien (Prince), 98, 165,
235 (n. 65), 244 (n. 10)
Muratori, Ludovico Antonio, 12

N

Napoleon I. *See* Bonaparte, Napo-
leon
Napoleon III. *See* Bonaparte,
Louis Napoleon
National Workshops, 59
Nice, 121–25
Nuova antologia, 197
La nuova Europa, 149
Il nuovo ricoglitore, 10

O

Oriani, Alfredo, 100
Orleans, Louis-Philippe of, 22, 36,
39, 48–52, 62, 63, 69, 70, 85,
86, 87
Orsini, Felice, 96
Ortega y Gasset, José, 205
Ott, Auguste, 25
Oudinot, Charles-Nicolas, 64, 75

P

Pantaleo, Giovanni, 246 (n. 2)
Papacy, 42, 43, 44, 45, 53, 55, 80
Papal States, 13, 14, 34, 78, 121,
126, 147, 151, 170, 178, 179

Parietti, Giuseppe, 141, 241
    (n. 31)
Paris Commune, 25, 88, 194, 196,
    197, 198
Parma, Duchy of, 114, 121
Party of Action, 96, 97, 204
Pavia, University of, 6
Perini, Osvaldo, 235 (n. 55)
La Perseveranza, 148, 200
Persigny, Victor Fialin de, 87
Le Peuple constituant, 52, 61, 69,
    87
Peyron, Amedeo, 22, 23
Pianciani, Luigi, 219, 246 (n. 6)
Il piccolo corriere, 98
Piedmont-Sardinia. See Kingdom
    of Sardinia
Pisacane, Carlo, xi, 79, 83, 96,
    160, 219, 233 (n. 12)
Pius IX (Pope), 54, 76, 162, 191,
    202
Plombières Conference (1858),
    95, 97
Il Politecnico, 29, 120
Porro, Alessandro, 20, 48, 50, 56,
    60, 228 (n. 64)
Porro, Carlo, 20, 60
Predari, Francesco, 224 (n. 20)
Proudhon, Pierre-Joseph, xii, xiii,
    47, 73, 83; interpretation of
    Bonapartist coup of 1851, 86,
    87; friendship with Ferrari, 87,
    88, 89; influence on Ferrari's
    economic thought, 89, 90, 181;
    Ferrari's influence on his anti-
    clericalism, 90, 91; views on
    Bonapartist foreign policy, 92,
    93; Ferrari's influence on his
    federalist thought, 94, 95; cor-
    respondence with Ferrari on
    Italian Question, 113, 114,
    115, 117, 119, 120, 124, 144,
    145
Provisional Government (1848):

French, 24, 56, 61; Lombard,
    57, 58, 60, 61

Q

Quinet, Edgar, 27, 35, 43, 49, 50,
    99, 100, 111

R

Radetzky, Joseph, 56, 57
Raffaele, Giovanni, 162
Ramorino, Girolamo, 235 (n. 63)
Ranke, Leopold von, 31, 39, 212
Rattazzi, Urbano, 121, 122, 129,
    147, 148, 149, 150, 155, 176,
    179, 193
Reformation, 33, 34, 35, 36
Rémusat, Charles de, 62
Renaissance, 12, 13, 14, 29, 33,
    34, 39, 40, 52, 53, 54, 100,
    102, 170, 205
Renan, Ernest, xii, 99, 111, 212
Repetti, Alessandro, 65, 66, 83
Le Représentant du peuple, 87
Restoration, 3, 4, 5, 10, 12, 44
Revue des deux Mondes, 23, 25,
    39, 42, 43, 48, 99
Revue indépendante, 39, 51, 52,
    101
Revue nationale, 25
Reynaud, Jean, 24, 56, 61, 225
    (n. 7)
Ricasoli, Bettino, 148, 157, 158,
    171, 172, 174, 176, 178, 220
Ricciardi, Giuseppe, xi, xii, 145,
    191, 226 (n. 20)
Riccio, Gennaro, 161, 167
Robespierre, Maximilien, 74
Rochefort-sur-mer, 32, 63
Romagnosi, Giovanni Domenico,
    9, 10, 13, 15, 16, 18, 19, 20, 21,
    24, 104, 152, 180, 206
Roman question, 172, 180, 192

Romano, Liborio, 161
Romeo, Stefano, 150
Rosmini-Serbati, Antonio, 13, 14,
 41, 42, 224 (n. 18)
Rousseau, Jean-Jacques, 72, 75
Ruemelin, Gustav, 205, 207

S

Sacchi, Defendente, 7, 9
Sacchi, Giuseppe, 7, 9
Saffi, Aurelio, 125, 150
Saint-Simonian movement, 9, 10,
 11, 24, 31, 35, 75
Sainte-Beuve, Charles-Augustin,
 23
Salvemini, Gaetano, 170
Sand, George, 23, 39, 104, 228
 (n. 2)
Sartorio, Michele, 7, 237 (n. 14)
Savarese, Giacomo, 161, 165,
 167, 244 (n. 11)
Savarese, Roberto, 161
Savonarola, Girolamo, 114
Savoy, Duchy of, 121, 123, 124
Savoy, House of, 45; Amedeo,
 202; Charles Albert, 57, 58, 60,
 61; Victor Emmanuel II, 98,
 112, 114, 120, 127, 145, 147,
 169, 170, 176
Schoelcher, Victor, 51, 67, 84
Scialoja, Antonio, 176
Scienza Nuova, 10, 17, 26, 29,
 205
Second (French) Empire, xiii, 87,
 92, 111, 180, 191, 192, 193,
 197, 198, 233 (n. 13)
Secondi, Giovanni, 241 (n. 33)
Secularism, 71–73, 170–72,
 201–2, 219. *See also* Ferrari,
 Giuseppe, secularist ideology
Sella, Quintino, 181, 183, 187,
 188, 202, 203
September Convention (1864),

151, 174, 175, 178, 179
Sineo, Riccardo, 127, 149
Sirtori, Giuseppe, 150
Smith, Adam, 73
Socialism, 23, 24, 25, 73–78, 80,
 89, 90, 113, 117, 119, 186,
 187, 188, 189, 219. *See
 also* Buchez, Philippe; Leroux,
 Pierre; Marx, Karl; Pisacane,
 Carlo; Proudhon, Pierre-Joseph
Società degli editori, 11, 20
Société des amis du peuple, 24
Sonnino, Sidney, 170
Southern question, 160–70
Statuto (1848), 145, 201
Strasbourg, City of, 24, 32, 33,
 34, 35, 38, 40, 41
Strasbourg, University of, 32, 35,
 39, 56, 57, 59, 60, 88
Strauss, David Friedrich, 212
Il Suffragio universale, 203, 204

T

Taillandier, René-Gaspard, 35
Tenca, Carlo, 98, 99, 115
Thierry, Augustin, 23, 27, 38, 152
Thiers, Adolphe, 100
Tipografia Elvetica, 66, 67, 68, 81
Tocqueville, Alexis de, 83, 86, 233
 (n. 16)
Tommaseo, Niccoló, 42
Tonello, Michelangelo, 176
Trasformismo, 200, 218
Treaties of 1815. *See* Congress of
 Vienna
Tuscany, Grandduchy of, 114,
 121

U

Ugoni, Filippo, 226 (n. 20)
L'Univers, 34, 36, 38
Université, 26, 33, 34, 36, 61, 64

V

Valerio, Lorenzo, xii, 22, 41, 225
  (n. 13), 227 (n. 45)
La Valle di Giosafat, 162
Vanini, Lorenzo, 225 (n. 5)
Vatican Council I, 191, 193
Ventidue marzo, 58
Verri, Alessandro, 12
Verri, Pietro, 12
Veuillot, Louis, 34, 35
Vico, Giambattista, 9, 12, 14–18,
  20, 23, 25, 29, 205, 207, 224
  (n. 23), 225 (n. 5)
Victor Emmanuel II, King of
  Sardinia and King of Italy. See
  Savoy, House of
Vieusseux, Gian Pietro, 224
  (n. 17)
Villafranca armistice (1859), 112
Villemain, François, 34–38, 40,
  227 (nn. 38, 39)
Visconti-Venosta, Emilio, 199,
  200, 201

Voltaire, François-Marie Arouet
  de, 72

W

Wallon, Jean Gustave, 191, 202,
  244 (n. 10), 246 (n. 5), 247
  (n. 30)
War of 1859, 26, 98
War of 1866, 183

Y

Young Italy, 19, 20, 60

Z

Zanardelli, Giuseppe, 134, 240
  (n. 16)
Zeller, Jules-Sylvain, 99

The Author

Clara M. Lovett, associate professor of history at Baruch College, City University of New York, is author of *Carlo Cattaneo and the Politics of the Risorgimento.*

The Book

Typeface: Mergenthaler V-I-P Sabon

Design and composition: The University of North Carolina Press

Paper: Sixty pound 1854 by S. D. Warren Company

Binding cloth: Roxite B Vellum 51565
by The Holliston Mills, Incorporated

Printer and binder: Braun-Brumfield, Incorporated

Published by The University of North Carolina Press

DATE DUE

GAYLORD			PRINTED IN U.S.A.